Confronting Evil

Confronting Evil

Two Journeys

Fred Emil Katz

STATE UNIVERSITY OF NEW YORK PRESS

Published by
State University of New York Press, Albany

For information, address the State University of New York Press,
90 State Street, Suite 700, Albany, NY 12207

Production by Marilyn P. Semerad
Marketing by Fran Keneston

Library of Congress Cataloging-in-Publication Data

Katz, Fred E., 1927–
    Confronting evil : two journeys / Fred Emil Katz.
        p. cm.
    Includes bibliographical references and index.
    ISBN 0-7914-6029-0 (alk. paper) — ISBN 0-7914-6030-4 (pbk. : alk. paper)
        1. Good and evil—Case studies.   2. Holocaust, Jewish (1939–1945)—Moral
and ethical aspects.   3. Good and evil—Social aspects.   4. Holocaust, Jewish
(1939–1945)—Causes.   5. Katz, Fred E., 1927–   I. Title.

BJ1401.K37 2004
170—dc21   2003052611

10 9 8 7 6 5 4 3 2 1

To those who, wittingly and unwittingly, shared my journeys:

Liat Jennifer; Trude; Herta and Justin Katz; Recha, Boris, Ted and Joan Levitt; my parents, Max and Jenny Katz. Amid the journeys, they sustained the bonds in my family.

Hertha Karger and Ida Field. They helped me discover that I could undertake journeys.

George Tracy, Harry Martin, Clyde and Betty Wilson. Their friendship gave me grounding and hope within my profession. This eventually led to the second journey.

Paul Rosenblatt and Amichai (Max) Heppner. Their friendship gave me constancy amid the turbulence of both journeys.

Renate. Whose affection keeps me grounded while letting me go on journeys.

And Ernestine, this Christian German woman, of blessed memory, who showed me that amid the horrors there were also persons of great courage and decency.

$\mathscr{C}$ontents

# Preface

Addressing Evil

This book continues the work of two of my previous books. It is an attempt to make a constructive and creative response to some of the major horrors of the past and present century. In the beginning of the first book the following approach to evil is laid out. This approach underlies the present volume as well.

> I define and use the word *evil* to mean behavior that deliberately deprives innocent people of their humanity, from small scale assaults on a person's dignity to outright murder. This is a *behavioral* definition of evil. It focuses on how people behave toward one another—where the behavior of one person, or an aggregate of persons, is destructive to others.
>
> Evil is commonly seen in religious, moral and philosophical terms: as violating higher commandments, as breaking valued constraints that bind us to other persons, or as making us depart from a benign deity in favor of following a malignant deity, a satan. I do not deny that these are important, even profound ways of considering evil. I shall not delve into them because it would distract from what I want to accomplish here; namely showing that a behavioral view of evil helps us confront it. We thereby lift evil out of the realm of the supernatural and place it squarely in the realm of day-to-day living.
>
> When I say that a behavioral approach to evil will help us confront evil, I do not mean to say that we will henceforth avoid evil, that evil will no longer happen. I mean, only, that it will enable us to know more realistically how evil is produced. And from this more realistic knowledge we will be in a better position to avoid traveling the road to evil, if we so choose. We shall see road signs where we previously did not see road signs.[1]

The present book makes its central concern the very real possibility that evil is something we humans may actually confront in our own ongoing behavior. As these words are written, in the wake of the terror attacks on the American World Trade Center and the Pentagon on September 11, 2001, Americans' confrontation with evil is only too real and, alas, too raw. It is too soon to see its long-term workings in this instance. In the following pages I shall demonstrate and examine some of these long-term workings using my own history, among others, in the effort to extract dispassionate lessons from the workings of evil.

$\mathscr{A}$cknowledgments

This book contains revised and adapted versions of the following items I have previously authored:

"Responses to the Holocaust: The Painful Birth of the Third Phase," presented at the International Scholars Conference at Oxford University in July, 1988, and published in the proceedings of that conference, *Remembering for the Future*, Pergamon Press; Oxford, England.

"On Surprises, Linkages and Separations" in Ilya Levkov, editor, *Bitburg and Beyond*. New York: Shapolsky Publishers, 1987. Copyright, Ilya Levkov. Used by permission of Ilya Levkov.

"Implementation of the Holocaust: The Behavior of Nazi Officials," in *Comparative Studies in Society and History* 24 (3); 1982. Copyright Society for the Comparative Study of Society and History. Reprinted with the permission of Cambridge University Press.

"A Sociological Perspective to the Holocaust" in *Modern Judaism* 2 (3); 1982. Used here by permission of Oxford University Press.

Use of this material is gratefully acknowledged.

Introduction

The challenge: We need better explanations of evil if we are to get past our impotence and vulnerability in the face of major horrors.

In recent times it has become increasingly clear that ordinary people—not emotionally deranged people, not social deviants, not zealots of any kind—are fully capable of taking part in great horrors, and of doing so with enthusiasm. In a book about German police reservists during the Second World War, Christopher Browning reported that these men, who were not crazed Nazis, carried out an entire campaign of exterminating innocent Jews in a region of Poland.[1] In the year 1994 we began to receive reports about recent events in Rwanda. In the course of one hundred days about eight hundred thousand persons had been slaughtered.

> ... the ruling Hutus did it to the minority Tutsis. Close to a tenth of the population was destroyed. ... How was the slaughter done? By machete and nail-studded club, mainly. By hacking and slicing and pounding, essentially. Who did the work? This is perhaps the most unimagined part. The killers, by and large, were ordinary people—not jack-booted representatives of the state. Neighbors did it—to neighbors. Pastors did it—to parishioners. Doctors did it—to patients. Schoolteachers did it—to pupils. In-laws did it—to in-laws. Workers did it—to fellow workers at the township office of the local tire factory.[2]

It is not enough to report such horrors. We need explanation. How is it that *ordinary* people would engage in such horrendous acts? This is the challenge to which I address this book. I maintain that we must confront evil from a

1

new perspective if we are to get past our impotence and vulnerability in the face of it.

First, I will offer some background about my own life and its bearing on the mission of this book. I am Jewish. As a child, I lived in southern Germany under the Nazi regime in the 1930s. I was sent to England under a children's rescue mission, known as the *Kindertransport*. My parents arranged it because we could not find a way to escape from our village as a family. The book starts with my return to the village forty years later. I had been terrified about going back, yet I was also strangely yearning to go back. I suppose I was trying to address the past in the hope of ending my lingering fears, such as those kindled during Kristallnacht and other assaults on our family. I needed to create some endings to that past so that I could have some new beginnings in my life. The trip to my village turned out to be the beginning of two journeys to confront evil.

Setting Out on Two Journeys

The first journey is that of a survivor wrestling with the past in order to get on with life; it is a journey to where the present is no longer debilitated by the past, and where the future can be embraced with some confidence and joy. Learning about this journey may help others struggling with survival. In my case, the journey eventually gave impetus and nourishment for the second journey.

The second journey is that of a behavioral scientist who was finally obliged, after a long period of psychological denial, to address the horrendous evil which still afflicts us in the repeated eruption of horrors we humans impose on one another. My starting point for this journey was the need for a new way of looking at evil. We need to acknowledge and understand that ordinary people, "good" people, healthy people, morally sensitive people, are fully capable of taking part in horrendous deeds. How does this actually happen?

In my second journey I look for clues to extremes of evil in human ordinariness—in how we make decisions in daily life, in how we attach ourselves to larger causes, in how we use our freedom, and, most especially, in our human need to live in, and contribute to, a moral context. It emerges that it is precisely in our moral humanity, that we are, first and foremost, moral creatures, that the basic clue to our susceptibility to participating in extremes of evil lies. Therein lies the greatest danger. And therein, too, lies great hope.

Paradoxically, when it comes to creating evil, we are often dealing with the best in us, with ourselves as moral creatures, not as cold monsters beyond moral reach. And, most hopefully of all, we are dealing with the ordinary human ways that are knowable and ultimately manageable by ourselves; we are not dealing with mysteries beyond our control. This is a new way of looking at evil: Evil as rooted in our ordinary ways of wanting to lead good lives. These human ways are not mysterious. We can understand how they work, and hence how they can go awry, to become the ingredients of evil. As we do so, we can throw off the shackles of mysticism about evil that have beset us far too long. For, stated a bit more intellectually, ". . . if evil . . . escapes the reach of our imagination, it will have established dominion over us all."[3]

The mission of this book is to contribute a quite dispassionate view of how evil can be produced by people who do not have horns on their head, who are not pathologically deviant. By people like ourselves. After we embrace this perspective we can gain freedom from dumb victimhood. We will no longer be ignorant of what produces massive horrors and we will gain the flexibility to become better masters of our destiny.

Some Background

Decades after the liberation of the death camp of Auschwitz we still hear the plaintive cry, "Never again!" But it is happening again. Genocidal actions have again taken place in our time; major horrors have taken place in the not-so-distant past in Bosnia, Rwanda, Cambodia. And there have been around fifty acts of lesser horror since World War II. All display utter disregard for human life and dignity. It seems that human beings are easily recruited to commit horrors against one another.

The political scientist R. J. Rummel estimates that in the twentieth century some sixty-one million persons were murdered in the Soviet Union; some thirty-eight million were murdered by the Chinese Communists; some twenty-two million were murdered by the German Nazis; and some ten million were murdered by the Chinese Nationalists. All these murders were over and above the thirty-five million deaths caused by the various wars of the twentieth century.[4] And these are merely the major horrors of that past century. The many lesser horrors include the ethnic cleansings in the Balkans and in Rwanda in the 1990s.

Each mass horror seems to catch us by surprise. What is more, we seem to be so callous that we are almost inured when we hear about new horrors. We end up focusing on numbers, as I have just done, rather than on human life.

Behind our surprise is a profound bewilderment when perpetrators of horrors claim moral justification for their deeds. The terrorist who blows up buildings or airplanes with innocent people inside, the ethnic cleanser who slaughters members of a designated ethnic group, the participant in genocidal campaigns all typically claim moral justification for their actions. To us, the bystanders or victims, this seems to be the crowning insult. Not only are the deeds horrifying beyond belief, but the perpetrators claim to have a high moral purpose for performing their deeds. That moral purpose may well be the keystone of the perpetrators' existence in general, as well as the guiding directive for their murderous actions.

Here evil operates under the guise of morality. It utilizes and twists the very human need to exist under a moral umbrella. Many other forms of human ordinariness also persist while individuals engage in horrendous activities. In the chapters ahead, I shall dwell on how so much ordinariness also persisted in the behavior of individuals who did extraordinarily evil deeds, such as Adolf Eichmann and Rudolf Hoess, the commandant of Auschwitz. We can recognize, in these individuals, the possibility that our own ordinariness—including the ordinariness that all humans are moral creatures—can lend itself to the production of evil.

When it comes to explaining outbreaks of horrendous actions, such as the Nazi genocide of Jews and others they deemed to be unworthy of life, an adequate explanation has thus far eluded us. But we have come tantalizingly close in the reignited debate about the involvement of ordinary people in entirely horrendous deeds, sparked by Daniel Goldhagen's *Hitler's Willing Executioners: Ordinary Germans and the Holocaust.* Before the Goldhagen book there was Christopher Browning's book, *Ordinary Men: Reserve Battalion 101 and the Final Solution in Poland,* and a book of mine, *Ordinary People and Extraordinary Evil: A Report on the Beguilings of Evil,* (published in 1993).

Goldhagen emphasized that a vast number of ordinary Germans not only knew about the Holocaust, but participated in it in one form or another. Browning gave us a case study of a unit of German military reservists. These reservists were not ideologically crazed Nazis; they had hoped to sit out the war in a non-combat capacity. But, to everyone's surprise, they became willing and eager killers once they were assigned the task of exterminating innocent people in Poland. Goldhagen's view is that such people, along with a majority of their ordinary fellow Germans, were poisoned by the virus "eliminationist anti-Semitism." In short, he maintains, they had a sickness, a sickness shared by millions.

In my 1993 book, I emphasized that individuals who carried out horrifying acts did so by harnessing very ordinary attributes, attributes we all share and, often, treasure. My message in that book is that in the quest for weapons against horrendous evil, we must cease the fruitless search for monstrosity, sickness, and other aberrations as the root of evil. Instead, we must look at how readily the attributes of our human makeup—the attributes we use in the most mundane activities of everyday life as well as in the pursuit of our most noble aspirations—can very readily be harnessed for entirely evil ends. We can understand how this process works. And, as we learn to do so, we can cease being the unwitting allies and impotent victims of such evil. My 1993 book is a start in this direction, and the present book is a continuation.

The forerunner of this entire debate, the person who set forth the still fundamental issue about ordinary human beings participating in great horrors, was Hannah Arendt. In her book *Eichmann in Jerusalem: A Report on the Banality of Evil*,[5] she produced the provocative insight that an individual who made a huge contribution to evil—the one who single-handedly masterminded the capture and transportation of millions of innocent people to their death—turned out to be maddeningly "banal." His greatest regret toward the end of his life was not his contribution to evil, but the fact that he had not achieved as high a rank as he thought he deserved. In Arendt's view, he was a terribly ordinary little man who, nonetheless, made extraordinary contributions to genocide. He did so, according to Arendt, through the vantage point of his own limited little world, dominated by small-time career aspirations. Through it he became a modern man, a specialist, an administrative specialist in the art and science of exterminating human beings.

The broader issue, Arendt tells us, is:

> ... that so many were like him [Eichmann], and the many were neither perverted nor sadistic, ... they were, and still are, terribly and terrifyingly normal ... this normality was much more terrifying than all the atrocities put together, for it implied ... that this new type of criminal ... commits his crimes under circumstances that make it well-nigh impossible for him to know or feel that he is doing wrong. (p. 276)

Arendt's message caused much consternation. Her shocked critics asked, how could one possibly regard an Eichmann as banal, or "ordinary" in any sense? His deeds spoke terribly loudly. His ordinariness, in the form of careerism and other small, day-to-day routines and aspirations must surely have been supplemented by deeply evil intentions and perversions. If not inherently evil, such a person must, at least, be profoundly sick or morally demented. An ordinary "healthy" individual could not possibly do what Eichmann did. To think otherwise threatens our own mental health.

Here, let me say that Goldhagen is returning to the earlier, pre-Arendt, thinking. He answers the ordinary-people's-participation-in-evil challenge by returning to the claim that such persons are profoundly sick. In the Nazi German case, this sickness was caused by a particularly virulent form of anti-Semitism. Browning, on the other hand, left us with an uneasy, disturbing, and far more challenging notion: Perhaps the doers of horrendous deeds were not sick, or in any way clinically different from any other people, Germans or non-Germans. Yet they performed horrendous deeds, and did so with considerable zeal. Browning, in the tradition of Arendt, leaves us with the agonizing question, how can human ordinariness account for such humanly perpetrated horrors as actually took place in the Nazi Holocaust—and, later, in Bosnia and Rwanda, and in many other places?

The Arendt's banality-of-evil thesis suggests to me that we must find the clues in the social psychology of ordinary human beings, not in aberrations from ordinary living, not in sickness, not in a search for monsters and monstrosities, not even in poisonous anti-Semitism (although the Nazi German anti-Semitism was indeed poisonous, and did indeed have great lethal impact). Arendt's pointing to Eichmann's infatuation with his own careerism leads us in the right direction. But surely careerism is not enough of an explanation for the massive evil that occurs so often in human history. People's tendency to obey authority—which was so prevalent in Nazi Germany and which, thanks to the electric shock experiments by Stanley Milgram, we know exists in many, if not most societies—is also not enough. After all, a good deal of the evidence, from Browning's and others' work, tells us that people will, under some circumstances, do horrendous evil with great willingness, even with zeal and joy and a sense of personal liberation. They will do all this not merely under duress of orders to do horrible deeds; they are not merely obeying orders from an authority.

Therefore we need a more adequate social psychology, one that lets us understand what it is in human ordinariness that is so readily harnessed for doing evil. How can one discover such a social psychology?

It seems to me that the clue comes from a peculiar inadequacy of Arendt's picture of the mental world of Eichmann. She describes that world as almost entirely fatuous, empty. A nothingness seems to prevail as Eichmann goes about his pragmatic, immediacy-focused little life. She states:

> Except for an extraordinary diligence in looking out for his personal advancement, he had no motives at all. And this diligence in itself was in no way criminal. . . . He was not stupid. It was sheer thoughtlessness . . . that predisposed him to become one of the greatest criminals of that period . . ." (pp. 287–88)

By contrast, I suggest that Eichmann, and many other Nazi adherents, lived in a distinct Moral Universe, one that provided a moral umbrella for their actions. It was far from empty. It was not fatuous. Arendt herself says, in regard to Nazi mass murderers, "What stuck in the minds of these men who had become murderers was simply the notion of being involved in something historic, grandiose, unique, 'a great task that occurs once in two thousand years.' " (p. 105) They had a sense of following a *moral* calling. They felt a *moral* justification for their deeds! Here I must point to a book by Peter

Haas; *Morality after Auschwitz: The Radical Challenge of the Nazi Ethic.*[6] Haas suggests that the Nazis created a distinctive morality for themselves, one that justified their deeds. And they did not regard their deeds as evil. We may find the Nazi morality abhorrent, but it was a morality nonetheless, and it served as the moral umbrella for the Eichmanns of the Nazi era.

There are no special human attributes that lead humans invariably to do evil and which, if found, would then liberate us from evil. There is no evil-generating virus, waiting to be discovered. There are only ordinary human attributes, such as (but not limited to) how we make decisions in everyday life, how we attach ourselves to causes larger than ourselves, how we pursue careers, how we try to protect ourselves against pain, how we make use of our freedom. All of these can be harnessed to produce a decent and humane life. Yet the same attributes can just as readily be harnessed to help the individual engage in horrendous evil when evil presents itself in a beguiling way. How can evil become so beguiling? By arriving under the guise of morality. This is the key, and the focus of much of this book.

We humans are fundamentally moral creatures. We get our sense of who we are, what we are, our sense of self, from our immersion in a moral community. A moral community can be one's family, one's ethnic group, one's religious group, one's country, one's professional peers, one's gang, or even what sociologists used to call one's "reference group." When we are immersed in a moral community we may derive profound rewards from it; they are fundamental to our sense of personal identity and our life's meaning.

However, our immersion in a moral community goes well beyond merely accepting, in an abstract way, the group's moral creed, its standards, its values, and its expectations from us. Quite concretely, in our daily life we derive a sense of our personal worth, what I shall call our "moral virility," from our own contribution to the moral community to which we see ourselves belonging. When I say, "I am a good citizen; I vote and pay my taxes," I am saying that I am contributing to the moral fabric of my country. In much of our day-to-day activity we see ourselves contributing to the moral fabric that frames and sustains our ongoing life. That fabric allows our own active participation in morally meaningful activity. It justifies us in what we are doing. It orients us. It makes us willing to undertake risks, do new things. And, alas, it can also support us when we engage in horrendous evil.

Within the confines of a moral community we may discover and participate in the most humane and life-affirming activities. Yet, also within a moral community (for example, a religious cult), we may find moral justification for the most inhumane activities, up to and including the sacrifice of our own and our children's lives. I am convinced that a majority of the Nazi Germans who participated in the genocide of Jews did so out of a sense of contributing to a noble moral cause. They were not merely part of a nation.

In their view they were a *moral community*, where the murder of undesirable people was regarded as a necessary prelude to a higher form of existence for the German people, and where one's own participation in murderous actions would help to bring about that grand future. One's own actions, even if they were occasionally distasteful, would make a vital contribution to realizing Germany's glorious future.

On a far smaller scale, but within the same perspective, the participants in Stanley Milgram's laboratory experiments, who were willing to inflict electric shocks on innocent people saw themselves as part of a distinct moral community while they participated in a "learning" experiment. I shall discuss the Milgram experiments in more detail later in the book. Here, suffice it to say, among the participants a distinct set of norms prevailed stating that making a contribution to science can involve having to make uncomfortable decisions. The participants were not merely obeying authority, as Milgram emphasized. Instead, and far more importantly, they saw themselves as actively making a contribution to a special and distinctive *moral community*. Here, their values outside the laboratory on which they were brought up— such as the one that says that you do not hurt innocent people—were declared totally irrelevant. In the laboratory, they were told—and they believed—their own actions produced something of benefit to the community that had asked them to participate. They were making a contribution to a community that represented a morally justified cause.

In short, moral communities have compelling influence on the behavior of their members. They constitute a Local Moral Universe that fills the moral vision of their members. The vibrancy of that moral universe depends on the ongoing and active contribution of the members toward converting the moral vision into palpable reality.

But it is surely evident that there are very many different kinds of moral communities, which nurture vastly different moralities. Behavior encouraged or supported by these moral communities can range from the contemplative and ascetic to murderous physical assault on innocent people. They are all advanced under the mantle of the particular moral community, with a sense of moral rectitude that can be highly enticing to members. The members are apt to believe, earnestly and unwaveringly, that the most basic meaning of their lives revolves around the moral sponsorship of the particular moral community to which they subscribe. Their highest goal, their noblest deed, is to contribute to their moral community.

∼

In summary, this book emphasizes that evil can become entirely beguiling because of its claim to have moral legitimacy. In *Ordinary People and*

Extraordinary Evil: A Report on the Beguilings of Evil, I emphasized that what facilitates this enactment of evil is that ordinary human ways are being used. For example, we routinely make decisions in small, incremental ways; this ordinary human *process* can be used, without alteration, to promote evil. The crux of this matter is that evildoing does not rely on fundamental changes in human behavior but, instead, makes use of many of our ordinary, mundane ways of behaving. This greatly facilitates the process of creating evil among ordinary people. I reiterate and further develop these ideas in the chapters "A Look at Implementation of the Holocaust" and "The Routinization of Evil" in this book.

In another book, *Immediacy: How Our World Confronts Us and How We Confront Our World,* I emphasized that the very nature of the *immediacy* in which we live our daily lives can also contribute to our doing evil. Immediacy, I argue, contains distinctive attributes that can be clearly identified and understood. These attributes can foster the emergence of the Local Moral Universe. The attributes of immediacy are not inherently evil or good; they are merely part of the nature of how we live in the social contexts in which we find ourselves. But they can contribute to the production of horrors. Fortunately, they need not remain mysterious. And with knowledge of the attributes of immediacy can come mastery over these attributes and, from it, more mastery over our lives.

Now, turning to a more practical matter, to understand how humans can be willing participants in communities that underwrite horrifying deeds we must depart from the seemingly obvious issue of trying to understand their motivation. Rather than ask, *why* do people do such things?, we must take the scientist's more productive approach of turning away from "why" questions and turn to "how" questions. How do humans come to participate in horrors? How do they "travel" to that point? What pathways do individuals follow that lead them to carrying out horrors? In this book I shall illustrate some such pathways, always (quite deliberately) emphasizing how very "ordinary" ways of behaving can constitute pathways to horrendous deeds—and how the turn toward evil is rarely marked with clear indicators.

This book reports on my two related journeys toward coming to terms with being a survivor of the Holocaust. The first journey deals with remembering. In my case, this came after more than twenty years of denying that the Holocaust had anything to do with me personally. Eventually I confronted the reality of what happened. I sought to *actively* remember by, for example, visiting the village where I was born. The second journey addresses shortcomings of the first journey; while remembering is a necessary part of the mourning process, remembering is not enough. There must be a new embracing of life, a moving beyond victimhood by somehow claiming an active role in shaping one's future. Intellectually, this means recognizing limitation of the popular notion that we must remember what happened so that it won't happen again. That notion is an updated version of George Santayana's dictum that if we forget what happened in history we are bound to have to re-experience that history. I believe Santayana's dictum is a sad illusion with which we still delude ourselves. Remembering, alone, is no vaccine against future horrors. In fact, if we take history seriously we must acknowledge that many horrors are committed precisely because past horrors *are* remembered—that generations sometimes engage in horrific retribution for horrors committed against their ancestors. Furthermore, I have come to fear that exclusive and passionate reliance on remembering may so restrict our capacity for dispassionate analysis that it can, inadvertently, prolong our impotence in the face of new horrors we humans inflict on one another. This is the incentive for undertaking my second journey.

I had an awakening. I realized that although extremes of evil may mystify us for long periods of time, they need not remain mysterious. Indeed, lessons we can learn from the Holocaust and other horrendous actions may enable us to contribute to a science of *ordinary human behavior* that is powerful enough to help us understand—and eventually bring under control—extremes of evil. For me personally, this has been a quest for meaning for my life, as both survivor and behavioral scientist (in the tradition of Viktor Frankl, who discovered his life's meaning at Auschwitz). I also fervently hope that in some way this quest may lessen our impotence in the face of recurrent outbreaks of extremes of evil.

The Journeys: An Overview

My first journey begins with my visit to the village where I was born. It produced an encounter for which I was entirely unprepared. I suddenly found myself in the role of a Jewish Holocaust survivor confronting Christians about the Holocaust; I had considerable repressed anger and lingering fear. Now, many years after that visit, I am discovering that the visit led to some tangible reconciliation and new personal freedom for me. It has produced healing. It has given my life a new dimension.

I also have learned that the past has disconcerting ways of re-emerging in the present, as I discuss in the section on the Bitburg Affair (see chapter 2). Yet there comes a time when we must permit ourselves an embrace of the future, where our present is not permanently fixated on the past. I address this in the chapter, "Surviving the Holocaust: The Pain and Reward of Confronting the Future in a Personal Way."

The remainder of the book, Part two entitled "Dissecting Evil," chronicles my second journey. It begins from the conviction that we must discover ways of addressing major horrors—such as the Holocaust—in ways that go beyond the search for monsters. We must do so not merely by proclaiming that ordinary humans are fully capable of engaging in horrors, but must show convincingly how this can happen. This requires an effort to foster dispassionate and scientific study of evil actions. For me, this began by my waking up to our appalling impotence in the face of repeated eruptions of major human horrors. The Holocaust is the best known instance, but it is by no means the only one. Until fairly recently many behavioral scientists have been stunningly unresponsive in the face of evil on such a massive scale. I can say this because I am one of them. We have pretended that evil is not real at all. We used to regard "evil" as a quaint religious concept. In our zeal to be pure scientists, we believed that we needed to escape being tainted by "religiosity," and we have tended to deny that there is such a thing as evil. As a result, we have ignored the issue of why people engage in evil—whether they may unsuspectingly contribute to it or, even, whether they may participate in evil with full awareness, knowing very well that their actions are evil. (I am defining evil as behavior that deliberately deprives innocent people of their humanity, their sanctity, ranging from assaults on a person's dignity to outright murder.)

It is not inevitable that we use our ordinary human ways to contribute to evil. Much of the time we contribute to evil inadvertently, assuming that our personal actions do not really matter. Or that if they do matter, we can limit and contain their impact. Sometimes our assumptions turn out to be cruelly wrong.

Contributing to evil inadvertently is not the whole issue. We humans are sometimes beguiled by evil. We can, and sometimes do, engage in evil quite deliberately, even joyfully, believing that by doing evil we are making a magnificent contribution to a morally justified cause. We can discern how this works and, to counteract that tendency, we can conform less to the seductions of evil when they come our way, particularly when they come to us under the mantle of a moral community. We can become less gullible.

Discerning how ordinary people's ordinary ways of behaving can produce evil is a lesson, indeed a gift, to be derived from the Holocaust. As we put this discernment to use—by being wary of the potential contribution to evil by ordinary, well-intentioned people—we can create a less violent, more peaceful, more sunny world. This is the grand long-range goal. It is the world we want to create. But the first and immediate present task is to produce more effective discernment of how horrendous evil can be sewn from the cloth of human ordinariness, including the ordinariness—and haunting necessity—of our membership in moral communities.

Part two of this book, "Dissecting Evil," incorporates responses I received to my book, *Ordinary People and Extraordinary Evil*. That book, published in 1993, actually was completed in 1987, so I have the benefit of responses over a relatively long period of time.

I hereby thank those individuals who responded. I rejoice in their willingness to engage in dialogue around the issue of creating tools for reducing our impotence in the face of massive horror. The best gift I can envisage in return for my efforts is more dialogue, dialogue that leads to better approaches and creates better tools for freeing ourselves from our lingering torment. To succeed, we must begin by moving beyond the quaint assumption that only persons afflicted with distinctive pathologies (be they psychological or societal)—monsters, really—can become evildoers.

I am particularly indebted to Carol Mann and Max Heppner, who read and gave insightful reactions to early versions of the manuscript. Max Heppner did so from the vantage point of both a professional editor and a fellow member of the Baltimore-Washington Child Survivor group that sustained many of us for many years and who, therefrom, knows my wrestlings with evil.

PART ONE

A Visit:
Beginning the First Journey

The first journey involved confronting my own survival from the Holocaust. It began with a visit to the village where I was born, forty years after I left there.

I went with vague yearnings. Perhaps I could find out something about the last days in the lives of my parents. But more honestly, I did not know what I was looking for or what I would find.

As I see it now, many years later, I went to begin my journey into learning how to live more effectively, how to stand upright as a human being. I vaguely felt that my village must be the place where this could and must begin. Yes, I was an adult with a family. Yes, I had already served as a professor at universities. But I still felt like a lost child. The visit might begin a journey that would grant me viable adulthood, including the glimmer of my second journey, of using my profession's skills to address our impotence in the face of evil.

CHAPTER ONE

All in One Day

Its name is Oberlauringen. It is located in southern Germany. I was born there. I spent my first eleven years there. It is my village.

I left in the summer of 1939. My parents had arranged for me to be brought to England under the care of a child refugee program *(Kindertransport)* when it became clear that they could not leave Germany.[1] I left behind my mother and father, our house and the yard around it, our synagogue and our cemetery, our neighbors and their daughter, Margot. I used to play with Margot.

My older half-brother, Ludwig, left home shortly before I did, expecting to emigrate to Palestine. He had joined a movement (Hachsharah) that was to train him to become a farmer, and this training was to take place in Holland. He was living in Holland when the invading Germans caught him. He was deported to the death camp of Sobibor in Poland where, I was informed, his life was ended immediately. Ludwig was my "half-brother" because his mother had died while giving birth to him. Hence, his life began and ended in horror. He was most gentle and loving.

I took with me to England memories of a fear-filled life in Oberlauringen. I wanted to escape, yet as I write these words, more than sixty years after my departure, I still do not know whether I ever really left Oberlauringen.

For years I did not think about Oberlauringen at all, but it lingered as a hazy mist about my childhood. I kept moving from place to place. I had moved thirty-six times when I stopped counting my movings. I hate moving. I tell myself that the only thing that makes moving bearable is the hope that the latest move is the very last move I shall ever make. But I have kept on moving. After moving from Germany I have lived—and moved—in England, America, Israel, and Canada.

Throughout these movings there remained anger and dread about Oberlauringen. Was Oberlauringen still my home? Was it my anchor in the world, the one place from which I should not have moved? I told myself I would never go back there. Oberlauringen was Germany, and it held the terror of being a Jewish child there in the 1930s. I would have a heart attack if I ever set foot on German soil again.

Then, over the course of years, the anger and dread gave way to a strange yearning. Perhaps there was something more I could learn about my parents, about Margot, about the other Jewish families in Oberlauringen. Perhaps there would be something else, something I could not quite put my finger on, something more. I must go back. There was so much that was unfinished and unclear. Oberlauringen was holding me hostage, and I had to seek release. This yearning gradually but unyieldingly overpowered the sense of dread I associated with that island in the world.

In 1979 my wife and I made plans to go to Oberlauringen. Without my wife's support I would not have had the courage. I told myself I would not stay overnight; darkness in Oberlauringen held a special terror. I would arrange to arrive in the morning and leave in the afternoon. All I had to do would be carried out in one day. And this is what I did. Except that the one day stretched backward, into the past, and forward into the rest of my life.

∾

Confronting Oberlauringen would not have been possible had I not, inadvertently, earlier confronted the German language. When I confronted the German language, I had to confront myself. This confrontation is ongoing.

From 1939, when I left Germany, up to 1972, I never voluntarily spoke German. In my early years as a refugee, when German-speakers—fellow refugees, relatives, friends—spoke to me in German, I replied as best I could in English. This was no conscious decision; I did not deliberately set out to stop speaking German. I simply could not produce words in German. I was unable; my inner being stopped me.

In 1972 we moved to Israel, my family and I. It was to be a permanent emigration. I had obtained a professorship—a tenured full professorship—at Tel Aviv University. As academic positions go, this was surely a grand prize (even though I was already a full professor at the State University of New York at Buffalo).

Two entirely unexpected things happened to me in Israel, and both relate to language. My German returned easily, and Hebrew proved impossible for me to learn. Upon meeting German-speaking relatives in Israel I found myself speaking German, as well as English, comfortably. I spoke with some ease, with a sense of being at home in the language. In the land of

Israel, I was speaking German for the first time in thirty-three years. During these intervening years I had felt that I was unable to speak German. I was now realizing that I could express things in German that I could not express in English. I could feel things in German that I could not feel in English. German was a rich and nurturing language for me. Yet, lurking in the background, German was also the language of fear and terror for me. I had spoken nothing but German up to the age of eleven and returning to that language, I was once again connected to that sense of terror. In some ways, I again became that terror-struck child. For many years I had guarded that child by blocking out the German language. I shall say more about my newfound terror in a moment.

In addition to not having been able to speak German, I could not sing. Up to the time I was married, in 1969, I had told myself that I was unable to sing. I could not produce a tune. The ability to sing had suddenly left me during childhood, when I was expected to join my classmates in enthusiastically singing the Horst Wessel song that goes "When Jewish blood comes spurting from the knife then all goes really well. . . ."

During my "non-singing" years—long after I had left Germany—I was occasionally the guest of friends at Passover Seder celebrations. There I heard certain Passover songs for the first time. I did not participate in singing because "I could not sing." I merely listened. Yet years later, during my marriage, when I conducted Seder services for my family, I discovered that I had learned these songs, and was able to sing them with much enthusiasm.[2]

Upon arriving in Israel, we moved to a residential *ulpan* where a very sophisticated program for teaching the Hebrew language to newcomers took place. Here our everyday needs—food, lodging, and child care—were provided for while we engaged in an intensive program of studying the language.

For most people this program works well. They learn the language. But the program did not work for me. I simply could not learn the Hebrew language. During three months of classes, as I remember it, I never once spoke during class. I froze. And without speaking, one obviously cannot learn to speak a language. Perhaps I was assuming that I could replicate my singing experience, that I could learn the language without speaking it. More likely, though, I was telling myself that learning a new language would open me up to frightening issues. The safest thing was not to learn it. At the time I had no understanding of what I was doing, at least not consciously.

German immigrants who came to Israel in the 1930s had a reputation for holding onto German as their chief language. These "Yekkes" did learn Hebrew, but they tended to feel superior to Hebrew-speakers, to regard German as a more dignified and sophisticated language. I, on the other hand, had the greatest difficulty learning any Hebrew at all, and not because I felt superior, but because I felt intimidated by and terrified of confronting this new language.

Because of my sense of terror I could not function well in the Hebrew language. I began teaching in English. No one at my university pressed me to teach in Hebrew, but I knew I should be—if not immediately, then surely within a few years. I did function minimally. I could buy a loaf of bread by asking for it in Hebrew. But I was nowhere near the level of proficiency that would allow me to teach in Hebrew.

I have since heard of studies of child-survivors of horrors who were transported to a country where they knew no one. They knew neither the customs nor the language of that country. Nonetheless, most of these children made a reasonably adequate adjustment. They learned the new language and operated within it successfully. But later in life, if they were called upon to make another major transition, including having to learn another new language, then all the trauma of the first transition broke out into the open. They suddenly reverted to being little children who had been unable to express their fears, forebodings, and terror.

This is what apparently happened to me in Israel. Here I was, an adult with a family of my own, holding a highly prestigious position. (In Israel, being a full professor with lifetime tenure is even more prestigious than it is in the United States.) Nonetheless, I felt like a frightened child who could not understand what people around him were saying. By not learning the language I was making myself into a child, one who felt terribly alone and lost and who could not function as an adult. Let me give just one example. At Tel Aviv University I was the only full professor of sociology. I was therefore the sociology faculty's representative on the University Senate—the governing body of the university. In the Senate deliberations, which were conducted in Hebrew, I could not understand what anyone was saying. To say that this was embarrassing would be an understatement.

My mounting discomfort caused us to change our plans, and we eventually returned to North America. By then, however, I had re-established a feeling of linkage between me and the German language. Without that feeling I could not have considered visiting Germany.

Why was I yearning to go back to Oberlauringen? What was I looking for? Was I trying to address my homelessness? Or, more accurately, my "placelessness"?

Place seems to be the key issue I was addressing. In no place did I ever feel at one with the world, and this nurtured the urge to move, move, move. I think I was looking for a place through which I could affirm that I belong here, on this earth. And where better to look for that affirmation than the place where I was born?

Perhaps I also was attempting to find a place, a physical location, where I could mourn my loved ones in a tangible way. In the United States, Vietnam War veterans and their families seem to have found that the Vietnam Memorial in Washington provides them with a place, a physical location, where they can start to focus their mourning for their loved ones who fell in that war. Here, at long last, grief could be expressed in a tangible way. So I seem to have sought a place where my mourning could begin to have focus and be expressed in a tangible way. In the case of the Vietnam mourners, this starting point means locating the name of the loved one inscribed on the memorial and then, literally and physically touching the name.[3] The memorial becomes the gravesite. Perhaps I subconsciously believed that Oberlauringen was such a gravesite, where my diffuse mourning could finally be focused and that I could thereby achieve greater inner peace.

While finding a tangible place to mourn is part of the story, it is not the whole story. At the time I seriously considered visiting Germany, there was a demon at work within me. When the Second World War ended, in 1945, I made inquiries about the fate of my parents and my brother to various search organizations, chiefly the Red Cross. I received information that they had been deported to Poland and were officially declared dead. But at the time I did not go to Poland or to Germany to look for them.

It seemed hopeless. And, I was only seventeen years old when I received confirmation that my family had perished. But some people, I have since learned, went to look for their loved ones despite such official reports. And in 1984, after attending a Holocaust commemoration event in Washington, I also resumed looking. To this day I make inquiries. Whenever I meet someone who was in camp Westerbork (in Holland), where my brother was briefly held before being sent to the death camp of Sobibor, I ask whether they knew a Ludwig Katz. Earlier, in 1967, I went to Holland and made inquiries. But I did not go to Germany.

My not searching for my parents was not accidental. Whenever I thought of looking for my parents—and I did think about looking for my parents— I was struck by a terrible fear that I might find them *alive*. I was terrified that I might actually find them, and that they were not dead. This was my personal demon, at work within me.

The first time I admitted this openly, to myself and to others, was in the year 1991, forty-six years after I had received official confirmation of my parents' death and long after my return to Oberlauringen in 1979. The expression of fear that my parents were alive came out of me, without warning, during a group session at a conference of child-survivors of the Holocaust. Did I want my parents to be dead?

As I mentioned previously, my parents had sent me to England in 1939 under the auspices of a child refugee program when it became clear that they could not leave Germany. After I arrived in England, I wrote to them only about four times during the three years when it was still possible to write to them, before they were deported to their death. (One could write letters until the war started, and twenty-five–word messages through the Red Cross during the war.) I knew full well that hearing from their child was one of the few things for which they lived. By not writing to them, was I trying to kill them? Or, at least, wish them out of my life? (My sister, I later found out, also wrote to them very rarely.)

The 1991 group session of fellow child-survivors was led by a very wise psychologist. His response to my outburst was a gentle question: "What did you want from your parents?" My answer came in the high-pitched tearful voice of a little boy: "I wanted them to take care of me." This awakening took place when I was sixty-three years old.

In June 1992 my personal demon raised its head again. I had read a book about persons who had saved Jews during the Holocaust. The book was much praised, yet I found myself becoming very upset—angry, in a state of turmoil, and feeling physically ill—in response to that book. For quite a while I was too distraught to understand why I was so upset. Why was I reacting so negatively to what others regarded as a story of glorious human courage?

Then it dawned on me what my issue was. Why had no one saved my parents? And, closer to me, why had I not done more to save my parents? In recent years I have heard of refugee children in England who persuaded adults they met to sponsor the rescue of their parents. I had failed to do so. It did occur to me, but I did not do so. This is why I was so furious. Suddenly it came to me: I must write about my visit to Oberlauringen. It would be my one effort to "do more" about my parents. This is how this chapter was born.

Memory

In preparation for my visit to Oberlauringen, I asked my sister for names of persons whom I might contact. She gave me the names of two of her former classmates. I wrote to them, saying that I should like to visit. They replied very warmly, saying they looked forward to the visit.

Why did I need to ask my sister for names? I remembered each Jewish person in the village. I remembered their names, their faces, the houses where they had lived. I remembered their personalities, their crazinesses and kindnesses. I remembered their seats in the synagogue, and how they said their prayers. I remembered their work. I remembered their voices.

I could not, however, remember a single Christian person. Not a name, not a face, not a house. Not a voice. Not a look. The world of non-Jews—of Christians—was void, and to enter into this void I had to ask my sister for names. I had to contact Christians because all the Jews, as far as I knew, were gone. I could not contact any of them.

Upon our arrival in Oberlauringen, my wife and I were greeted very enthusiastically, and even affectionately, by the two women to whom I had written. But I did not remember them, and I did not remember a single other person I met that day—not even a man who came up to me, saying, "Don't you remember me? We were the two smallest ones in class and we always sat together." I did not tell him so, but I did not remember him. During my visit no memory of individual Christians in the village came back.

I can now speculate about this selective amnesia of mine. When it happened, however, I did not understand what was going on. Clearly one's subconscious mind can speak honestly and directly, even when one's conscious mind is indirect, fearful, and dishonest. That entire day I adopted a friendly posture toward the villagers, smiling and listening. After I left, the next day and for weeks thereafter, I felt utterly furious. Perhaps my selective amnesia—with its not-so-subtle expression of hostility—was the one honest part of my visit.

The recollections recounted by the villagers centered on their own hardships during the Second World War. They told me at length about the shortage of food and other basic necessities they had suffered. They told me about so many of their sons who had died. More than half of the villagers' sons had not returned from the war. They grieved for them to that day. They had erected a plaque in the center of the village, bearing the name of each one who did not return.

Where were the names of the Jews? Where was my brother's name? He, too, did not return. He, too, was young and had yet to live his life. I did not have the presence of mind and the courage to ask about the absence of Jewish names on the plaque. (Some months later I wrote to one of the women who had so warmly hosted my visit and I mentioned the absence of Jewish names on the plaque. I never received a reply.)

During my visit the villagers did not ask me about my life after I left the village. Not one question. They, too, had selective amnesia.

The villagers did remember that shortly after the war ended—that is, thirty-four years before our conversation took place—a Jewish girl, slightly older than I, returned to the village one day. She had left the village with her family shortly after I had. When she returned, she had a camera and took pictures. And she talked to no-one. After thirty-four years the villagers remembered that she talked to no-one! Her silence was loud enough to be heard thirty-four years later. It remained a haunting memory. Perhaps this was fitting punishment for their own silence during the time of moral challenge.

Yet we must face the fact that memory can also be very complicated and bewildering. The Holocaust has generated an immensely powerful literature. It captures some of the essence of the horrors. From the diary of Anne Frank to the writings of Elie Wiesel, our hearts are torn asunder as we read and remember. Ellen Fine, an American professor, draws a bead on this issue. In discussing the French writer Myriam Anissimov, Fine comments:

> She poignantly portrays the inner landscape of the haunted and the hunted—those who have lost their official status as persons, those forced to live with the perpetual threat of a death sentence, and those innocents who finish by believing in their own guilt.[4]

Fine goes on to give us a clue about the bewildering limitations of memory in observing that "Myriam Anissimov cannot rid herself of the past. Writing and remembering are forms of bearing witness, but they do not set her free. . . . The wounds do not heal but only deepen in time."

Much of Elie Wiesel's work suggests the same thing. With time, the wounds only get deeper.

Since my trip to Oberlauringen I have come to realize that memory—even when expressed by superbly gifted artists—is not enough. It is not enough for the task of producing safeguards against future horrors. Shocking us about the past by revealing the horror of the horrors is not enough. To be sure, hallowing the memory of the innocent victims is an important part of the mourning process, but mourning is not enough.

While we should encourage and preserve the artist's version of the events and their aftermath, we desperately need, in addition, the scientist's creative efforts to help us move beyond the impotence we still have in the face of the monstrous evil that humans repeatedly inflict upon one another. This is what I have been trying to do in writings since 1982; it is my "second journey."

I firmly believe that scientists who analyze human behavior can help free us from our ignorance about the workings of human nature that bear on the production of evil. Yes, we already have a vast amount of information about the horrors we inflict on one another. But our level of comprehension, our understanding of this information, is about where the physical and biological sciences were a thousand years ago. The issue is not that human behavior is more complicated than other phenomena in the natural world. The issue is that we have barely begun to develop the scientific tools—the ways of looking, the ways of dissecting what we see, and the mental constructs with which to do these things—that will move us beyond mysticism and impotence when it comes to horrendous human behavior.

Einstein is reported to have said that God has not made the task of understanding nature easy, but that God does not play games with us. That is, God does not act capriciously and arbitrarily. There is order in nature, and the human mind can understand much of that order. (Many believers in religious mysticism who believe in a God contend that God's ways are entirely beyond human understanding. I do not agree with that mystic view.) It takes courage and imagination and discipline to discover the order in nature. When it comes to massive human horrors, we have been terribly unsuccessful at discovering how this portion of nature's system works. Yet I believe we have been given the capacity to discover it. We need to use this capacity. As we do so, we must be prepared not only to honor memory, to pay attention to what has actually happened; we must also be prepared to dissect memory, to look at memory dispassionately, rigorously and imaginatively, to ask uncomfortable questions. Memory will thereby help us serve our future.

Jewish prayers can teach us something relevant here. They frequently distinguish between Knowledge, Understanding (or Insight), and Wisdom. The role of science is to transform Knowledge—raw information—into valid Understanding of how things work. This requires far more than assembling raw information. Facts do not speak for themselves, contrary to the popular saying. We need the role of Wisdom, the wise uses of valid Understanding. This goes beyond the realm of science into morality, religion, and faith. If we succeed in improving the *science* of human social behavior we will then be faced with ever-more challenges of Wisdom—how to make morally justifiable use of that Understanding. In this book I concentrate on the previous, the developing-science phase.

Primo Levi, himself a Holocaust survivor, ably demonstrated the role of science. His writings exemplify the dispassionate and insightful thinking of the scientist when he wrote about his experiences at Auschwitz in his books *Survival in Auschwitz* and *The Drowned and the Saved*. His other books, such as *The Periodic Table* and *Other People's Trades*, give us a glimpse of an Auschwitz survivor re-embracing life with some joy, vitality, and the intellectual vigor of scientific thinking. While Levi's ultimate suicide raises discomforting questions, these questions cannot diminish this scientist's challenging contributions to life and the living, and his legacy. We must continue what he began: the transformation of Knowledge into Insight, with a glimpse of Wisdom at the end of the tunnel. Sometimes Insight comes to us from a single event that can become a critical incident for illuminating our social landscape, for showing us a piece of reality we did not recognize before, for casting a shadow over the future.

Events as Critical Incidents

President Reagan's visit to the German cemetery at Bitburg was one such critical incident event.[5] It illuminated the lingering bearing of the Holocaust in the life of American Jews while, at the same time, showing the vulnerabilities and strengths of American Jews. I shall discuss this more fully in a later section.

Similarly, near the end of the nineteenth century, the Dreyfuss Affair[6] was a critical incident that illuminated widespread and deep anti-Semitism in France. It brought into the open the second-class status of Jews in France at that time, a condition that had been comfortably hidden away. But the Dreyfuss Affair went beyond clarifying a state of affairs in France at a particular time.

It also cast a long shadow over the future. The anti-Semitic actions of the Vichy regime during the Nazi German occupation of France was but a replay of the Dreyfuss Affair some forty years earlier.

Critical incidents characteristically cast a shadow over the future. They become *riders* that make an imprint on the future. Pearl Harbor, for example, has become a rider; it has left an imprint on much of America's political life since the time of the Japanese attack on this American port.

From my years in Oberlauringen, the events of Kristallnacht stand out as a critical incident. In one sense Kristallnacht was the culmination of a series of earlier harassments of us Jews living in Oberlauringen. But it was also a singular event that transformed everything, that cast a permanent shadow over the future and made it abundantly clear that Jews had no future in this village of Oberlauringen, or in this country of Germany.

The event that foreshadowed Kristallnacht for my family took place shortly after Hitler came to power in 1933. One night all our windows were smashed. To my knowledge ours was the only house so attacked. My father went to the police. Since there was no police force in our small village, he went to the county authorities located about an hour's bicycle ride away. At that time the police were still friendly to us and supportive. The police encouraged my father to go away from the village for a while, and they said they would advise him when it was safe to come back.

My father went to the town of Mellrichstadt, where he was born. His older brother and his family still lived there in the family's home of generations of Katzes. We felt fearful. But the authorities seemed to be on our side despite the actions by what everyone regarded as Nazi ruffians, who did not represent the government. Needless to say, no one who participated in the attack on us was identified or caught. After some weeks my father returned.

By 1938, when Kristallnacht took place, Jews could no longer count on support from the police or any other agency of the government. We also did not receive any support from the non-Jewish people of the village. We were alone.

There were many rumblings which foreshadowed that day of destruction. A Jew had assassinated a German embassy official in France, and the Nazi propaganda machine began full-blast attacks on Jews. They claimed there was a Jewish "plot." We felt very fearful and apprehensive.

On November 9, the day before my eleventh birthday, there was a roundup of all Jewish men in the village. My father and my brother (who was seventeen years old) were among those picked up and driven away. The women and children were left behind.

In the evening, my mother and I went to stay with our neighbor, the village baker—actually with his family, because the baker himself had also been taken away. We joined his wife and daughter, Margot, who was about seven years old, and with whom I often played. We hid in the attic. After nightfall we heard a great deal of commotion: cars driving up, men breaking into the house, things smashing, and much yelling of "Where are the Jews?"

We were terrified. Were they going to find us and kill us? Would we live through the night? After what seemed like an eternity, they left. We stayed in the attic, huddled together, until the morning.

When we finally did go downstairs, we had to climb over shattered glass and broken furniture. When my mother and I went over to our own house, we found that the front door had been smashed. All windows were broken. All the furniture—high European furniture with glass fronts—had been toppled over and smashed. The feather beds had been ripped open. Broken glass was everywhere. It was eerily quiet as we climbed over the rubble of what had been our belongings and that had, in the past, given us a measure of privacy and joy.

The nearby synagogue had been desecrated. The sacred Torah scrolls had been taken out of the synagogue and thrown onto piles of manure (remember, this was a farming community).

At some subconscious level, awareness of this came back to me on my visit to Oberlauringen in 1979. During that visit I went into our house, into the Jewish cemetery, into the house of the Christians who were our hosts. I was free to go wherever I wanted to go. But there was one building I was unable to enter. It was the synagogue. It was now a bank. I stood in front of it, paralyzed, unable to move.

Why did this metamorphosis of the synagogue shatter me? I had thought I had left religion behind. After leaving home in 1939 I had lived in a very secular, and rather anti-religious, boarding school in England. After finishing school, I had cut off most of my ties to religious Judaism for almost thirty years. Yet standing in front of the former synagogue in 1979, I was reacting in stunned pain against the desecration of sacred Jewish religious symbols. Turning the synagogue into a bank desecrated it a second time. It shattered me since, in my heart, this synagogue was still my synagogue—where my Hebrew name was inscribed in a Torah wrapping to celebrate my birth and my membership in this community, where my father and mother each had a fixed place (being an orthodox synagogue, men and women were separate) where they worshipped and where I, as a child, had eagerly joined them, feeling sheltered and comforted.

Some weeks after Kristallnacht the men in our family returned. My father and brother, it turned out, had been held at a regional prison some sixty miles away. Others, those who still owned some property (among them Margot's father), had been sent to concentration camps. Upon their return some time later, I could not recognize Margot's father. They did not talk about their experiences, but they did not need to talk. Their haunted look, from their hollowed eyes, spoke louder than words.

During my 1979 visit I learned about Margot's fate. I was told that there had been a Christian family in the next village who helped to save some Jews. They had offered to hide Margot, but Margot refused to leave her parents. When the roundup for deportation came, in 1942, Margot's father committed suicide. Margot and her mother—together with my parents—were sent off to their death.

They did not survive. Those of us who did survive face burdens. In a fictional story about a Holocaust survivor, *Enemies, A Love Story,* Isaac Bashevis Singer tells the tale of how a man carries with him his hayloft hiding place for the rest of his days. It shows up in the fact that he keeps manufacturing turbulence for himself. He has three wives simultaneously, and tries to keep each one matrimonially happy and unaware of each other. He is also unable to obtain and hold onto work that is anywhere near his intellectual capacity.

I do not adopt this particular method of keeping my life in a state of turbulence, but I do manage to produce and retain turbulence for myself, as my movings and escapings from success demonstrate. Am I still carrying the attic (where I hid during Kristallnacht) around with me? Or am I finally transforming my attic into a laboratory that contributes to a more potent science of human behavior? I hope it is the latter.

Encounters

My first impression on arriving in Oberlauringen in 1979 was rather disconcerting. The place was much larger and more prosperous than I remembered it. The rough unpaved streets I remembered were now neatly paved. Main Street, where we had lived at number fifty-seven, no longer stood out as the only paved street. Now there was running water in every house, while I remembered the hand-operated pump some distance from our house where the women used to get water for their families. Now there were telephones in every house, while I remembered only one telephone, located in the post office. Now there were cars. Now there were television sets.

The houses looked neat, prosperous, and caringly maintained. There were a lot of flowers. Yes, there were still a few of the very old buildings I remembered, but most of the village looked like a birthday cake with the words "1960s suburbia" sprayed on it in yummy sugar letters. Along with the indoor plumbing, individuals commuting to jobs in nearby towns, and people having contact with American troops, came a touch of worldliness that was different from what I remembered. It was no longer a rural village.

I suppose I expected to find drabness and decay. Instead I found Western-style comfortable living combined with Germanic neatness and love of good housekeeping. This triggered positive responses in my reluctant heart.

It was also vexing to see the villagers living so well and seemingly achieving some of the dreams I still have about how to live a contented life.

My own Germanic habits came out in the fact that I was rigidly following a very tight, preplanned time schedule in my visit to Oberlauringen. I arrived in midmorning and planned to leave that same afternoon. I only left time for meeting "older" people who might be able to shed light on my parents' last days. I left no time for meeting children, or current school teachers, or priests and ministers, or young farmers and factory workers.

I also left no time to follow up when I heard that our family physician, Dr. Heusinger, was still alive. Dr. Heusinger was the caring family doctor who lived in the next village and who had overseen my birth and everything else connected to our family's medical history. He is the one Christian whose name came back to me during the visit. I remembered him with fondness, awe, and unlimited trust. In retrospect, it would have been valuable to have talked to him. He died shortly after my visit to Oberlauringen.

The two women who were our hosts were most pleasant and helpful. They introduced us to people. They guided us, showing us what was new and what was old. They encouraged us to stay longer. They could not have been friendlier and warmer.

I went to my former house. The outside was virtually unchanged. It still served as a family home and a butcher shop, although the sign "Metzgerei Max Katz" was gone. I had assumed, somehow, that the sign would still be there. Or, at least, that beneath the current paint there would still be a faint indication of where the sign had been. But no, there was no indication that this had been the Katz butcher shop, the Katz home.

The people who now lived in the house were not the ones who had taken our house away. They were from another generation and from another locality. They had moved to Oberlauringen just a few years earlier and had not been involved in displacing my parents. They were uncomplicatedly friendly and open. They let me roam around the house in any way I wished. And roam I did, from the attic to the cellar.

The cellar, I recalled, was the place where my father stored meat. (We had no refrigerator. My father also kept meat in cold storage in a cave in the mountains, just beyond the village.) The attic had been my favorite play area. I found myself automatically—and with some desperation—looking for things with which I might have played. But I found none. There were no remnants to link me to my childhood. My childhood was not being returned to me.

Both attic and cellar were unchanged from what I remembered. The house owners told me that I was fortunate to have come when I did because they were about to "modernize" the cellar. The rest of the house had already been thoroughly modernized, with running water as the harbinger of modern bathrooms, a modern kitchen, and all sorts of electrical appliances. My home had been transformed into modernity.

In the afternoon we were invited to the home of an elderly woman. I estimate she was in her mid-eighties. We sat down for coffee and cake. Here, in the *gemuetliche* setting, we were told about the hardships they had endured during the war—the shortage of food, of clothing, of fuel.

In this conversation, and throughout the day, no-one asked me about my hardships during this period. I, too, had gone through a period when I did not have enough to eat. It happened in New York, after my arrival in America. I had no job and not enough money to buy food. I lived on stale bread.

The elderly woman said that she had been very kind to my mother. She had given my mother food, in exchange for her silver. As I heard this I kept on listening attentively and smiling. The impact of what the woman had been saying did not hit me until the next day, when I had already left the village. It had not occurred to me earlier that this woman was proud of the fact that she had given my mother food as an excuse for robbing her of precious belongings. And it did not occur to me until very recently, two decades later, that the word "silver" might not only have included silverware—knives, forks, and spoons—but also any jewelry my mother might have had. Perhaps my mother still had a silver necklace, or a brooch. And the woman took it. And I had just sat there and smiled.

A number of the conversations throughout the day centered on the hardships the villagers had endured during the war. I heard them make the identical statement they had made in the 1930s, forty years earlier: "We are just little people. What could we do? It's the government."

As I see it now, they were really asking for forgiveness. They wanted me to absolve them of responsibility. Despite my attentiveness and my frozen smile, I was in no mood to forgive and to absolve. I was deeply furious with these people. They had stood by when innocent Jews, who had lived among them for generations, were hounded and, eventually, murdered.

During my visit I was compounding my own fury by not expressing it. If I had expressed it, perhaps we might have been able to reach some sort of meeting of minds. This could have contributed to mutual healing. But I was not ready. I just listened and smiled, and vaguely felt boiling inside.

Several persons mentioned that I must see Ernestine. Ernestine, they told me, had helped the Jews. It turned out that Ernestine had been the one person who had not distanced herself from the Jews. When Jews had already been deprived of their livelihood and their houses and had been forced to move together into one house (this happened after I was sent to England), Ernestine brought them food. As best she could, Ernestine stood by the Jews, surely a very unpopular thing to do at that time.

I went to see Ernestine. Although I did not recall it, she had apparently worked in our household when I was young. She reminded me that she had diapered me when I was a baby. Despite this intimacy I had not remembered her, but I had the good sense not to tell her so. Although Ernestine was not sophisticated with words, she spoke eloquently. She said what the Nazis did was not right. She talked about my parents. She gave me pictures of herself with my family and with our neighbors. She wept. She made my visit to Oberlauringen worthwhile. She added dignity and decency.

I went to the Jewish cemetery. It was the first time I had ever been to this cemetery. My family are "Cohens," supposed descendants of the priests, who are not allowed to be in the proximity of the dead except when one's immediate family is involved. Cohens are not allowed to go to cemeteries unless members of their immediate family are buried there.

Since my parents were observant orthodox Jews, we had observed this rule while I lived in Oberlauringen. As a child I had many fears and nightmares about death. I knew that death happened but that I must not come near dead persons, lest I be defiled. It did not make matters easier that the special black hearse, used in all Jewish funerals, was parked in a yard behind our house. It constantly reminded me of the frightening face of death.

During my visit to Oberlauringen, I felt that it was perfectly in order—actually, it was absolutely crucial—for me to enter the Jewish cemetery. For one thing, I was no longer an observant orthodox Jew, and therefore forbidden to enter this cemetery. For another, I felt that this cemetery was *my family* cemetery, even though my parents were not buried in it. Since I do not know precisely where and how my parents died, I was, in a way, free to choose where they are buried.

This was my second "burial" of my parents and my brother. While I held my first academic teaching job, in Lubbock, Texas, in 1960, I bought a burial plot and marker for my parents and my brother. It was not a Jewish cemetery. I was then entirely dissaffiliated with, and alienated from, all things Jewish. It did not occur to me at that time that my parents and my brother would have been very pained by the thought of their burial in a non-Jewish cemetery.

The Oberlauringen Jewish cemetery is located about a half mile from the village. It was in immaculate condition. The grass lawns were beautifully maintained and the gravestones were all in place. Apparently the German government was scrupulously tending to the upkeep of Jewish cemeteries that are no longer under the guardianship of a local Jewish congregation.

Since both of my parents had moved to Oberlauringen from elsewhere, I knew that I had no grandparents in this cemetery. The one close person whose grave I located was that of Lilly Schoenfeld, my father's first wife, who died while giving birth to my brother Ludwig. Her grave was in a conspicuous place, near the very front. Perhaps women so often died in the course of childbirth that a special place was reserved for them. Or she was in a location reserved for the families of Cohanim, the priests.

We took pictures of the cemetery.

Beyond Survival: There Is Life beyond Oberlauringen

I returned to Oberlauringen to find out just how much of me had left and how much of me was still there. Am I still running from—and to—Oberlauringen? I have the scars of incomplete survival. Yet the visit to Oberlauringen gave me hope and renewed faith in being able to survive survival.

The great sociologist Emile Durkheim taught us that human beings derive their sense of themselves—who they are, what they are, what their life is about—from the fact that they are part of a larger moral entity.[7] A country can be a moral entity; a community, a village, a town, can be a moral entity; a professional association can be a moral entity; a religious congregation, a church, a synagogue, can be a moral entity; a family can be a moral entity. These entities have a twofold bearing on our lives. From them we derive values and a set of cultural tools for living, including language and symbols. Equally importantly, all this comes in the form of people to whom we are attached precisely because they embody the things we treasure most; our values and culture tools for living.

While Durkheim taught us how moral entities shape our sense of social community, he did not, to my knowledge, pay enough attention to the fact that when people are defined as being outside our own moral entity, we often treat them with total disdain and irreverence. Their lives are not worth living, as the Nazis explicitly put it. When we encounter ethnic wars, or religious wars, or nationalistic wars, we are seeing the consequences of the distinction between those whose values are valued and those whose values are scorned; between people whose lives must be honored and people whose lives must be dishonored; between us and them.

The Nazi credo defined Jews as being outside of the German national moral community. After visiting Oberlauringen, and after reflecting about the early years when I lived there, it seems to me that Jews really were treated as being outside of the German national moral community. The villagers seemed to accept the Nazi credo.

Yet here was Ernestine, teaching me that a German Christian in my village refused to exclude Jews from her moral community. She thereby taught me that I do not need to give Hitler a final victory by accepting his credo that Jews are outside the pale of German or, for that matter, outside the pale of any, moral community. I need no longer carry the burden of the homeless wandering Jew. I can stop moving from place to place, and from job to job.

Ernestine had nursed me when I was a baby. She nursed me again when I came to her fifty years later as an adult, who still felt raw hurt. But the human mind moves slowly. My meeting with Ernestine took place in the summer of 1979. Only as I write these words, in the year 2000, do I realize the meaning of the gift Ernestine gave to me. Sadly, she died in 1987, before I could tell her what her gift means to me.

Other non-Jews also demonstrated that they have included Jews in their moral community. In the French Huguenot village of Le Chambon Sur Lignon, five thousand Christian inhabitants saved about five thousand Jews. Several of my friends, who belong to a Holocaust child-survivor group to which I also belong, bear testimony to the fact that individual Christians saved them. These caring persons took great risks, for themselves and their families, to save the lives of Jews to whom they had little or no previous relationship. These persons teach us that there are humane, decent, and courageous human beings in this world. These persons also teach us that we who were cast out are not outcasts. We were persecuted, but we do not deserve a life of rootless wanderings.

The issue for the survivor is how, then, to get on with life, how to live beyond survival. Viktor Frankl, a psychiatrist who survived Auschwitz, tells us that the fundamental element of one's living is the meaning one finds in one's life. Such *meaning* is not simply handed to us. It must be discovered, by each one of us, by oneself. One may find meaning in adoring nature, or in doing creative work, or in love relationships to persons. According to Frankl, meaning can also be found in suffering, as he personally discovered in his Auschwitz experience. In his book *Man's Search for Meaning,* Frankl tells us that, "In spite of all the enforced physical and mental primitiveness of life in a concentration camp, it was possible for spiritual life to deepen." He continues: "even the helpless victim of a hopeless situation, facing a fate he cannot change, may rise above himself, may grow beyond himself, and by doing so change himself."[8]

I would add, in the tradition of Durkheim, that the individual must find meaning in a way that links one to a human moral community, where that community can provide an individual with spiritual nurturance. It can also lead to reality testing. An entirely private meaning, on the other hand, can sever the bond between the individual and his society, and human societies have a limited tolerance for "private worlds." Persons living in extremely private worlds are shunted to mental hospitals.

Raymond Federman, a novelist, sees creative writing as a way of extracting meaning, and life-sustaining vitality, from the horrors of the Holocaust. In his own literary writings he specifically addresses Holocaust issues. He does so with an emphasis on creativity:

> The fact of being a survivor, of living with one's death behind, in a way makes you free. . . . it is no longer through the functions of memory that one will confront the issue [of the Holocaust], but with the power of the imagination.[9]

My writings since 1982 have built on these perspectives, that one can derive life-sustaining meaning from the Holocaust, in the sense that Frankl has shown us, and that creativity is needed as we confront the Holocaust, as Federman has shown us. But I have chosen the posture of the scientist. I do not question the unique contribution of the artist, such as Federman. But there is another dimension to the Holocaust, much neglected and barely explored. It is the dimension of what science can contribute.

The philosopher Emil Fackenheim contributed a famous dictum to Jews: Do not give Hitler a posthumous victory by giving up on your religion.[10] I hope one can develop and justify a related dictum: When it comes to combatting human horrors, do not give up on science. Despite the disgraceful contributions to the Holocaust by many a scientist and despite the failure thus far to discover effective predictors of, and antidotes to, the extremes of human evil, I say, *do not give up on science.*

Above my desk I keep a sign that reads, "606." It is a reminder about Paul Ehrlich, a pioneering biochemist and Nobel Prize winner who lived early in the twentieth century. He developed the first effective drug against syphilis. Ehrlich named the drug Salvarsan 606. Why 606? Because he had had 605 failures before he found the one that worked. Let us not be discouraged by our failure, thus far, to devise an effective scientific theory about massive evil. Let us continue until we discover one with the power to actually change human behavior.

The ashes of the Holocaust may yet reveal the process by which ordinary humans can be brought to practice horrendous behavior and, from there, lead us to understand how to prevent human horrors of the sort practiced by the Nazi regime. This would be a real victory over Hitler. It would also amount to extracting a gift to humankind from so much horror.

PART TWO

Beyond Surviving:
More of the First Journey

After my visit to Oberlauringen, I gradually began to realize that long after physically surviving a horror one needs to learn how to live again, how to survive surviving. To do so, survivors must not only confront the past, they must confront the future. And they must do so in two ways; as members of a people and as individuals.

To illustrate the concept of surviving as members of a people, I shall discuss the Bitburg Affair. This event suddenly awakened Jews to the realization that, as a people, they had unresolved and still very real issues about their survival to confront. Among Jews, fear for their survival had been kindled by the Nazi Holocaust. Following the West's victory over Nazism and the establishment of a Jewish state, it was assumed that Jews no longer feared for the survival of the Jewish people. But the Bitburg Affair demonstrated an entirely different reality, namely that these fears had persisted in dormant form, subject to dramatic reactivation by events such as President Reagan's plan to visit the German military cemetery at Bitburg. The Bitburg Affair caused dormant memories to erupt and created unanticipated political alignments and pressures. It also demonstrated that, since the Holocaust, Jews had learned something about the power of social activism.

As an individual, given a traumatic experience in one's past there is much incentive to remain locked into that past and its crippling debilitations. The challenge is to find ways to confront the future in a spirit of openness to new opportunities and embrace of life. In my case, I began to confront this fact only about forty years after the Holocaust ended.

CHAPTER TWO

The Bitburg Affair

Initial Impressions

The Bitburg Affair began with the announcement that during his official visit to West Germany in 1985, President Ronald Reagan would visit the German military cemetery at the town of Bitburg. The visit was to be part of the process of cementing relations between the United States and modern West Germany, a solid ally of the West in its political struggle against the Communist world during the Cold War. Within days of the announcement, major newspapers reported that the Bitburg cemetery contained not only graves of ordinary German soldiers, but also graves of SS men—notorious enforcers of the most gruesome parts of the Nazi agenda. These reports produced gasps of surprise, followed by a wave of shock that was deep, widespread, and profound.

American veterans were greatly offended, especially when President Reagan clumsily tried to defuse the issue by saying that all Germans who took part in the war, soldiers and SS alike, did so pretty much against their own will; that these individuals, just as American soldiers, were themselves innocent victims.

Those who really knew World War II were not assuaged by this sort of reasoning. They remembered the mass murder of captured American soldiers by the SS in that very area of Germany the president was planning to visit. Perhaps the murderers themselves now rested in the Bitburg cemetery. The National Commander of the American Legion wrote, in an editorial in the newspaper *USA Today* (on 15 April 1985):

American veterans—and not only those who fought during World
War II—have spoken with one voice in response to President Reagan's
plan to honor German war dead at West Germany's Bitburg cemetery next month: Don't do it . . .[1]

The greatest shock of all was felt by American Jewry, and they responded in kind. They saw a most odious sign in the indiscriminate honoring
of SS men alongside ordinary German soldiers, to be undertaken by an
American president at the request of the West German chancellor, Helmut
Kohl. Here, all of a sudden, they said, was an effort to whitewash the Nazi
past. Here, they said, the Holocaust's perpetrators were being forgiven, even
honored. Here, Germany's ghoulish war against the Jews was being side-
stepped in favor of modern realpolitik, where today's friends are prepared to
ignore yesterday's deeds, however horrendous these deeds were.

One Jewish leader, an official of the Anti-Defamation League and himself a survivor of the Holocaust, stated:

My first reaction was disbelief—it was impossible. No president
would honor Nazi SS murderers by placing a wreath on their graves.
Not 40 years or 400 years after the Holocaust . . .
The shock. How could he do this? What motivated him?[2]

A Critical Incident

As I discussed in chapter one, in the course of a community's ongoing life
there may occur an event that has far-reaching meaning. Such an event can
serve as an indicator of the real content of the social order under which we
exist. It can thereby clarify fundamental characteristics of that social order. It
can bring out into the open things we do not ordinarily notice, or prefer not
to notice. And it can produce profound changes. We call such an event a
"critical incident."

President Reagan's proposed visit to Bitburg was such a critical incident.
For American Jews, here was an American president who was, and remained,
a very good friend of theirs, and yet he seemingly trampled upon the victims
of the Nazi Holocaust. He appeared to show gross disregard for the suffering
Jews had endured during that era. Further, he appeared to show a lack of
awareness of just how deeply and personally Jews still felt about the Holocaust.

It mattered little that President Reagan later added a visit to a former
concentration camp to his German itinerary, and there made a most moving
speech about the Holocaust. It also mattered little that, while at the Bitburg
cemetery, he made no public speeches and that the visit, itself, was deliber-

ately short. The damage was done, irrevocably so, and to such an extent that the visit became a critical incident that aroused in Jews profound questions about their security in a Christian world.

Not only did Jews remember the Holocaust, with its millions of Jewish victims. Perhaps more poignantly, those who were old enough suddenly remembered Jewish helplessness in the 1930s, the years leading up to the massacre of the Jews. They remembered that the Roosevelt administration—so humane in many of its social policies—was tardy and recalcitrant when it came to providing practical help to the endangered Jews of Europe. Many American Jews suddenly saw themselves, again, as a vulnerable minority group.

To the credit of American Jews, the Bitburg critical incident galvanized them to action. They energetically made their concerns known. They did so far more effectively than their parents had done in the 1930s. The president, on his part, demonstrated more realistic concern for Jewish sensitivities and fears than did Franklin Roosevelt. After all, we were not back in the 1930s when Jews were fearful of expressing themselves publicly and politically, and when an American president could quietly brush off requests made by Jews (they did tend to be "requests" rather than demands).

After the Bitburg critical incident, life for American Jews may not ever be the same again, much as the Dreyfuss Affair in France at the turn of the twentieth century altered the mind-set of French Jews. These critical incidents demonstrated to many Jews in modern Western countries that even when anti-Semitism was not on open display, subterranean anti-Semitism might be quite pervasive. Such subterranean anti-Semitism might, on occasion, be available for gruesome activation. They remembered the "assimilated" Jews of Germany before the Hitler period, who believed that in a modern sophisticated country such as Germany, anti-Semitism had been largely eliminated. Bitburg brought Jews back to a reality they had preferred to ignore. Perhaps, they now seemed to say, there are some Jewish concerns that even the most well-intentioned non-Jews of America do not share.

Is this Jewish paranoia? Or is this a basic aspect of being a minority group in a land of minority groups, where each group retains some memory of its particular history, and therefrom holds on to some perspectives, commitments, and concerns that other groups do not share? Perhaps even in a melting-pot society, such as the United States, each ethnic group retains some elements in its historic identity that other groups do not share, and can never share.

About Surprises: A Matter of Linkage and Amalgamation

Let us now take a deeper look at the surprises that accompanied the Bitburg Affair. We need to go beyond merely describing how the surprises manifested themselves and ask why Jews and veterans were so surprised. And why, in turn, the Reagan administration was so surprised by the response to its announcement of the planned visit.

The answer to these questions lies in a process of linkage and amalgamation among four different issues:

1. For the Reagan administration, the Bitburg visit was meant to underscore West Germany's role as a strong ally in the West's forty-year-long and steadfast Cold War confrontation with the Communist East European bloc of nations. Since World War II, this confrontation had become a core ingredient in the political life of Europe and America. In the wake of becoming the dominant economic power of Western Europe, Germany also had become a very staunch political component of the Western alliance, despite occasional pointed reminders, by its erstwhile Western enemies, that her past required some atoning.

    Right before the time of the Bitburg Affair the German government had, once again, proven its political loyalty to the United States by permitting advanced American weaponry—including, presumably, nuclear weapons—on its soil. Other Western allies, and quite a number of vocal German citizens, regarded these weapons with undisguised misgivings. For his political loyalty to the United States, Chancellor Kohl, personally, needed to be thanked and supported. In short, the issue here for the Reagan administration was fundamentally one of thanking Chancellor Kohl for his support of the Western Alliance and courting Germany for further support in the future.

2. For Chancellor Kohl, the president's visit represented a move toward a "new" Germany, a Germany resting squarely on its considerable economic accomplishments and consequent stature as a world power. It was time to look ahead, rather than to a past that the present generation had not been guilty of creating. The president's visit would underscore that war dead were war dead, regardless of the side on which they fought, and regardless of the particular unit in which they served their country. Germany had been snubbed long enough when it came to honoring Western war dead. She had paid her dues politically (in her help to the Western Alliance), as well as economically.

    Personally, for Chancellor Kohl, the president's visit offered valuable support in the forthcoming German elections. Kohl could use the glory of standing beside the American president, on German soil, honoring Germans who had given their lives for Germany. (In light of the subsequent events, this calculation backfired.) In short, the issue for Chancellor Kohl was that a new era for Germany was being recognized publicly and internationally.

3. For American Jews, the Bitburg Affair took on gigantic proportions because their minds were still centered on the Holocaust as a palpable terror.
For surviving victims, for families of victims, and for all contemporary
Jews, the Nazi Holocaust remained a burning issue. It was not something
they could readily lay aside. In particular, the SS units were regarded as
unforgivable and unforgettable for the part they played in the Holocaust.

When viewed as a critical incident, the Jewish response to the Bitburg
visit demonstrates that the Holocaust remains a terribly raw wound not
easily healed with time. It may never heal. For Jews, the possibility that
Germany's responsibility for the Holocaust—and the SS culpability in
particular—might be sloughed off is especially repugnant. President
Reagan's proposed visit to Bitburg seemed to ignore this repugnance.
The issue for American Jews was that President Reagan seemed to say,
let us forget the past, including the Holocaust.

4. For many American veterans who had fought against Germany, to honor
the notorious SS indicated profound blindness to the mass executions the
SS carried out of American prisoners of war, as well as the mass executions of Russsian prisoners of war and of Jews.

To be sure, since the end of World War II, we have occassionally seen
a perverse sense of camaraderie among former enemies. We have seen
"reunions" of airmen. I recall one such reunion between British and German airmen who were former enemies. The participants from both sides
toasted one another as good-old-boy gentlemen, basking in wasn't-it-grand-
sport celebrations of their past deadly encounters. But the deeds of the SS
went beyond this level of glorification of war. The deeds of the SS went
beyond any rules of war that even some perverted gentlemen could accept.

The issue for many veterans was that honoring the SS dead did utter
violence to their fellow American soldiers, their buddies, who were victims of the exorbitant brutality of the SS.

For the members of each of these four interest groups, theirs was the all-
important issue for which the Bitburg visit was a critical incident. The Bitburg
visit was a drama that highlighted and revitalized their particular interests and
concerns. Yet the viewpoint of each of the interest groups became linked. The
Bitburg visit became an amalgam of the vital interests and concerns of these
interest groups. This amalgam was not a new alloy, where all the parts coexist
in harmony, forming a new homogeneous entity. Quite the contrary. The new
amalgam consisted of centrifugal forces, each retaining the possibility of quickly
going off into a different direction, since each was ongoingly nurtured by a
different interest group.

Because of this unpredictability, the amalgam represented a particularly difficult predicament for the American government. Internally, none of the four interest groups fully accepted the others' priorities, although the veterans and Jews were roughly in agreement that the Bitburg visit should be cancelled, and the Reagan administration agreed (publicly, at least) with Chancellor Kohl that the visit should go ahead as planned. Externally, as a totality, the amalgam represented a marriage of convenience among fairly uncongenial partners, whose only bond was a passionate conviction that a vital nerve had been touched.

This marriage was potentially explosive because few constraints were in place. Future behavior of each group was highly unpredictable and, therefore, potentially dangerous to those in charge of keeping the nation on a fairly stable course.

~

When the Reagan administration first announced the Bitburg visit, its officials may have been aware of the sensitivities of Jews and American veterans. But they assumed that these concerns could be overridden and kept far in the background. They assumed these issues were not actively linked to the administration's need to reassure the Germans of American political gratitude and support, which the Bitburg visit would symbolize. The Reagan administration officials were wrong. They were surprised by the linkage, and they were forced to take it into account.

Chancellor Kohl, from his vantage point, was not merely concerned with his political priorities (for Germany as well as for himself). He also assumed that President Reagan could pull off the feat of helping to detach the Holocaust memories, once and for all, from the contemporary political and economic realities in which Germany so clearly excelled. Kohl himself had tried to do this in his speeches on a "new" Germany. He welcomed President Reagan for what, he believed, would be some very valuable help in cutting the linkage to the past—a past which he, Kohl, preferred to forget. Kohl was surprised to find that President Reagan, personally, was not quite so ready to forget the Holocaust. He was surprised, too, to find that many citizens of his own country were sympathetic to the issues raised by the American veterans and Jews.

For American veterans, the Reagan administration represented friendly and congenial offialdom. Many of the issues favored by the traditional veterans' associations were favored by this president. These included emphasis on America's military strength and on honoring its armed services. The president's catering to these issues made him attractive to official veterans' associations. The president was their kind of man.

The surprise of the veterans was great when this president, of all people, showed ignorance and insensitivity to some harsh military realities of World

War II. The memory of the murderous activities of the SS was still very much alive to veterans who had had contact with the SS. Although many veterans shared the president's political posture of strong anti-Communism, they were unprepared to renounce the memories of the ghastly deeds of the SS to modern realpolitik, which saw West Germany as a fine, untarnished ally against the Soviets. They were surprised that President Reagan could fail to see, and accept, the linkage between the deeds of the SS and the pain and heroism it had taken for the American military to prevail against such a foe. It had happened during the president's lifetime. How could he have forgotten? How could he disconnect it from his policies?

For Jews, the president's concentration on modern realpolitik seemed to disconnect him from a reality where many American Jews live. Despite the president's expression of support for Jews on many occasions, particularly his strong support for Israel, his Bitburg visit seemed to separate him from a most fundamental Jewish historic and psychological reality. It was not only neglect of the specifics of the Holocaust (and its deep and ongoing meaning for Jews) that Jews found so surprising. For some Jews (I do not know how many) the president appeared to dissociate himself, and his administration, from American Jewry.

The Holocaust is very central to contemporary Jewish life. To many Jews it is as basic an event as the Destruction of the Temple or the Covenant at Sinai. The Holocaust calls some Jews' entire religiosity into question; it reaffirms the religiosity of others. However, it is very vital for all Jews' sense of identity as Jews. When President Reagan announced his Bitburg visit he seemed to separate himself from this core phenomenon in Jewish identity. Jews were surprised that the president could find it in his heart to separate a current American political activity from a reality that is so pervasive, so raw, and so immediate to themselves.

When Jews expressed this sense of linkage of Holocaust memories to current American Jewish life, they found a surprised president. He had not wanted to hurt Jewish sensitivities. He had believed that the Bitburg visit could be separated, benignly, from the Holocaust concerns.

Surprises do not arise out of thin air. They have their roots in social realities. In the case of the president's visit to Bitburg, the surprises themselves were vital indicators within a critical incident that illuminates real differences of political pluralism within which the American president, the German chancellor, American veterans, and American Jews operate.

The Bitburg Surprises: Two Explanations Suggest Themselves

Dormancy

Stated abstractly, a particular item in our sociocultural repertoire exists in a dormant state. Its potency—including its size and potential impact—may be misjudged precisely because it exists in a dormant state. That is, since it is not *active* it is thought not to exist at all or, at least, not to be particularly relevant or dangerous. But once the item is activated it turns out to be far more potent than had been anticipated.

In the case of Jewish sentiments about the Holocaust, the Reagan administration may have been misled by the fact that Jews were not actively and loudly clamoring about a current threat of deep and widespread anti-Semitism in America. Indeed, most polls at that time suggested that anti-Semitism in America was in decline, as seen by both Jews and non-Jews. To be sure, American-Jewish sentiments about the most extreme forms of anti-Semitism, such as the Holocaust, were known to be strong and deep. But it was not believed that the Jews still thought that the Holocaust represented a direct threat to their very existence as Jews.

Little did the Reagan administration realize that, beneath the surface of their public posture, American Jews still thought of the Holocaust as a terrible threat to their very existence—just as, in a personal psychological sense, an individual who was once traumatized may carry the trauma and its accompanying sense of danger to one's very existence—for a lifetime.

For American Jews the Holocaust existed as an event that still had bearing on their lives. It existed as an awesome threat to their identity and survival as Jews. Yet these fears were largely dormant. In the Reagan era they were not being expressed in public ways.

In 1967, threat to Israel's survival in the days leading up to the Six Day War provoked a vital Jewish response. This should have given the message that Jews believed that—because of the Holocaust—their very survival was precarious and easily placed in terrible jeopardy by new events. But Israel had won the Six Day War very decisively and, with it, Jewish survival fears seemed to have dissipated.

In short, Jews still saw the Holocaust as a threat to Jewish survival, but in a dormant mode. Since this concern was not publicly and openly expressed, officials in the Reagan administration discounted it. (Similarly, I suspect that among African Americans the issue of slavery still occupies a powerful, though largely dormant, place. It may yet be capable of profound arousal.) The Reagan officials believed that American Jews had largely come to terms with the Holocaust as a horrible, but past, episode in their history. American Jews were now ready, the officials thought, to get on with their relatively prosperous, well-supported lives and put the Holocaust behind them. Therefore they would raise no objections if their government moved toward a reconciliation with its formerly notorious enemy who had become an ally.

Small Quantity

Alternatively, a small item in our sociocultural repertoire can exist, and persist, in an active state, even though it stands in disagreement with the dominant policies of the country. Since it exists in a small quantity, or it is located in an inconspicuous niche, it may be deemed trivial and nonthreatening to the country's dominant policies. Yet that "small item" may become the catalyst that totally transforms existing behavioral practices and commitments. This is particularly likely to happen when a new *rider* arrives and sponsors a new set of priorities among the existing behavioral practices and commitments.

More concretely, the Reagan administration realized that the Holocaust was important to American Jews. But in the 1980s, only a very small number of Jews seemed to seriously involve themselves in "Holocaust matters." An even smaller number seemed to link it to any active and ongoing American political concerns. Holocaust issues seemed to be quite trivial on the contemporary American scene.

The Reagan administration had friendly relationships with its Jewish constituency. It had nurtured that relationship through its very active help and support of the State of Israel, a major concern to American Jewry. The Republican Party of President Reagan had a number of prominent Jewish supporters in its ranks. Given this situation, the Reagan administration operated on the belief that it was considered well disposed to American Jewry. It felt sufficiently well connected to American Jewry to know the concerns and wishes of that constituency. From the information it was getting from its Jewish supporters, the Reagan administration had no indication that the Holocaust was still a burning issue for many American Jews. If it was of concern it was of concern to only a very small number of individual Jews. Hence, it was believed, Holocaust issues could safely be ignored as a serious component in the contemporary politics of East-West relations.

~

A very unanticipated thing happened when the Bitburg visit was announced. The announcement gave rise to a sudden and highly emotional series of activities. Among Jews, the small band of Holocaust-remembrance activists suddenly found themselves energized and listened to as they had not been in a very long time (not, in fact, since the Six Day War). Suddenly far more Jews took a stand than the Reagan administration had anticipated in what had been a politically sleepy atmosphere.

Among veterans the same thing happened. Following the announced Bitburg visit, there was an upsurge of activity by veterans' organizations and an unanticipated degree of public interest in the views of veterans.

All this was made possible because the Bitburg visit by the president became a new rider to public discourse. It offered an overarching theme that impinged on a whole range of activities. A rider can elicit new priorities among these activities, spelling out what is important and what is not important. The Bitburg rider provided a mandate for new alliances: liberal Jews with conservative Jews; all Jews with veterans' organizations. These were short-term marriages of convenience; they lasted only long enough to shake up the Reagan administration's faith in their realpolitik toward Germany. The Bitburg rider also provided a mandate for creating new priorities among the existing practices: The political hard line of Reaganite anti-Communism had to confront some limits when it came to memory of what the SS, and the Nazis, had done, and when it came to Jews comfortably keeping quiet in the face of reminders of the Holocaust.

Quite unexpectedly, Bitburg became a marker on America's social and political landscape. The incident demonstrated the powerful potentials of dormant components in a society's heritage. It also demonstrated the swirling action of a strong democratic system which, amid the flux and fury of ongoing events, exhibited both a distinctive orderliness and a moral rectitude of its own.

Stated differently, the Bitburg-related linkages and amalgamations show us some of the dynamics of political forces in a democracy. It includes temporary and relatively long-lasting linkages among a society's component parts; it includes separations that may begin as slight fissurs and end as wide chasms; it includes overarching riders that may transform a society's customs by rearranging the priorities among their component parts. In short, in the Bitburg Affair we have a manifestation of a virtual catalogue of societal capacities for re-arranging its component parts. Perhaps even more importantly, the events illuminate ways of mobilizing societal effort.

For me, a bystander with a personal stake in the Holocaust, the Bitburg Affair affirmed that the Jewish community spoke for me. It spoke on my behalf. It fought my fight. The larger American community, in the person of its president, was listening to "our" vehement declarations, our pain, our anger. It replied, saying, "We are with you." I felt, yes, I am an American. I am on a journey of survival through citizenship in this nation. I had moved forward in my first journey.

At about that time I joined a Holocaust survivor group—the child-survivor group in the Baltimore-Washington area. Earlier I had been most reluctant to associate with Holocaust survivors. This, too, was part of my first journey.

CHAPTER THREE

Surviving the Holocaust: The Pain and Reward of Confronting the Future in a Personal Way

For those who survived the Holocaust, or other horrors, there exist two challenges: to keep the past alive and come to terms with that past, including one's own survival; and, beyond it, to recognize that one can still embrace vitality and new purpose in life, that for elderly persons there are unique opportunities to discover new vitality and purpose.

A message to survivors:

We are sometimes afraid to embrace the future, thinking that we are thereby ignoring the frightful memories of the past; that, by embracing the future, we might be dishonoring the memory of loved ones who did not survive. Yet we can embrace the future without desecrating the past. Indeed it is by both remembering the past horrors and embracing the future that we do justice to a message from the past: That we must not allow life's spirit to be extinguished by remaining exclusively locked into the horrors of the past.

By contrast, we may continue to live our lives with the past horrors still so overwhelming that they dominate much of our entire being in the present, and become disabling to our future. We may thereby live in permanent victimhood, enslaved to the past. This can begin when we tell ourselves that we have a sacred obligation to remember the horrors for the sake of our loved ones who perished in the horrors. This is a most noble and justified conviction. It can reach an extreme when we tell ourselves—consciously or unconsciously—that we must try to relive the horrors in order to keep alive the reality of the horrors and thereby, perhaps, protect against future horrors.

We hear the mantra, "We must not forget, so it won't happen again." Sadly, there is very little historical or psychological evidence that remembering will serve as a prophylactic against future horrors. I believe the George Santayana adage that those who forget history are bound to have to re-experience it is cruelly inaccurate. Many horrors are committed by individuals as retribution for horrors they remember against their own ancestors. In the 1990s, Serbs murdered Croats for what Croats had done to Serbs fifty years earlier.

Yes, we must remember the horrors—for the sake of our loved ones, for our process of mourning, for educating the next generation that extreme horrors actually did happen. But let us not be deceived into believing that remembering horrors, and reminding others of the horrors, is by itself a prophylactic, a vaccine against future horrors. Remembering is not enough. Shocking people about horrors is not enough. In the following pages I suggest some ways of moving beyond remembering. You, the reader, may come up with additional ways.

One component of the we-must-not-forget perspective can be that we tell ourselves that we must somehow capture and retain the horrors that our loved ones endured to reduce their loneliness. We tell ourselves that if we, in bountiful love, try to share their suffering, we will diminish their suffering. Yet we know all along that what we are doing is doomed to fail. We cannot capture, we cannot retain, we cannot diminish the horrors that fell upon our loved ones. They endured the horrors and they retain them. No amount of love from us will change that.

By attempting to share the horrors, we give a double victory to those who produced the horrors in the first place. They caused us suffering and we now continue their handiwork by ourselves, upon ourselves, and upon the loved ones in our present life. Adapting Emil Fackenheim's well-known admonition, "do not give Hitler a posthumous victory by giving up on the Jewish religion," we must recognize that when living exclusively in the horrors of the past we are giving Hitler a posthumous victory by giving up on life.

There is an alternative. We can create a real future for ourselves. We can look to the past to enhance life rather than stifle and suffocate life. We can do so by regarding the future, our own future, as rich in possibilities for living an effective life. And we can help transform these possibilities into realities. We do not need to remain victims forever.

This alternative requires that we move beyond the early phase of mourning. We must, and can, once again embrace life. Viktor Frankl, a psychiatrist and Auschwitz survivor, has shown us a way. He tells us that those of us who have survived the Holocaust can discover *meaning* for our life from the horrors of the Holocaust. This meaning can serve us as a vehicle for getting on with life, for embracing the future with a sense of personal mission and gratification, and, even, joy. This discovery of meaning is an entirely personal journey; each one of us has to discover our own route. The book you are reading illustrates my route to discovery of meaning. Others travel by different routes. To clarify such routes it will be well to consider how individuals frequently react to bereavement. (I am relying heavily on Elizabeth Kuebler-Ross' book, *On Death and Dying* [N.Y.: Collier Paperback, 1982].)

Very commonly, the first response to the death of a loved one, especially a sudden death, is utter shock and emotional withdrawal. In this first phase of bereavement the individual tends to turn inward, giving little outward reaction while suffering great unfocused inner pain and turmoil and, not uncommonly, denying to oneself that the death has really happened. This most rudimentary form of mourning is typically followed by a second, and very different, phase, a sort of confrontation. It often is an openly grief-stricken confrontation, sometimes an angry confrontation, but always an explicit confrontation—and it always includes a recognition that the bereavement is real. This phase can be followed, eventually, by a third phase, where the bereaved individual becomes reintegrated into life, comes to terms with the loss, and may even derive some sustenance from the loss for facing the future.

Among survivors and others closely connected to the Nazi Holocaust through family and ethnic ties, a very similar pattern of response has taken place. In this case, the sequence has been drawn out over more than fifty years, and many an individual has not yet been able to make the transition to the third phase, the reintegration into effective living, including a confident embrace of the present and the future. That third phase is still in its infancy among this group. There are many groping efforts toward it. Indeed the Holocaust conference for which this chapter was originally prepared, in the year 1988, was one such effort. Yet as a group, we have not come very far in the journey back to life. Perhaps fifty years is a short time when it comes to an event as life-denying as the Holocaust.

The first response to the Holocaust was stunned silence. After the earliest news reports described finding the camps and the survivors, and confirmed the worst fears about the fate of millions, the news accounts slowed to a trickle. This was followed by virtual silence. Little was heard from the survivors themselves or from sheltered Westerners. During an interview in 1987, the writer Aharon Applefeld described a response that typifies the early period: "The Holocaust belongs to the type of enormous experience which reduces one to silence. Any utterance, any statement, any 'answer' is tiny, meaningless and occasionally ridiculous. Even the greatest of answers seems petty."[1] This statement is intellectual and rational, the result not only of anguish but of serious thought over a considerable period of reflection.

A more passionate and emotional outpouring came from Elie Wiesel. His powerful words are known to the entire world. In the first years after 1945, however, Wiesel remained in stunned silence. Then he became the *shofar* of anguish, the purest voice for the eloquence of silence, the voice that said that no words can possibly convey what happened, yet speak about the events we must.

Each survivor has his or her own version of the early stunned silence, of withdrawal from emotional encounter with the events. In my case the withdrawal lasted thirty years. It was a time during which, beyond ascertaining that my parents and my brother had in fact perished, I denied the existence of the Holocaust to myself. I listened to no voices about the Holocaust. I avoided associating with Holocaust survivors. I read nothing about the Holocaust. I dissociated myself from Judaism and lived among Christians. I occasionally attended Quaker religious services while I was a student at a Quaker college, but I attended no synagogue services. I did not observe Jewish religious practices although my parents had been Orthodox Jews and they had trained me to be an observant Orthodox Jew. During my thirty years of withdrawal, I was violating virtually every orthodox ritual and commandment to which my parents had adhered very strictly and which, in my child's mind, had done nothing to protect us from lethal harm.

I mentioned in the first chapter that in 1979 I visited my native village in Germany. I went to the Jewish cemetery. I went into the house where I was born and where I had lived until I left Germany in 1939. I went into a number of other buildings, but I found myself unable to enter the synagogue. It had been converted into a bank. I stood in front of it, paralyzed. Only now, many years later, do I realize that here was a critical moment in my return to Judaism. Only now do I see that I was revolted by this second desecration of our synagogue, seeing it used as a bank. The first desecration had taken place during Kristallnacht, in 1938, when our synagogue's Torahs had been dragged from the building and thrown onto piles of manure. That deed fills me with raw grief to this day. The visit in 1979 was the beginning of my confronting the Holocaust in an emotional way. It was my entry into the second phase.

In the Jewish communty in general, in the 1950s and 1960s there emerged a drastically changed pattern of Holocaust response. It stands in stark contrast to the early silence and has dominated thinking about the Holocaust to the present time. That response has taken many forms, all of which revolve around a central theme: The events of the Holocaust must be confronted; silence is no longer the most appropriate response. At the very minimum, the events must be described with great specificity. They must be made known publicly. They must be taught to those who did not themselves experience them. Perpetrators of the horrors must be identified, apprehended and punished.

In this second phase the Holocaust is not to be regarded as mere pedantic history, as wanting the facts to be known because some people simply do not know them. Far more importantly, there is passionate commitment to teaching about these events. It is a sacred duty in partial payment of an eternal debt to those who did not survive; it is restitution for one's surviving when so many loved ones did not survive; and, additionally, it is an act rooted in the conviction that by actively remembering the past we are seeing to it that such things will not happen again. Whether this conviction turns out to be valid—whether remembering the Holocaust events will in fact serve as a vaccine against future horrors—is quite another matter. It has not been proven, but nevertheless, the conviction that remembering will prevent future horrors is embraced fervently by many persons.

These responses are profound and visceral. They have energized the processes of remembering. They have galvanized an unparalleled outpouring of historic scholarship, literary and poetic productivity, commemorations, and building of memorials.

A central theme of all these second phase remembrances is that the Holocaust is ineffably unique. Its objective, the specific and total destruction of a people, and its scope and level of degradation have no parallels in human history. Being without parallels in history, they are beyond comprehension, beyond our power to understand. All we can do, and must do, is to remember what happened.

On the personal level, in the second phase the suffering remains raw and unhealed. An Auschwitz survivor writes, in the year 1991 (forty-six years after Auschwitz!), "Now as I remember that terrible time, my feeling is that I have never actually left Auschwitz. I go to bed with it and get up with it."[2] Another survivor writes, in the year 1992, "Most of my relatives and friends perished in death camps. I have survived but have lost my previous capacity for love and happiness."[3]

The second phase also includes explicit and vehement *expressed* anger, whereas the first phase concentrated on *repressed* anger. It includes an attempt to locate the remaining perpetrators of atrocities and bring them to justice. It includes an attempt to get bystanders to atrocities to accept some responsibility. It includes emphasis on the payment of restitution money. And it includes an attempt to understand, through scientific studies, the pathology of individuals who participated in the morally degenerate deeds—despite a haunting message, from many nonscientists and many survivors, that it is really beyond human capacity to understand this behavior.

The earliest of these scientific studies was the depiction, by Theodore Adorno and his colleagues, of German fascists as authoritarian personalities, as persons who, due to their childhood upbringing, developed into rigid, authority-worshipping brutes, capable of monstrous acts in obedience to authority. A more recent study in this tradition is Robert Lifton's depiction of a particular "disorder," which he calls "doubling," among German physicians who willingly and actively participated in horrors. Lifton describes "doubling" as a tendency of these physicians to develop a separate self, which allows the individual to keep intact some traditional humane medical values while concomittantly engaging in monstrous behavior.

In the sphere of religion, the second phase generated a wide range of responses. At one end of the range, we find total rejection of a God who could permit the Holocaust to happen, as expressed in Richard Rubenstein's book *After Auschwitz*. At the other end, we find various efforts to reconcile Judaic theology with the horrors, including works by the theologians Steven Katz, Emil Fackenheim, and I. Maybaum. As part of contemporary Jewish religion, the Holocaust has become a major rallying point on a par with other catastrophes in Jewish history, such as the Destruction of the Temple and the Exile, which form the framework of much Jewish religious ritual and worship. It is these efforts to make the Holocaust not only an element of Jewish history but an element of continuing Jewish religiosity that enable Jewish religiosity to continue into the future—a link to the third phase.

∼

The third phase of response to personally experienced horrors differs profoundly from the second phase. In the second phase one operates from the standpoint that torment, pain, and suffering of the past define one's life in the present as well as in the foreseeable future. The third phase, by contrast, places the past in the past and permits a new future to enter our view of our world. As survivors, we can then entertain the possibility that there can be joy in our life; that we can have some control over our life; that there is dignity in our life. This does not mean that one forgets past horrors, or forgives the perpetrators. Rather, it denies them the opportunity to totally define our future life. It means that we see the future as something that contains new options for ourselves, which can be grasped and incorporated into our life, here and now.

Placing the past in the past does not mean either that one denies the past or that one ignores horrors that were profoundly and totally real and ought to be remembered. Instead, it places horrors in an appropriate niche, where they will assuredly be remembered, but where they cannot dominate the present and future lives of ourselves and our loved ones.

At the time I write these words, Holocaust survivors have become what we call "elderly," "past middle age," or, even more euphemistically, "mature." We are not deemed to be youthful. This ties in with the prevailing American cultural dogma that old people have little more to offer, and little more to expect, as they quietly await their final ride in a hearse. All we have is the past. And that, by definition, is past. It does little for our future.

This is true only insofar as we believe it. If we do not believe it, we can transform it into a piece of folklore that we can ignore. Indeed, we must ignore it if we want to get on with our lives, and do so vitally, productively, and joyfully. We can seize opportunities that exist precisely because we *are* "elderly" and may not need to concentrate on issues that weighed so heavily in the past, such as the quest for financial security through a job or, stated more formally, through an occupational career. Here, then, to start with, I am talking about opportunities for elderly persons altogether, not merely Holocaust survivors.

Opportunities for elderly persons? A newly retired person with interests in science may be able to enter an area of scientific work that is clearly unpopular. It may not have even the remotest chance of "being funded" by the existing grants agencies or of being appreciated by those in charge of career opportunities. A young, newly minted scientist just out of graduate school would be loathe (and imprudent) to enter such a field. Our "elderly" scientist, however, may enter it merely and only because he or she is excited by its intellectual challenge.

Where are the funds going to come from for a laboratory and the equipment it requires, or paid assistants? One can do a great deal of scientific modeling with just a computer, and do it by oneself. Mathematical work is particularly suited to such individualized work habits, as is computer-based modeling as a replacement for laboratory experimentation.

What holds in unpopular and monetarily questionable areas of science holds even more for the humanities, such as painting, composing music, and writing. Here the individual can go vastly beyond college courses geared to appreciating past accomplishments ("music appreciation," etc.) and, instead, become an active, even creative, participant. One can be guided by a sense of creative participation, where one's "future" is grasped right here, in one's present life. To be sure, one may need to obtain new skills, and one may need help that goes beyond a one-shot art appreciation course. But the individual can be an active and creative participant, building upon life experiences but going further into creative ventures.

Folklore, with some truth attached, has it that in some fields, notably mathematics and physics, only the very young are really creative, as was the young Einstein. Yet in some fields, such as philosophy, the rather old are sometimes the most creative, as was Alfred North Whitehead (who did his most productive philosophical work after he had reached his mid-sixties). The book you are now reading is my third one since reaching the age of sixty-five. The second one, *Immediacy*, advocates and plunges into a largely new paradigm. It was self-published and has, thus far, been a lonely voice. In that book I indulge in the luxury of delving into a zone of science that has little attention in the present climate governing the behavioral sciences.

The sociologist in me says that creativity is often nurtured by being an outsider. The young scientist and mathematician may benefit from being a newcomer. Either is still an outsider to the career constraints and ways of thinking imposed by membership in a profession. He or she can still think outrageously and irreverently—if one's graduate school training has not destroyed one's mental flexibility and playful creativity.

Similarly, an older person may again be able to think outrageously and irreverently as he or she is removed from the ongoing career hurdles, political infighting in one's profession, and economically motivated (and necessitated) myopia. The "creative" Whitehead of his late sixties had just retired from his mathematics professorship at his British university and had left both his university and his country to join the philosophy department at Harvard University. He had become a new outsider.

Our culture's definition of old people as being "outside" the mainstream may turn out to be a bonanza for those who are willing to grasp their unique, age-driven opportunities. We outsiders may turn out to be creative and productive human beings if we give ourselves a chance to do so by refusing to accept the stereotypes that hold us back—and retire us to the golf course. Those of us who are both older *and* survivors of horrors are in an extraordinary position to reinvent lives for ourselves.

The third phase of response to the Holocaust is still in a state of emergence. We do not know yet what its total configuration will be. We do know that it includes decidedly new steps and some reassessments of cherished items of the second phase.

One starting point for the third phase is that knowledge of the horrors of the Holocaust has not prevented additional genocidal actions from occurring in many parts of the world. Survivors are discovering to their dismay that remembering the Holocaust is, by itself, no vaccine against future social horrors. But confronting the horrors in our past can provide us a Holocaust-inspired sense of shared grief for the suffering of others, as exemplified by Elie Wiesel's visit to Cambodia after the genocidal horrors were going on there in the 1970s. This points the way to a universalism, a moving beyond the earlier, very understandable, inward-looking orientation toward the Holocaust.

A powerful perspective for the individual's entering the third phase comes to us from Viktor Frankl, the psychiatrist and Auschwitz survivor I mentioned previously. Frankl tells us that perhaps the most fundamental phenomenon of life, for each one of us, is discovering some meaning in our life; that one can find meaning in various ways, such as through love of nature or through love of another human being. One can also find it through suffering. Frankl personally found his life's meaning in and through Auschwitz.[4] It became the fundamental vehicle for getting on with his life after the Holocaust, leaving behind the second phase, and giving him enrichment and an anchor for living.

For me to operate in the third phase, I must adopt the posture of a behavioral scientist to help me understand the actions of people who do horrendous evil. That posture includes abandoning the fruitless search for monsters in order to explain monstrous actions. It includes abandoning, even, the search for unique sicknesses to explain outlandishly sick behavior. To the contrary, it includes—it requires—looking at the ordinary in order to explain the extraordinary. It also includes the conviction that we can understand, and thereby eventually control, such actions.

My first recognition of the second phase, and a glimmering of a third phase, took place in Israel. I was teaching sociology at Tel Aviv University in the early 1970s, after about twelve years of teaching at American universities. I had written books and articles about a variety of sociological topics, but remained totally oblivious to the Holocaust. Israel removed my blinders. There I was having daily encounters with persons who had my kind of personal history. Many of these people were no longer afraid to confront the Holocaust and face the future. They were building a nation in response to the Holocaust. I could no longer remain in fearful hiding.

I awoke to a peculiar fact. The Holocaust was real. This was supported by a vast amount of documentation. Yet my colleagues in the field of sociology, many of whom are Jewish, had been almost totally silent about the Holocaust. Some of them may have shunned the Holocaust for personal emotional reasons, as I had done. Others may have felt that the Holocaust was not an appropriate secular topic, not a topic for dispassionate sociological research. At any rate, despite the publicity about the Holocaust—the commemorations, the teachings, the outpouring of professional and popular historical writings—there was a virtual conspiracy of silence about the Holocaust among my fellow sociologists.

In later years, thanks to the excellent scholarship of sociologists like Helen Fein (especially in her book *Accounting for Genocide*[5]), this situation has changed somewhat. But by and large sociologists were for a long time reluctant to confront the Holocaust with their particular expertise. Instead, they were bystanders to the work of psychologists, historians, and political scientists (many of whom have done important work), and have left largely unchallenged the search for monsters and unique sorts of pathology among perpetrators of horrors. Sociologists have not responded to important challenges. I am not the only sociologist who thinks so. Zygmunt Bauman has expressed the same opinion.[6]

The search for monsters began soon after World War II and culminated in the war crimes trials. The idea behind the trials was to find the criminals, hold them up to full public view, and then punish them appropriately. The rationale for this is rooted in a commitment to preserving respect for law and human decency. Brought to trial were individuals who had committed deeds of incredible horror; they often did so at their own discretion, surely bearing responsibility for what they had done. They could not convincingly sustain their claim that they were merely following orders. They demonstrated to us, through the process of the trials, that they, actual human beings, had committed monstrous deeds.

Yet there were some serious shortcomings in this search for identifiable monsters in human clothing. First, it absolves the bystanders, the millions of citizens—from little burghers to major social figures—who surely knew what was happening but did not act to stop the horrors. By isolating and punishing a few major evildoers, the rest could sleep in peace. Those who had seen their Jewish neighbors rounded up and dispatched to distant death factories could console themselves with the belief that the perpetrators of the misdeeds had been appropriately punished. They could tell themselves that their silence was justified. My fellow sociologists (and I) have been very reluctant to address how such large-scale silence could happen. In fact, we matched it with a silence of our own.

A second shortcoming in the search for monsters is more subtle, but perhaps even more important. Rather than revealing themselves to be the clearly recognizable monsters people were looking for, these individuals looked and acted like average citizens. The search actually seemed to backfire. To be sure the actions of the accused, and later convicted, perpetrators were utterly beyond belief. Yet the more the accused were made to talk in court by their accusers, the more alarmingly ordinary they appeared to be. In many of their personal habits and dispositions they were uncomfortably similar to their fellow countrymen. To be sure, most were authority loving and rigid, but so were many others who shared their upbringing. Some were officious and pedantic, but so were millions of other Germans. Some even had a sense of humor. They did not seem to have horns on their heads.

This was hard to accept and acknowledge openly. Hannah Arendt, acting as an observer at the Adolf Eichmann trial, blew the whistle on this issue. She did so, first, in a series of articles about the Eichmann trial in *The New Yorker* magazine and, later, in the book *Eichmann in Jerusalem: A Report on the Banality of Evil.* When she pointed to Eichmann's banality, people responded with considerable anger, anguish, and pain.

This response was also based on Arendt's somewhat crude assertions about the functioning of the Judenraete—the Jewish Community Councils—through which, she claimed, the Jews cooperated in their own demise with unnecessary alacrity. But even putting this issue aside, the public response to Arendt was a case of wanting to shoot the messenger who brings bad tidings and raises very painful issues: If the Eichmanns of this world are ordinary, banal persons, where does this leave the search for evildoers? What do we do with our—very justified!—anger? Where does it leave personal accountability for one's actions? And if the Eichmanns are not terribly and terrifyingly different from the rest of us, where does this leave the rest of us?

Here we have the rudiments for third phase responses to the Holocaust. Certainly it is appropriate to bring criminals to justice, and the Nuremberg and subsequent trials did indeed bring horrendous criminals to justice. However, we are beginning to realize that the search for monsters is not going to clarify how evil is produced, no more than did the search for witches and other monsters clarify how evil was produced in the Middle Ages. *Monstrous* attributes do not seem to form the basis for horrendous behavior, but rather *ordinary* human attributes form that basis. They are the raw material that can help to produce evil.

Every human being seems to share and value a repertoire of ordinary behavior. The ingredients of this repertoire can be used in horrendous activities just as readily as in humane activities. We must learn to identify how ordinary behavior can be harnessed to accomplish horrendous deeds. I have tried to do so, in articles on Nazi bureaucrats and in the book, *Ordinary People and Extraordinary Evil*. Others have also made this attempt, notably Stanley Milgram, in his experiments on ordinary people's willingness to inflict pain on innocent people,[7] as well as Israel Shahak, of whom I shall say more in a moment.

Painful questions arise when one demonstrates that ordinary people's ordinary behavior can lead to active, even enthusiastic, evil. It includes willing participation in horrendous deeds, not grudgingly or reluctantly but, often, intelligently and creatively. For instance, without wanting to start a crusade against medical research, in other writings I have pointed out that a passionate commitment to doing medical research is but a hair's breadth away from engaging in the most immoral practices, as some research-minded SS physicians did. I have explained that dedication to an occupation can be a source of moral blinders, as can the effort to provide for one's family. In doing so, I hope I am contributing groundwork for seeing how we must look for the potentials for thorough evil in entirely noble human efforts. The potential for evil lies in the very same areas where there are potentials for cherished behavior. Just as ordinary characteristics of cells and DNA structure can contain the potentials for good health, they can also contain the potentials for suffering and pain. As we learn more about the ordinary nature of cells and DNA, we will learn more about ill health and disease, and gain weapons against disease.

Taken unemotionally, these conclusions can help guarantee a new universalism. To begin with, they require a redefinition of the "uniqueness" of the Holocaust. There can be no doubt that the Holocaust contains unique elements. These include its explicit effort to totally annihilate a people, its scope and use of systematic murder technology, and, finally, its almost exclusive impact on the Jewish people. Yet the focus on uniqueness has proven to be an intellectual and emotional straitjacket; it has prevented us from learning things from the Holocaust that might help safeguard the future more effectively. It has blinded us to some facets of the Holocaust.

In a provocative article, Israel Shahak has pointed out that upon seeing and hearing of the horrendous deeds by the Nazis, Jews in the Ghetto responded very much like Poles outside the Ghetto.[8] Both sought to create some "normality" for themselves in the face of unspeakable horrors. This was not a matter of the Poles being callous toward the Jews, or of Jews being callous to the suffering of their brothers and sisters. Shahak, who suvived much of the Holocaust in the Warsaw Ghetto, sees this merely as human nature asserting itself. All people tend to behave this way. Poles and Jews alike had a small minority of people who behaved brutally in the course of the Holocaust. Each also had a minority who behaved heroically, who risked their lives to save others. The majority among both sought some sort of accommodation. They sometimes struggled against the wickedness of the minority, but mostly they simply tried to preserve a measure of normality amid a world of horrors.

Shahak points to similar reactions during other large-scale extermination programs. He cites the well-known case of extermination of the Armenians by the Turks between 1915 and 1917, as well as the less-publicized but equally cruel extermination of the Tasmanians by the British and a cadre of specially recruited Aborigines in the second quarter of the nineteenth century. Finally, he points to the also-neglected extermination programs in China throughout much of Chinese history. Shahak uses these examples to attack the claims to the Holocaust's uniqueness. I tend to agree. There surely is much similarity in the human capacity for participation in massive evil in all the situations Shahak cites. And we can, and must, understand this capacity more fully.

Yet there is also a reality in the victims' experiencing the Holocaust as utterly unique, and the experience of uniqueness is a legitimate and necessary part of the mourning process during the second phase. What happened to our personal loved ones—what happened to my parents and to my brother—is totally and utterly unique for me. But this should not become the end point of my life's journey. If there is anything stronger than the obligation to mourn our dead—by concentrating on the uniqueness of their and our tragedy—it is the obligation to confront the life in which we and our children now find ourselves. This requires moving beyond a focus on the uniqueness of past events. It requires moving into the future, into the third phase, with an active heart and mind.

For me personally, this constitutes my "second journey," the effort to use my professional skills to attain more insight into the nature of massive evildoing. In the sense in which Viktor Frankl taught us, this gives meaning to my life. I am concentrating on one dimension of a larger agenda, namely that relatively sane and ordinary people may skillfully and energetically take part in outlandish brutalities, and often do so by making use of a most human attribute: the conviction that one is acting under moral directives, what I am calling the Local Moral Universe.

Knowledge of the ways in which human ordinariness can manufacture horrendous evil may help us forge weapons against the manufacture of evil in the future. We do not need to remain unwitting helpmates of evil because, in our ignorance, we do not know how the process of manufacturing evil works. That is the practical side. The first step in this enterprise is to clarify how that process works and, to do that, we need to craft more effective scientific tools. This is the objective of the next section of this book.

Dissecting Evil: The Second Journey

Ilya Prigogine, a Nobel Prize winner in science, told us: "Our [twentieth] century is a century of explorations: new forms of art, of music, of literature, and new forms of science."[1] Dissecting evil can produce knowledge that will improve our lives. But the process of creating this knowledge *demands* a new form of science, one that treats evil as dispassionately as it treats other aspects of our ordinary ways. This requires an orienting vision about what is distinctive in human behavior. That vision, I suggest, is that human life operates under a moral venue: We are moral creatures. We derive our sense of worth from the moral community to which we belong and to which we actively contribute in our ongoing life.

The new science requires a search for underlying orderliness in how we act under a moral venue. And this, in turn, requires that we create some tools in the form of new constructs, so that we can discover orderliness more effectively. This section attempts that task.

Ilya Prigogine reminded us that new sciences are constantly being created. They lead to new perspectives on old issues, new answers and, also, new questions and new uncertainties. Will the new knowledge be used responsibly? A new science is an act of faith in a venture of the mind.

CHAPTER FOUR

Unpleasant Surprises

We seem to be impotent in the face of mass horrors. There are myths we must discard before we can come to grips with mass horrors. We need not remain so impotent!

In the recent past, we were once again surprised by humans doing horrible things to one another on a massive scale. This time, in the 1990s, the horrors took place in the Balkans. We heard that in Bosnia, Croatia, and Serbia people turned against one another with utter disregard for life; human beings slaughtered human beings. Some time later a new series of mass horrors—mass slaughter—was reported. This time it was in Rwanda, in central Africa. We were again confronted with unspeakably violent activities by human beings. We were again appalled by what human beings could do to one another. Being appalled, we told ourselves that we must put an end to such activities.

We are repeatedly appalled, but we have not put an end to such activities.There is little likelihood that if we continue on our present course we will ever put an end to such activities. We are victims not only of recurrent social horrors, of human beings doing brutal things to one another on a large scale. We are also victims of our own mental shackles of outmoded ways of thinking about large-scale social horrors. These keep us from developing effective weapons against the horrors. Yet I am convinced that we need not remain victims who impotently live with recurrent social horrors. We need to, and we can, shake ourselves loose from our mental shackles.

After the end of the First World War, in 1918, many people thought that the gruesome trench warfare of that war would sicken humans of killings forever. There, on many a single day, in direct face-to-face combat, thousands upon thousands of men slaughtered one another. Virtually a generation of young men of several European countries bled to death, just as Americans had during the Civil War.

Let us be clear and explicit what face-to-face combat means. It means that you affix a bayonet, a kind of pointed, two-edged knife, to the front of your rifle. You shoot at the opposing soldier from a distance, and, if you do not succeed in killing him with your shots, you storm toward him and plunge your bayonet into him before he plunges his bayonet into you. You do this to someone whom you have never met. He is a human being who is likely to be as innocent of crimes as you are; he is a human being whom you kill because someone has defined that person as your mortal enemy, someone you must kill. And you do it in the most direct, physically uncompromising way.

After the First World War many believed that this was surely a temporary throwback to uncivilized times that could not, must not, happen again.

Thirty years later, when the Second World War ended, similar sentiments surfaced. People were sickened by the saturation fire bombings and atomic bombings of cities, each of which extinguished around one hundred thousand lives in a single day or night, to say nothing of the Nazi Holocaust itself. All these, surely, would awaken us to the reality of massive inhumanity and so shake our conscience that we would put an end to such social horrors.

Our conscience was shaken, but we did not put an end to such horrors. We have tried to do so. In the political realm, we tried to put an end to brutal wars by creating international arrangements that would substitute discussion and debate for warfare. After the First World War we created the League of Nations. After the Second World War we created the United Nations. There were efforts at creating a world government by an organization called World Federalists. There was also an effort (begun in 1887) to create Esperanto as a world language that would unite people through one common second language. Although these efforts had some successes (they did arouse many people to the need to do something about the horrors we periodically inflict on one another), they did not prevent resumption of massive social horrors.

We have pointed out how horrible the horrors were, and still are. But it did not help to point out the horror of the horrors. Doing so did not inhibit subsequent behavior. Those who committed the horrors in Cambodia in the 1970s remembered and mentioned the horrors of the Nazi Holocaust, but it did not stop them from committing horrors of their own. Those who committed horrors in the former Yugoslavia in the 1990s also remembered the Nazi Holocaust; it has not stopped them, either.

We are surprised when massive social horrors happen again. Each time new horrors arise, as they were doing in Serbia and Bosnia in the early 1990s, we are surprised. How could it happen? And, most surprising of all, how could it happen among these people who had been living peacefully with one another for many years? How could it happen among these "civilized" Europeans, who had a history of living as one nation, particularly during the forty years after the Second World War, and who had, surely, overcome ethnic tribalisms a long time ago? How could this happen?

Our first response, usually, is disbelief. It cannot be true. It had better be ignored. It will go away if we just don't overreact. This was the American government's early response to the events in the former Yugoslavia in the 1990s. That response probably reflected what many of the rest of us, ordinary citizens, felt.

The second response, by the American government and by many of us, was to look for monsters, for evil people who must be behind the horrors. There must be evil people who are getting ordinary people to do things which these people would not ordinarily do. We told ourselves that behind the visible horrors there were a few evil people who either personally committed acts that the rest of us would never commit, or who got innocent people to commit horrors that these innocent people would not ordinarily commit. This, to some extent, took care of our sense of outrage and our surprise. The surprise, in particular, is taken care of by assuming that evil people, somewhere, somehow, get good people to do horrible things. We no longer call such evil people devils, but this is pretty close to a devil's theory of human behavior. We no longer speak of devils among us, but we might as well. (As I write these words, America is once again in the throes of identifying a devil, this time it is Saddam Hussein of Iraq. He did commit horrible deeds. But he could not possibly have done so without a great deal of help from many people.)

It comes down to this: When we try to understand how horrible events can erupt and flourish in our time, we are no nearer to reliable knowledge than were our ancestors who, six hundred years ago, tried to understand the Black Plague. They, too, were appalled. They, too, looked for monsters to help them explain horrible events. They did so because they felt that here were events beyond the realm of the ordinary, beyond understanding in terms of day-to-day living. In religious terms, they told themselves that here were actions that were surely contrary to God's will, and therefore showed the handiwork of a devil.

Our ancestors' horror about the Black Death has long been replaced by reliable knowledge of how infectious disease processes work. From that knowledge we have been able to get on with the task of protecting ourselves against such horrors, rather than waiting until the horrors strike. But when it comes to massive horrors created by humans, of human beings brutalizing one another on a huge scale, the harsh reality is that we are still in the Middle Ages. We are repeatedly surprised by these horrors because we are still terribly ignorant of how such things can happen, and because of our ignorance we remain impotent against them.

Upon his return from Bosnia in 1992, a distinguished public health physician was interviewed about the conditions there. A longtime member of the Johns Hopkins University's School of Public Health, Dr. Carl Taylor remarked, "When I was there, the thing that came through every hour of every day was the intense hatred among people who would normally have been friends"[1] (*Baltimore Sun,* 29 December 1992). Surprising, is it not, that friendly people had turned into hate-filled enemies? What caused Dr. Taylor particular anguish was

> . . . (t)he intensity of the hatred, and the psychological trauma to children. That gripped me in a way that I had not anticipated.
> It was particularly bad because these were very cultured and presumably civilized people doing it to their neighbors' children.

Our explanations for such behavior, when we have any at all, are primitive, in the worst sense of this term. We are virtually impotent and helpless when it comes to understanding, let alone predicting or preventing, social horrors on a huge scale, such as the Nazi Holocaust and some forty additional mass horrors that have taken place since then (for example, Cambodia in the 1970s). In our appalled shock we tell ourselves that here are events that are beyond comprehension—human beings cannot be acting in this way and remain human beings. At the very least, we tell ourselves, the people who carry out the horrors, if they are not simply acting under duress, under orders from a depraved leader, are, at least, mentally or morally sick, or social deviants who are entirely different from the rest of us.

Let us listen to, and learn from, the man who was in charge of the United Nations refugee program in the former Yugoslavia when the horrors of the 1990s began, Mr. Jose-Maria Mendiluce. He was personally greatly traumatized (to the extent that his own health broke) by the events he saw. He states that ethnic conflicts, such as those in the former Yugoslavia, could easily take place in other parts of Europe. He tells us that he has learned that "people can be transformed into hating and killing machines without too much difficulty."[2] It is very easy, in his view, for cynical leaders to activate this process. His focus is on the leaders, and the ease with which they can instigate horrors, carried out by their people. Doubtless there is much truth in what this courageous and sensitive man says. But let us not dwell on the leaders alone. Let us ask ourselves how it is that "people can be transformed into hating and killing machines" so readily. Why are they so easily deceived and manipulated by leaders? Is the role of leaders a sufficient explanation for what is happening?

We must challenge our assumptions about those who actually carry out horrendous deeds. There occasionally are evil-intentioned leaders who deliberately try to produce an evil course of action. There was a Hitler, and a Stalin, and some others too, who belong in the category of evil leaders. But to focus solely on the intentions and plans of such leaders does not take into account the decisive contributions of followers, who do far more than follow orders. It does not take into account (1) the contribution of people who *design programs* for implementing the horrific dreams of leaders, from lawyers who design increasingly repressive legal measures against designated persons to individuals who design incarceration, torture, and extermination procedures; (2) the contribution of people who *solve problems* along the way, the Eichmanns who exercise great ingenuity and incredible persistence to make sure that there are trains to carry victims to their final destination in the gas chambers; (3) the contribution of people who, as regular functionaries within the system, *invent their own ways of contributing to evil* over and beyond the evil that was envisioned by the murderous, and perhaps crazy, leader;[3] and (4) the contribution of ordinary people, who are neither functionaries in a national system nor personally brutalized, yet who *actively take sides and participate in the process* of escalating estrangement between themselves and those who have been defined as alien "others." During the conflict between Croatians and Serbs in the Balkans, Croatian and Serb communities in the American city of Chicago became actively alienated from each other, after years of shared cultural activities. These people, thousands of miles away from the manipulations of local Balkan leaders, now actively contributed to the further estrangement and hostility toward their Chicago neighbors; they will, in all likelihood, contribute to its perpetuation by implanting it in the thinking of their children.

Some Myths We Must Discard

Our difficulty in coming to grips with horrendous human actions springs at least in part from the ways in which we think about massive horrors. They constrict our thinking, distort our vision, and prevent effective understanding of what is going on. Here are five myths that still plague us.

Myth Number One: Ordinary, normal human beings—people who are not mentally unbalanced, or suffering from a disorder, or poisoned by a vicious creed (such as German "eliminationist anti-Semitism")—could not possibly engage in mass murder and other forms of horror against entirely innocent persons.

In the subsequent pages of this book I shall emphasize, again and again, how even doers of the most horrendous deeds tend to make use of very normal, nonpathological human ways in the course of doing evil. Indeed, it is from within the normal, the ordinary human ways, that we discover clues of how horrendous evil is actually produced.

Myth Number Two: Horrendous evil, especially on the scale of the Nazi Holocaust and the horrors in Rwanda, cannot be understood. After all is said and done, says many a Holocaust survivor, the Holocaust is beyond human comprehension. Words cannot do justice to it. Analyses cannot do justice to it. It will forever remain a mystery.

I am proceeding under the assumption that, to be sure, many things about the great horrors will remain unexplained, and unexplainable. But I am also convinced that we *can* explain a great deal more than we have done thus far. In part, what we explain depends on the outlook we adopt to begin with, whether we go into the enterprise thinking that we can indeed discover new insights or whether we think that, underneath it all, there is mystery. This makes a great deal of difference.

Myth Number Three: Facts will speak for themselves, and assert moral rectitude. When the stark facts of what happened during a particular mass horror are made known, this will, then, lead to such revulsion that comparable horrors will not be repeated. Humans can be shocked into renouncing evil.

Anyone familiar with history knows the folly of such thinking. Yet much current scholarship about the Nazi Holocaust still operates under the belief that if these horrors are fully known, they will not be repeated. I am not saying that such scholarship should cease. But I am saying that it is sheer folly to assume that historic information, alone and by itself—even if it is thorough, complete, and accurate—will produce an end to horrific deeds by human beings. Facts do not speak for themselves. Facts must be spoken *to*; they must be dispassionately dissected and analyzed if they are to yield useful information. If horrendous deeds are to yield information that will produce some potentially prophylactic information, we must go beyond reciting the horrors that happened.

Myth Number Four: The closer we get to reproducing the actual experiences of what happened—somehow portraying what they were like as authentically as possible, even if one portrays only one tiny fragment of that reality—the more valid the insights that are then produced.

This has great intuitive appeal, and it is certainly a very worthy thing to do, particularly as part of the early process of mourning for lost loved ones, and of reminding the political community that horrific events did really happen, and some people bear responsibility. Yet in this book I have a different agenda. It is the agenda of the scientist. When a biochemist studies DNA material in order to try to discover causes of cancer, that scientist does not attempt to portray the actual experience of having cancer. It is not his or her intention to somehow do justice to the full manifestation of the horror of having cancer, or even the full horror of one single individual who suffers from cancer. To the contrary, the biochemist tries to look at some aspect— the specific structure and dynamics of the relevant DNA material—that is abstracted from the total horror we know as cancer. One hopes that, if the right items are being abstracted and rigorously and imaginatively examined, they may yield answers to horrors now afflicting very many cancer patients. We have here a distinctive perspective—a posture toward the world of information—that is radically different from the perspective of the person who seeks to completely portray a particular experience. In a sense the difference is that between the artist (the poet, playwright, painter, or, even, the social historian) who tries to fully portray a particular experience as against the scientist, who tries to develop knowledge that is precise and generalizable, even though it deals only with selected aspects of concrete reality.

In the following pages I am trying to abstract some items that relate to horrendous human behavior in the hope that this will produce some useful knowledge that goes beyond portraying the full reality of one particular horror. My approach will never take the place of artists or historians addressing the same issue. Theirs is a different agenda, addressed to the very worthy objective of portraying how and what actually happened. Mine is the objective of dissecting and abstracting from concrete reality in order to produce generalizable knowledge of people's capacity for taking part in horrors.

The particular items to which I am addressing myself are those that show the follower at work, one who participates in horrors, who makes use of ordinary human attributes to produce horrors of major proportions.

Myth Number Five: There is just one way of doing science: collecting new data. (This is a variation of the facts-speak-for-themselves myth.) If you collect more data you will get more knowledge.

Actually, there are many ways of doing science. For example, some physicists are primarily experimentalists, whether by temperament, by choice, or by accident. These individuals concentrate on devising experiments, where they organize, manipulate, and focus data and events in particular ways and, then, interpret the resulting findings. Other physicists are primarliy theorists, who may be utterly inept and clumsy in any laboratory and who conduct no experiments, except imaginary "thought experiments," and who collect no new data. They concentrate on what the mind brings to existing data. They are likely to reassess other scientists' findings and, thereby, devise new ways of seeing and interpreting existing data.

I am closer to this theorist category. My "reassessments" include, but are not limited to, a different way of understanding the well-known Milgram experiments and some of Hannah Arendt's writings on the banality of evil.

The background to reassessment is that in science there can be a huge gap, a chasm, between an intriguing discovery and an appropriate explanation of that discovery. Consider the proverbial hare chasing the tortoise for thousands of years. Intellectually, we have not found a formulation for allowing the hare to overtake the tortoise. In practice, of course, the hare overtakes the tortoise very quickly and decisively. But as long as our mind-set is fixated on the notion that for each leap by the hare the tortoise also makes a leap, albeit a tiny one, then the hare can never overtake the tortoise. We are here dealing with intellectual ineptitude, where the obvious "cannot happen." Does this sound familiar? Consider how our entrapment in mystical thinking, of the sort I mentioned above, keeps us from understanding how ordinary people can be doing horrendous things.

Let us now get on with the task of reassessing how people, ordinary sorts of people, can be major participants in horrors. To do so, let us first take a serious look at the fact that most of us, most of the time, see our lives in terms of some moral context. We humans are moral creatures. I am calling this the Local Moral Universe in our existence as human beings.

CHAPTER FIVE

The Local Moral Universe

It is . . . what normally innocent people do that concerns us; and if Joan [of Arc] had not been burnt by normally innocent people in the energy of their righteousness her death at their hands would have no more significance than the Tokyo earthquake, which burnt a great many maidens. The tragedy of such murders is that they are not committed by murderers. They are judicial murders, pious murders. . . .

—Bernard Shaw, *Saint Joan*

Cults

It is hard to understand that a moral context can justify mass murder and cruelty, yet it does happen. The SS men who carried out mass killings during the Holocaust and the individuals who carried out ethnic cleansings in the Balkans fifty years later all believed they were acting under high moral purpose, as did many other slaughterers of innocent people. The issue is the moral sponsorship of horrific behavior. How can it come about? How does it actually operate? To clarify this issue let us first examine cults, their leaders and followers.

Cults sometimes provide a particular version of moral sponsorship, namely activities by their members that the larger society's citizens find unacceptable, even appalling. Look, for example, at the mass suicide of members of the Heaven's Gate religious cult near San Diego, California, in

1997, and the strikingly similar mass suicide by members of a cult at Jonestown, in Guyana, in 1978. At San Diego, thirty nine persons killed themselves. At Jonestown, the number of suicides was nearly one thousand. "Mass suicide" strikes us as beyond belief. We cannot grasp how large numbers of people can possibly kill themselves of their own free will. We prefer to believe those who kill themselves and their families must be brainwashed so totally that they do not know what they are doing. They must be zombies, operating in a trancelike state. Or, alternatively, they must be acting under extreme coercion, where someone has forced them to abandon their will to live and, under extreme threat, obliges them to kill themselves. Or, perhaps, a few zealous functionaries must be going around and murdering these people.

The reality of these cult members' behavior near San Diego and Jonestown is perplexing. We just cannot understand how they went to their death willingly, cheerfully, even joyfully. It is hard to believe that this happened. Yet that is what indeed seems to have happened. The challenge before us is to explain such behavior.

We must begin, surely, by pointing to—and decrying and denouncing— the malevolence of the cult leaders and the ways in which they victimize a group of earnest and well-intentioned followers, just as we must denounce the top instigators of Nazism in Germany. These cult leaders deliberately created and, then exploited, people's vulnerabilities.

Yet if we are to make sense out of the horrors, if we are going to understand how mass suicides could happen, we need to go beyond concentrating on the malevolence of the cult leader. It may seem harsh, but we need to pay attention to the contribution made by the followers themselves.

At both Jonestown and San Diego a new moral community had evolved. At Jonestown, for example, the People's Temple community was strongly bonded around the values of racial justice and human equality in their life as an agricultural community. Their highly idealistic humanitarian focus was combined with some traditional Christian prophetic teaching that the kingdom of God could be promoted here on earth through active apostolic community. In this community mass suicide was not a sudden aberration, for which members were unprepared. In fact mass suicide was repeatedly rehearsed. It was part of the community's repertoire of treasured options for members to live up to their sacred calling.

To the members who embraced it, their moral community guaranteed access to a world of sublime meaning and destiny. That community assured one's transcendence beyond the impurities and ugliness of the rest of this world. It did so by shutting out that world and, in its place, substituted an entirely complete and unique system of moral life within that community. This community was the local and immediate embodiment of a new moral universe which members adopted. Here, in the members' Local Moral Universe, many of the outside world's moral standards, including contacts and obligations to friends and loved ones on the outside, were treated as totally inappropriate and irrelevant to one's current vibrantly moral life. Entreaties by family members on the outside were disregarded, as were entreaties by the larger community and the government. The members of the cult community believed that their own local community was the horizon to all that mattered, and it constituted the center and core of their moral obligation. They obeyed a leader unto death. They acted as a unified community, going to their death with apparent willingness, and possibly even with joy.

The outside world found that it had lost conrol over the San Diego and the Jonestown compounds. These (especially Jonestown) became closed communities, with very limited communication to the outside. Internally, each community developed a total system of allegiance and dedication to a particular lifestyle. Outside pressure served only to heighten the resolve of the members of these communities—from their leader on down to the lowliest follower—to assert their uniquely separate character and identity. Pressure from the outside culminated in an action which that outside world found totally abhorrent but which insiders saw as the ultimate sacrifice they needed to make in order to reach the dream of ultimate fulfillment in their lives.

In analyzing what went wrong, outside observers once again overemphasize the culpability of the leaders, James Jones in the case of Jonestown and Marshall Applewhite in the case of San Diego. These leaders did have immense influence on their followers, and they may have been self-intoxicated scoundrels who had little regard for the well-being of their followers. But they had followers who wholeheartedly embraced and enacted the cause which the leader presented to them. This made a world of difference. Cult members saw their cause as important enough to give up most of their previous moral commitments, including marital vows and responsibilities to their children. They went so far as to donate to the cause their very lives, openly and willingly.

The followers played an enormous part in the denouement of these communities. Let us be clear: The difference between a leader who has people willing to die on his behalf and a "leader" who is committed to a mental hospital is that the one has followers and the other does not. The followers make or break the kind of system that Jones, Applewhite, and their ilk try to construct. Leadership is validated by followers. Without followers there can be no leader. Jones and Applewhite had followers who validated their murderous demands.

Conventional wisdom is wrong in calling cult members brainwashed zombies, who follow their leader unthinkingly and mechanically. It is wrong to assume that cultists no longer have any will of their own, that they lack all autonomy. Only ousiders think like this.

Ask a cult member whether, as a cult member, he or she feels free, whether he or she has choices. The cult member is almost certain to answer that he feels exceedingly free, that he is making choices all the time, and that they are leading a creative and bountiful life. And, the cult member will add, they feel free and liberated precisely because of, and through, their membership in the spiritual community and through their adherence to this community's spirituality. An unprejudiced view of the community reveals a moral universe that totally fulfills the expectations of the cultists, as the cultists see it. What is crucial is that their sense of fulfillment is fostered by their very active participation in, and contribution to, the community's spiritual life. What they themselves contribute, what they give—even their own lives—heightens the spiritual bliss.

Many a cult member believes that salvation is directly at hand, not something that will happen remotely in the distant future, in another life. They are utterly convinced that their own efforts, centered on their spirituality as spelled out by the leader, inevitably brings the process of salvation to its grandly culminating conclusion. It will happen, not at a time far off, but here and now. The leader is seen as the supreme catalyst for the cultist's personal, and communal, salvation. This salvation is not a bland, zombie matter. It is an exciting and holy venture. Members actively participate in it in unison with all the other cultists in the community, the people in the world who matter most of all.

Social scientists have long been aware that people conduct much of their lives under the influence of those in their close, immediate social circle. People are influenced by immediate friends and neighbors in varied ways, ranging from decisions involving voting to decisions about buying consumer goods. This insight can be applied to the enactment of horrors, to humans doing terrible things in unison with other humans. At Jonestown and at San Diego, we saw people cheerfully go to their death in unison with their immediate circle of fellow believers. We, the outsiders to the world of cults, are brought face-to-face with a new, local system of morality that can be totally alien to the morality of our world. That system of morality is supported and underwritten by an immediate social circle of individuals in a close-knit community, one not unlike the social circles that influence the actions of most people, most of the time.

On this point, a return to Christopher Browning's book about a German reserve police battalion in the Second World War is instructive.[1] Members of the battalion were not zealous Nazis. They were persons who tried to more or less sit out the war in a noncombat niche. They were neither riffraff, picked for their peripheral place in their community, nor youngsters without life experience. On the contrary, they were people with stable occupations, such as tailors and mailmen, that gave them respectability in their community. They were not religious or political fanatics.

Unexpectedly, the reservists were activated and ordered to do service in Poland. Upon their arrival, they were ordered to carry out mass killings of civilians. Most of these men, despite misgivings expressed by some of them, actually went ahead with the task presented to them, the mass murders. This is the shocking message Browning presents to us. Ordinary men, with little or no commitment to Nazi ideology, became mass murderers. They did so without great duress. In fact, at the beginning the men were offered the opportunity to decline to participate. Few individuals declined. There and then, murder was the thing to do, and they did it.

Browning's stunning documentation of these "ordinary" men's participation in horrors is profoundly moving. While he provides no really convincing explanation of how this could have happened, Browning leads to the right question. Ordinary men were doing the horrors; they did so without being overly coerced to do it. Further, there is no convincing evidence of the sort of poisonous "eliminationist anti-Semitism" within the group that Daniel Goldhagen claims to have pervaded Germany during the Nazi era. Hence we are left with the obvious question; Why did they do the horrifying deeds? Or, more accurately, how did it come about?

It seems that in the intimacy of acting with other men, the reservists stopped asking the larger community's moral questions. Once removed from their home community and thrust into intimate comradeship with a particular group, they accepted an entirely immediate and local definition of right and wrong. After they arrived in Poland they operated in a myopic, locally defined moral universe, just as did the cult members at San Digo and Jonestown. Here, among these men, a new system of behavior, a new morality, prevailed.

What I am saying is that immediate, local circumstances can create a beguiling climate for behavior that most of us—and even people who might later participate in horrors—would ordinarily regard as abhorrent. Such generally regarded abhorrent behavior can be generated by a catalyst, such as a cult leader. But the catalyst does not, alone, implement the horrors. At My Lai in the Vietnam War, the catalyst was the extreme frustration of the U. S. soldiers in the months and days leading up to the military action there. Among the German police reservists, the catalyst may have been the fact that they were removed from their home environment, coupled with new intimacy among these men as they traveled together from Germany to Poland, and felt exhilerated by embarking on their first "field" assignment. Some catalyst, whatever it may be, obviously is at work in encouraging people to do evil. Often a leader plays the part of catalyst. Yet the catalyst merely sets the stage. It does not carry out the horrors alone.

The point I am emphasizing is that the "followers," the rank-and-file participants, *donate* their own active contribution to the cause. Their contributions are vital. A Marshall Applewhite without followers would be just an ordinary little scoundrel, in and out of jail for trying to trick people, or in and out of mental hospitals for believing in crazy visions. With followers, his insane cause gains legitimacy and impetus. It is the followers who give content and substance to a Local Moral Universe that sanctifies and implements the leader's insane message.

What Is a Local Moral Universe?

A Local Moral Universe can play a large role in distracting people from an otherwise generally shared sense of morality. As it is an important concept, we need to ask what, precisely, is a Local Moral Universe?

For my answer I shall go back to the well-known Milgram experiments, where persons showed themselves to be willing to inflict pain, in the form of electric shocks, on entirely innocent individuals who were, supposedly, taking part in a learning experiment.[2] It seems to me that the most important lesson to be learned from these experiments is not that these persons were obeying authority. While obedience to authority was Milgram's own explanation for what he found, we need not stop there.

Milgram's experiments were carried out in the aftermath of the horrors of the Holocaust. It was then the conventional wisdom that the horrors could only be explained by (1) the horrifying plans of the Nazi leadership—Hitler, most specifically—and (2) the German proclivity to obeying authority, even when that authority has a horrifying message. Surely Americans are less obedience-prone. They would never carry out horrifying orders. To test this assumption, Milgram conducted the experiments. He wanted to determine whether Americans were as prone to obeying authority as were Germans. Contrary to his, and others', expectations, the Americans were also very prone to obeying authority, even when that authority was making horrifying demands.

I believe that Milgram's experiments were carried out with great ingenuity and that his findings are real and valid. (The experiments were replicated in many different places, even in different countries, with roughly comparable results.) The findings show how people really do behave under such circumstances. I also believe that Milgram's own explanation of his own findings is too limited. It does not get to the heart of the matter.

I believe that Milgram created the circumstances—through his ingenious research strategy—where the participants in the experiment were made to believe that the moral standards of their personal lives were entirely irrelevant and inappropriate to their behavior in the experiment. They were made to believe that the moral standards presented to them by the experimenter should fully govern their behavior in the experiment. These standards were presented as an entirely complete and self-contained system; they comprised a moral universe of their own. Here was a system of morality that answered all questions from a particular local point of view. That point of view emphasized the importance of the participants' contribution to science, and therefore the need to be absolutely resolute in obeying the instructions to the letter, so that the scientific objectives could be achieved. But obeying instructions, let me repeat, was merely the by-product of a more profound reality, that *here was a local and self-contained moral universe that precluded the morality of the participant's personal private world.* The Local Moral Universe prevailed. It dictated behavior totally at variance with the ideals in which participants had been brought up to believe. A high priority in each participant's upbringing must have been the proscription against hurting innocent people. Yet here all reference to that belief was cut off by a locally defined, self-contained set of strictures.

This is also what happened among the troops that made up the German police battalion described by Browning and among the American troops who participated in the massacre at My Lai. In each case a Local Moral Universe came into existence. It prevailed over any misgivings that one's personal upbringing might have introduced. The idea that you don't murder innocent people—which was surely part of the civilian upbringing of both German and American troops—was ruled out as irrelevant to the immediate, local circumstances in which one found oneself.

A Local Moral Universe also prevailed in both the Jonestown and San Diego cults. In each of these the members were surely brought up to abhor suicide, as are most members of the society to which these individuals used to belong. Yet in each place there prevailed locally a moral imperative that denied admissibility of this value. It replaced it with the value that suicide can contribute to the highest state of grace, to one's salvation. This was accomplished amid a distinctive moral climate, where a total system of answers to all human yearnings was being presented. And, in the minds of the faithful, that system was being implemented.

A Local Moral Universe is most easily understood when it is practiced by a particular group of persons who are in close proximity and interaction with each other. Here the persons directly reinforce each others' localized moral strictures. We saw it among the troops in the German police battalion and among the American troops at My Lai, and, surely, we saw it among the cult members.

However, a local moral universe can also exist in a larger format. It can exist as a system of ideology, where no outside beliefs are permitted and where one particular system of belief claims to have an answer to every human need and concern. We encounter such large moral universes among early adherents to Marxist Communism, among some adherents to Freudian psychoanalysis, and among many adherents to religious orthodoxies. Such moral universes are "local" in that they claim to have answers and directives covering all circumstances, here and now, that individual adherents might encounter. Take, for example, the early True Believers in Stalin's Marxist Communism (those living in the West as well as those living in the Soviet Union). They either excused the murderous deeds of Stalin as necessary adaptations to great external dangers, or they simply denied that any such massacres had happened. When True Believers were told that the Stalin regime deliberately starved to death about thirteen million kulaks in the 1930s, the Marxists shrugged off the news as capitalistic lies. The outside world's evidence was simply and totally rejected as irrelevant.

I have also encountered Local Moral Universes in the "cultures" of graduate students undergoing university preparation for doctoral degrees. Here, given the students' high dependence on a particular mentor (usually the professor who is the source of their research funds), there tends to be total immersion in a particular school of thought. Rival schools of thought, which may be represented by other professors in the very same university, are either unmentionable or referred to only with utter scorn and cynicism.

Moral Universes beguile because they are so very complete. They offer an answer to all important issues, so what need is there to go elsewhere? Why should one be open to other points of view?

The thinking often seems rational, but it is not really a rational matter. A Local Moral Universe can easily take on the trappings of a moral crusade. Adherents can readily manufacture moral ardor for what they are doing. Among the SS engaged in mass killings it was not uncommon to invoke the sacred cause of Germany's quest to become racially pure. For them, the mass killing they carried out was a moral crusade. Among American troops in Vietnam, that war was regarded as the only means of overcoming Communism, which was seen as a scourge, an affliction, that must be eradicated before it totally engulfed and destroyed the American way of life. It, too, was a moral crusade for the participants.

In both cases, a purportedly moral theme became the central guidepost—the catalyst—that focused and gave justification to the actions in which individuals were engaged. It gave meaning to the lives of these individuals while they were engaged in killing. It consolidated these individuals into a community of persons with shared values, for which adherents were fully prepared to give their lives and take the lives of others. It congealed their Local Moral Universe.

Personal Responsibility

Within the type of Local Moral Universe I have described—as, for example, in the cult situation at San Diego—"outside" values, values learned before a participant joined the Local Moral Universe, are declared to be totally irrelevant and inadmissible. Where, then, does personal responsibility come in? Remember that cult members sacrificed not only their own lives but the lives of their young children. Do these parents not take responsibility for their actions? Are they not culpable for these actions? Have they really lost all will of their own, and have they abdicated responsibility for their actions?

Similarly, what about the "ordinary" German soldiers whom Browning describes, who willingly and personally murdered hundreds of totally innocent people? What about the American soldiers in Vietnam, so full of zeal while they went about slaughtering the unarmed villagers of My Lai? Are these people not aware that they are responsible for their actions? Or, more accurately, can we as outsiders assess their responsibility? Can we evaluate where and how they are responsible?

The issue of responsibility rests on an individual's personal autonomy. But autonomy is a very subtle matter. (I have been studying and writing about autonomy for many years, and still find myself discovering new features in it.[3]) As a starting point, I posit that an individual who has autonomy—who has the capacity to make choices, and who actually makes choices—bears responsibility for these choices. Does this axiom apply to cult members? Do cult member have autonomy? More subtly, but more importantly, what kind of autonomy do these people have?

Two different kinds of autonomy need to be considered here: personal autonomy which is legitimized by the wider society, and personal autonomy which is not legitimized by the wider society.

First, consider the personal autonomy which is legitimized by the wider society. A surgeon has autonomy in regard to performing an operation. After obtaining the patient's permission to perform a particular operation, the surgeon has autonomy to devise surgically appropriate strategies for carrying out that operation. In addition, the surgeon usually has the right, indeed the obligation, to make necessary decisions while actually performing the operation. If unexpected conditions are encountered during the operation, he or she does not have to ask for further permission from an outside agent.

In short, a society establishes zones of human behavior within which individuals can act autonomously and which the wider social order accepts and supports. Within that zone the individual is allowed to act autonomously and is exempted from culpability when exercising the sanctioned autonomy.

This type of autonomy has limits. To take a ludicrous but illustrative example: a surgeon does not have the autonomy to take off his or her sterile clothes and perform a striptease dance in the middle of an operation. To do so would disgrace the surgeon and lead to serious repercussions, including possible sanctions against the surgeon. In other words, a surgeon has considerable autonomy, but only in a certain specified zone of behavior; while in the role of surgeon he or she has no autonomy at all in certain other zones.

This first type of autonomy applies to much of our lives. Autonomy is "structured"; it is built into niches in the social order in which we live. There are many such niches. There are occupational niches (such as the autonomy of a surgeon), there are age-related niches (such as rights incurred upon becoming an adult), there are sex-related niches, there are citizenship niches, and so forth. In each niche there are distinct zones where the participant has guaranteed autonomy, and other zones to which autonomy does not extend.

Since autonomy is structured, the individual remains accountable to the wider society. To be sure, there is some unpredictability. One cannot be completely sure which surgical measures a particular surgeon will adopt when there are unexpected complications during an operation. But the surgeon is expected to exercise autonomy only within medically legitimate ways. This means that, although the surgeon has discretion as to exactly what will be done, the surgeon is autonomous along *medical* criteria. The autonomy is circumscribed. At the same time, the surgeon is freed from being held accountable for any tragic outcome resulting from his autonomous judgments, as long as the judgment falls legitimately within the zone of accepted medical autonomy. (If the surgeon makes mistakes because he is drunk, then these mistakes would fall outside accepted medical autonomy, and the surgeon would be liable for the results.)

In this first type of autonomy, then, responsibility is clearly defined because it is known in which zone of behavior the autonomy lies. In order to discover where responsibility lies, we must find out where autonomy lies— where it begins and where it ends.

The second kind of autonomy is the type *not* legitimized by the wider society. Individuals who act out of the second type of autonomy find that the wider social order does not endorse their autonomy at all. In the first type of autonomy there is a trade-off with the wider social order. In return for receiving some guaranteed autonomy, the individual must accept the norms and laws of the wider society that touch upon his or her social niche. In turn, the individual obtains a specified zone within which he or she is freed from culpability for autonomous actions, provided he or she is clearly acting within the accepted limits. One is then operating autonomously within a protected zone.

Inside a cult, there is no such trade-off with the wider social order, since its norms and laws are considered irrelevant. Here the second type of autonomy prevails. An individual's autonomous behavior is therefore no longer socially protected by the wider society, although it is recognized and protected within the Local Moral Universe. An individual's every act can be considered as a possible violation of the wider society's standards. At the same time, the individual cult member may act with virtually no external moral constraints, except those imposed by the cult's Local Moral Universe that prevail in the immediate situation in which the cultist operates. External world beliefs and practices are ruled out by the cult and, in turn, the wider society does not, and usually cannot, identify or condone the cult member's zones of behavioral autonomy.

Cult members do have specialized zones of behavior in which autonomy, in the form of innovative and creative activity, is encouraged and rewarded. They may produce new ways of venerating and worshipping the person and the message of the cult leader. They may develop creative ways of serving the leader and the cause for which the leader stands. They may have a sense of imminent salvation and great personal freedom by donating their autonomy to the shared grand cause. Specifically, cult members have donated their personal belongings, their time, their work, their sexuality, their children, even their lives. There is every indication that these gifts are donated freely, lovingly, even joyfully. The giver feels vibrantly alive and free while actively contributing to a venerated cause.

This type of autonomy, which is not mandated and constrained by the wider society, constitutes the second type of autonomy. It can lead to great extremes, such as donating the very life of young children. As far as the wider society is concerned, the cult, and its constituent Local Moral Universe, is seen as an illegitimate mutation of the society's moral system. The cultist's sense of personal freedom is not acceptable to the larger society.

A cult member's autonomy somewhat resembles the autonomy members of orthodox religious communities have. Members of both are apt to believe that they are participating in a richly creative life, even while adhering to tight strictures over personal conduct. To an outsider, members of both communities may appear to be totally controlled by their community. Yet the members are apt to feel that they are gloriously free.

There is a crucial difference between cults and orthodox religious communities, such as most orthodox Jewish communities. Typically, the orthodox Jewish community makes some sort of accommodation to the larger community and society. It accepts considerable accountability to the outside world. This factor places their members' behavior within the first type of autonomy. In fact, in Israel the orthodox religious community has been able to have a powerful influence on the government at large by exercising its swing votes in a political situation where the ruling party usually has only a slim majority. Quite obviously, most (but not all) orthodox groups in Israel accept the sovereignty of the state.

By contrast, extremist cults typically do not in any way accommodate to the larger society. Hence, in cult behavior there may be total breakdown of moral accountability, as the members of the larger society see it. The Local Moral Universe appears in complete control over the behavior of cult members.

For example, the larger society did not in any way grant the San Diego cult members the autonomy to murder their own children. When the cult members in fact murdered (or "sacrificed") their children, the larger society held them morally culpable. Cult members may have believed they were acting under moral autonomy granted to them by the cult movement which superseded the larger society's moral codes, but to the larger society this was unacceptable. It regarded cult members as morally responsible for their personal acts, and they stood ready to punish acts that violated the standards of the larger society, such as the murder of children.

In practice, when cult members have committed morally repugnant deeds and themselves live to be held accountable, the larger society is apt to demand that they be treated as criminals, and punished accordingly. Or they are defined as so mentally deranged that they must undergo deprogramming before they are permitted to return to regular participation in the society. In both ways, the larger society holds the cult accountable for illegitimate use of autonomy. The Local Moral Universe in which cult members operate is treated as an illegitimate mandate for personal behavior.

When it comes to strange Local Moral Universes, such as the one that prevailed during the massacre at My Lai, we tend to protect our sensibilities by pretending that, in that universe, the soldiers did not really "enjoy" the killing, that the soldiers were under great stress and did not know what they were doing, that a few leaders misled them. All these distortions are a way of saying that, surely, there cannot be a Moral Universe that differs so drastically from the Larger Moral Universe we know and venerate. How could such an alien, cruel culture appeal to the soldiers who are our own flesh and blood, our sons and daughters, our brothers and sisters?

Sad to say, a new Moral Universe, whose content is diametrically opposed to everything we value, does occasionally arise and gain allegiance from people like ourselves. In their localized allegiance, the sense of personal responsibility of those involved can come to stand in violent opposition to the responsibilities we treasure in the wider society.

In different words, there occasionally emerge Local Moral Universes that are a mutation from the Larger Moral Universe to which most of the society adheres. That mutation can constitute a great threat to that Larger Moral Universe that makes up the moral core of the society. It may be the beginning of a transformation of the larger social order, where personal responsibility is judged in frighteningly new ways. This, after all, is the reason why that larger social order attempts to crack down on militant cults, seeing them as nascent change of the moral core that may get out of control.

At the present time, we do not know when new Local Moral Universes may arise, what circumstances and beguilings are apt to produce them. We do not have a definitive formula that tells us when, after such mutations have arisen, there is a fertile social climate for them to flourish. In Darwinian terms, when do mutations survive? If societies are to avoid moral roller-coasters and, possibly, moral disasters, we need to find answers to these questions.

The Role of the Local Moral Universe in Genocides

The past century has seen the repeated rise of Moral Universes that have sponsored grotesque levels of social horror. Some of the worst of these are the modern nation-states, whose governments claim total moral authority over their citizens. The scholar R. J. Rummel writes in his book, *Death by Government*, that in the first eighty-eight years of the twentieth century almost 170 million men, women, and children were put to death by their own country's government.[4] The anthropologist Pierre van den Berghe begins his book, *State Violence and Ethnicity,* with the following statement:

> Since its inception some 7,000 years ago, the state . . . has been the primary killer in human history. Killing is, in fact, the very nature of the state. . . . Most states have outkilled all freelance murders by one or more orders of magnitude.[5]

The other side of this picture is that within the modern nation-state, the citizens regard the state as the major moral module within which they exist, and from which they obtain their sense of identity and life's purpose. When modern individuals speak of their "society," they usually refer to their country, the nation-state in which they reside. Its moral dimension is uppermost in shaping their thinking of themselves as part of a human community.

The great French sociologist Emile Durkheim emphasized that human societies are *moral* entities.[6] He taught us that societies contain people who share values and customs, language and symbols, history and traditions. These become fundamental social bonds among the society's members; they are what anthropologists later lumped together under the term "culture." These bonds, and the society that embodies them, define much of the personal life of the members of a society.

A society, as a *moral* entity, gives profound meaning to one's personal life. It nurtures the individual while, at the same time, it transcends that individual and links him or her intimately to something larger, to which the person owes *moral* allegiance, and whose values and traditions are believed to be most vital to the person's existence. Most importantly, the individual tends to accept that the society is larger and, in many ways, more fundamental than the individual. It is the source of the individual's identity and moral compass. Furthermore, the individual tends to accept that one belongs to this larger entity, and the moral reality it represents. For Durkheim, a society plays much the same role for the individual as God does for many religious believers. It is the source and embodiment of all that is morally and ethically most fundamental to one's makeup, including one's linkage to something larger than one's own life.

This may sound complicated and esoteric, but it is something for which many people have been willing to die. It is something that has often seemed very clear, immediate, and compelling. It is also something for which people are sometimes prepared to do horrendous deeds, even to their fellow citizens, their own children, and themselves.

Here is an example of one's moral attachment to one's society. It was at work (though it was not clearly understood) during the war crimes trials at Nuremberg after the Second World War. In these trials, the defendants, accused of horrendous crimes, usually stated that they were merely following orders. The prosecutors replied that some orders are so gruesome, so totally evil, that they should not have been obeyed. What the courts usually failed to highlight was the defendants' second statement. After claiming that they were merely following orders they typically stated, in one form or another, that, to them, *it was unthinkable to do otherwise*. After all, the German officer had "sworn an oath" to carry out all orders. How could one possibly break one's oath! It was simply unthinkable. This is how that society's moral business was accomplished. The officer's obedience was based not on coercion, but on moral conviction: what it meant to be a German officer; what it meant to be a German citizen. One's oath captured the very essence of one's bond to what was most sacred, the core of one's moral universe. It was unthinkable to go against this moral universe in which one was embedded, in which one's very identity was rooted, through which one was personally connected to a grand entity, the state. (Remember Durkheim: the state, the society, is virtually deified. One's attachment to it is the highest moral imperative.)

Helen Fein, a contemporary sociologist, took Durkheim as her starting point for analyzing the Nazi genocide.[7] She compared the fate of Jews in different European countries that were controlled by the Nazis during the Second World War. Her central thesis is that Jews fared worst in countries where they had been essentially excluded from the "universe of obligations" of the dominant culture. Jews were murdered in the largest proportions when they lived among people who regarded them as strangers who did not share in the common values of the society.

Fein goes beyond Durkheim's insight that societies are believed to be moral entities. She posits that persons who are regarded as being outside one's moral community can be regarded as not being human beings at all, and can be treated accordingly. They can be terrorized, even murdered, without this action arousing the moral conscience that would be aroused if such deeds were committed against one's "own kind." Going further, the populace easily supports individuals who attack outsiders, the potential infidels. The attackers are seen as defenders of the purity and virtue of the moral community at large.

Thus commission of mass murder can come to be seen as satisfying a country's need for internal moral purification. Under the incitement of manipulative charismatic leaders, citizens of a country are sometimes encouraged to join in internal moral "cleansing" operations. Deeply venerated, shared values, and the people holding them, are seen as coming under moral assault, and even death is deemed too light a punishment for the supposed transgression against the very essence of the society's moral order. Hitler's Germany was surely an example, as was Stalin's Soviet Union and Pol Pot's Cambodia, to mention just a few. The leader's claim to stand for a moral mandate becomes the rallying point for zealous cooperation and participation by followers in the most gruesome murder of fellow citizens.

However, a Moral Universe is not necessarily permanently fixed and stable. New Moral Universes can be created, and old, existing ones can change. Let us reexamine some of our examples of moral upheavals in the light of the proposition that Moral Universes can undergo drastic change.

1. Under the Nazi regime Jews were defined as being outside the German Moral Universe. Many, perhaps a majority, of German citizens—including most of the villagers around me during my childhood—accepted this formulation. But before the Nazis came to power, German Jews had been relatively well integrated into German national life. They participated, and were accepted as participants, in many dimensions of the German culture, and the Moral Universe it represented. The Nazi regime introduced a drastic change in what was regarded as the German Moral Universe.

   This points to a need to adjust Helen Fein's formulation, that Jews were most likely to be persecuted if they were regarded as being outside the "universe of obligation." In Germany, where Jews were comparatively well integrated into that universe, the Nazi *reformulation* managed to *transform* Jews into outsiders.

2. In the United States, Japanese Americans were well integrated into American national life. By 1940 many ethnic Japanese were native to the United States, were educated in American schools, and lived as active participants in American communities. Yet with the advent of the war with Japan, these persons were suddenly defined as strangers who were potentially disloyal and might operate outside the American Moral Universe. Based on this reassessment, Japanese Americans were driven from their homes and communities and interned in camps, as though they were real enemies.

3.   In our day and age the nation-state is not the only basis of Moral Universes. The rekindling of ethnic wars in the Balkans in the 1990s and the
tribal wars in parts of Africa in the 1980s alert us to this fact. Yes, as
R. J. Rummel reminds us, the history of nation-states contains ghastly
episodes when it comes to the protection of humane values and human
life. But amid the modern scenario of the nation-state, ethnic and tribal
loyalties continue to reemerge and reassert themselves as the moral
modules within which groups of people may identify themselves. Full-
blown lethal hatreds reemerged among people of different ethnic back-
grounds who had, for a period of time, lived together in harmony in a
nation-state like Yugoslavia after the Second World War.

Similarly, the periodic pogroms against Jews in Eastern Europe suggests that fanatical levels of moral zealotry can emerge in support of a
claimed moral community. After a long period of quiet coexistence among
groups that are ethnically different, former enmity turned out to have
been merely in a state of surface accommodation, hiding in a storehouse
of dormant social explosives. It required only the arrival of a catalyst for
the reigning moral compact—the system of values, loyalties and allegiances—to be reorganized and refocused and new moral priorities to
emerge. And these new priorities can claim fanatical intensity.

In the case of the Balkans of the 1980s and 1990s, the catalyst was the
collapse of the central Yugoslav government and the rather hasty international recognition of the earliest break-away provinces. Outside support emboldened the ethnic fracturing and the reemergence of dormant
allegiances to various ethnic groupings. The restructuring that followed
was dramatic, quick, and fundamental. A surprising level of murderous
inter-ethnic brutality emerged.

I have just repeated part of the discussion from the previous chapter. I do
so to make a new point: *Fundamental changes need not require totally new
components in the package of values and behaviors to which people subscribe.*
Instead, the changes can come about merely through reorganization of the
existing content of the package. The total tenor of the package can be set by
one new rider, a new theme that becomes all-pervasive. This theme can generate new priorities among the values and behaviors that make up the existing
package, and thereby totally transform the package. As a result, people feel
suddenly empowered to do things to their former neighbors which would have
been unthinkable to them before the reorganization of the package.

The switch takes on a personal face if we turn to the case of Dr. Eduard
Wirths, a previously humane and decent German physician. Dr. Wirths took
great risks to serve Jews as their physician during the early part of the Nazi
era, yet he became a major contributor to the Auschwitz program of system-

atic, genocidal murder[8] (I describe his case more fully later in this book). His fundamental commitment as a physician, surely, was that he was a healer. Being a healer is central to the outlook, training, and professional focus of most Western physicians, including the German physicians of the Hitler era. The Nazis managed to convert Dr. Wirths into a killer by convincing him that, by joining the Nazi program at Auschwitz, he would not only remain a healer, he would become a healer in a far more fundamental and magnificent manner.

Under the new rider, Dr. Wirths would become a healer of the German nation, the German Volk and the Nordic, Aryan race by contributing his expertise to the supreme purification process being carried out by the Nazis. The Nazis rearranged the priorities in Dr. Wirths' existing package of values and commitments. He was not being asked to drop his fundamental existing value, that he was a healer. Instead, he was asked to rearrange his values so that he would be a healer on a far grander scale, giving him an opportunity to make a far more important contribution to his society.

The lesson to be learned from the conversion of Dr. Wirths is that a rearrangement of the components of existing packages of values can be extremely seductive and beguiling. One is not giving up one's existing values. One is merely *revitalizing* them by setting different priorities among one's existing values.

It is important to realize that horrors can be generated within moral realities. People who commit genocidal activities believe that what they stand for and fight for represents what is morally most fundamental to their human existence. Some defend this moral "reality" with intellectualized passion, as did Dr. Wirths when he claimed that his participation in horrors was necessary for the greater genetic good of the German people and their racial composition.

Another key factor is the pure joy—the unvarnished pleasure—in contributing to a great cause. I am convinced that much genocidal killing is done with joy—not by sadists who pathologically enjoy killing but by individuals who believe they are actively contributing to a new vitality and cleansing of their moral community. Many SS officers believed this sort of reasoning. By murdering Jews, they believed they were actively cleansing Germany of racial impurities and helping to usher in a revitalized German nation. This line of thinking led to murderous activities done with creativity, joy, and moral fervor.

~

Obviously there are many loose ends in this analysis of moral aberrations. For instance, when is peaceful coexistence among people of very different ethnic background based on real peace and mutual acceptance of a Joint Moral Universe (as, we hope, is the case in the United States of America)? And when, by contrast, is apparent coexistence merely glossing over fundamental antagonisms that can be reactivated amid a mere rearrangement of the values underlying one's Moral Universe? We need the answer because we saw how moral restructuring can result in limitless violence that can reach genocidal proportion. How are dormant hostilities perpetuated, sometimes retaining their destructive moral force from generation to generation?

∼

Moral Universes profoundly energize human behavior and impassion people. All of us know that moral forces can generate profound bonding among persons, and result in the most generous and loving behavior. Yet I have been suggesting that moral forces can also generate and legitimize dangerous and destructive excesses. The two may be made out of the same cloth, namely membership in a Local Moral Universe. I am convinced that we must, and can, understand Moral Universes of all kinds—how they come into existence and how they operate. What I have done here in this section of the book is just a bare beginning. I hope it is enough to open up the examination of Local Moral Universes in earnest. I hope this will bring them under more intelligent and more effective control. I hope this will give us more weapons to face the morally mandated horrors we humans periodically inflict on one another.

CHAPTER SIX

A Look at Implementation
of the Holocaust

I started to piece together a theory of evil around 1981. I focused on the underbelly of that perverse moral universe called Nazism, namely, the individual participants in the Nazi horrors. I began to realize that these individuals not only saw Nazism as a distinctive moral umbrella—a source of values, beliefs, and rewards—but they also saw it as a venue where they could participate in a morally meaningful life. In Nazism, they felt they could be active contributors to a grand cause and, through it, discover meaning and fulfillment in their personal life.

By the year 1981, I had been a practicing sociologist, a researcher, and a college teacher for twenty years. I had been a Holocaust survivor for forty years. Until then, I had kept these two facets of my life very separate. For much of that time I did not admit even to myself, let alone confront in a practical way, my history as a Holocaust survivor. I saw no way for my Holocaust background to have any bearing on my "real" work, the work of a social scientist trying to understand human behavior. As I now see it, my level of blindness and self-deception was quite amazing. I had been immersed in the academic community and regarded it as a distinctive moral domain for my life, with its own rules, content, and rewards. I lived in the world of scholarship and college teaching, comfortably focused on research that had little bearing on painful matters in my personal life. Or so I thought.

I began my new quest from a viscerally felt conviction that different ways of thinking were needed in order for us to understand what caused the Holocaust. At the start I lacked a clear sense of what sort of thinking should

87

take place. I had rather recently left Israel and, with it, a senior professorship at a great university, largely because I was suddenly and belatedly and fumblingly confronting my personal Holocaust history.[1] I returned to the United States unsettled, and this state of mind was probably a major reason why I failed to obtain an academic position upon my return. I obtained, instead, a research position at a veterans hospital. But in 1981 I was failing in that position because I had committed the most dreadful sin a modern researcher can commit: I had failed to obtain research grants. One reason probably was that I had begun to focus my mind on other things.

I realized I was dissatisfied with the conventional wisdom that stated that the Nazi era was a time of monstrous deeds committed by monstrous people. That line of thinking does not explain very much. It urges us to find the monstrous persons and, then, render them harmless by killing them or incarcerating them. This may do something to lessen our heartfelt and justified rage at these perpetrators of evil. Yet I became increasingly aware that this line of thinking does not prevent the next round of horrors, nor the arrival of new generations of humans who do monstrous things.

I also was dissatisfied with the notion that the Holocaust was so unique that it defied understanding. This idea has compelling emotional appeal, but it enfeebled us inellectually. We remained not merely emotionally shattered—this I could accept—but we also remained intellectually shattered, impotent to understand the Holocaust events scientifically. This I could not accept.

Our lack of understanding of the Holocaust was taking place while we were being inundated by large quantities of information about the Holocaust's raw horrors. The Nazi universe was revealed to be so horrendous, so shocking, that it became increasingly difficult to recognize any moral coherence in its perverse content. It became impossible to take seriously its moral appeal—yes, *moral* appeal—to millions of ordinary people. Yet to fail to take that appeal into account is to deceive ourselves, and to deny ourselves the opportunity to understand its actual implementation.

Understanding that implementation requires dispassionate ways of thinking, and applying them to events that are drenched in private horror and personal trauma. Dispassionate thinking about horrors requires grinding some new lenses so that we might see a little better. The lenses I began to offer concern (1) the ways in which people make decisions, especially immediacy-focused incremental decisions; (2) the "packaging" of values into composite amalgamations; and (3) the ways we use our freedom: the social location, the context, and functions of our autonomy. These led to the book, *Ordinary People and Extraordinary Evil*, and will be developed more fully in the following pages.

∽

Historical research has supplied us with extensive information about the stark facts of the Holocaust. It includes efforts both to document the full extent of the horror and to maintain a degree of objectivity and avoid undue sentimentality. The historical work points to unresolved, and possibly unresolvable, questions, such as the nature of the involvement and the responsibility of European Christians. That issue includes, at one end, the accusation that Pope Pius XII was, at the very least, inactive in the face of a supreme moral challenge. It includes, at the other end, acknowledging courageous rescues of Jews by some individual Christians, at considerable risk to themselves.

My own odyssey pointed in both directions. My visit to Oberlauringen, the German village where I was born, eventually taught me that the actions of a single individual—the courageous Ernestine—can shine brightly amid the darkness produced by a host of moral delinquents. But one still has to ask how millions of persons could be harnessed to implement a program of utter horror. How did the harnessing work?

Social Dimensions: Scope, Cooperation, and Perversion

Historical research on the Nazi era illuminates not only the extreme brutality but the immense scope of the murderous campaign. It shows the highly complex administrative processes, vast material, and extensive human resources needed to accomplish the extermination of millions of people. In Germany, the existing administrative structure of the government was effectively adapted to that task. Ideological antecedents to Nazism, such as the dream that there once was a pure Aryan race that formed the basis of the German nation, were also adapted to the task. Highly systematized indoctrination of the young was also in place, ready for cooperation. In short, here was a nation transformed into a perverse moral community, where the existing machinery of the state was fully utilized in the service of that moral perversity.

We must, however, recall that we are not only dealing with the nation of Germany. During the Second World War Germany overran and occupied most of the countries on the European continent. In each of these countries there was a Jewish population. And in each of these the German government attempted to implement its policy of exterminating the Jews.

As discussed in chapter 5, sociologist Helen Fein examined how the different German-occupied countries responded to Nazi pressure to carry out extermination policies against their Jewish populations.[2] The extent of their collaboration with the Nazis and in carrying out their plan to exterminate the Jews varied greatly. Accordingly, the fate of Jews varied in the different occupied countries. In some, most of the Jews survived. In most, the large majority were murdered, after or while being sent to death camps in Poland.

Fein asserts that the difference among countries is attributable to the following factors:

1. The degree of German control in the country. Where there was a lack of resistance to the Germans, where there was much cooperation with the Germans, victimization of Jews was extensive.

2. The degree of social solidarity—cohesion, absence of strife—in the country before the war. If, before the German invasion, there was strong solidarity, there was little victimization of Jews after the German occupation.

3. The extent to which the Jews had been included in a common "universe of obligations" before the war. Where such inclusion of Jews was the general rule, there was little victimization during the German occupation.

In short, in this study we have an attempt to show the bearing of a nation's social structure upon genocidal actions.

We must also keep in mind that the Nazis conducted extensive extermination programs against a variety of peoples, not only against Jews. Gypsies, Poles, Belorussians, and Ukrainians suffered on the order of ten million killed through Nazi atrocities, in addition to those who died in military action. The scholar B. Wytwycky[3] reminds us that genocide—efficient killings of entire categories of persons—was a highly exportable method. It was applied to different peoples, in different geographic regions, of Europe. Although the present chapter concentrates on the genocidal persecution of Jews, it raises considerations that go far beyond the fate of the Jews.

Social Dimensions: Toward Sociological Dissection

Sociological research on the Holocaust has developed surprisingly late and, even now, is not plentiful. The just-mentioned study by Helen Fein is one of few in the field. As late as 1979, B. M. Dank, a sociologist, wrote that there was no sociology of the Holocaust.[4] Apparently, when it comes to explaining extraordinary events, social scientists operate under a severe handicap. We are inclined to look to the ordinary, rather than the mysterious or the unusual, and this isn't always seen as helpful in explaining the extraordinary. We should have been able to accept the possibility that routine and mundane behavior could produce morally monstrous consequences; we should have seen that "extremist movements are not primarily the product of extremists," as sociologists Seymour Martin Lipset and Earl Raab pointed out after they studied various extremist movements in the United States.[5]

Looking to the ordinary to explain the extraordinary is inherent in the outlook, and the paradigms, of the scientist. But this outlook can become highly suspect, even repugnant, when applied to events that are morally outrageous and uniquely abhorrent to the general public. For many who suffered in the Holocaust, or whose kinsfolk were victims, the Holocaust is an evil that is utterly ineffable. For them, focus on the "ordinary" cannot do justice to the Holocaust's uniqueness. Insights into the routine, the mundane, cannot compare with the soul-searing insights offered through poetry (such as that by Nellie Sachs) or fiction (such as by Elie Wiesel), or the numerous auto-biographical reports that dwell on the uniqueness of the Holocaust and the impossibility of comparing it to any other event.

There obviously is need for reconciliation between the two realms, that of the social scientist sifting the ordinary for clues to creating the extraordinary, and that of the morally outraged human being, crying out in wrenching anguish about the immediate urgency of the extraordinary that actually happened. Both are justified responses. Both have a mighty claim on our attention.

This very reconciliation is a major aim of my efforts. On the one hand, I attempt to develop scientific explanations, where the "ordinary" is the start-ing point for understanding how horrendous actions can happen. On the other hand, I attempt to link these explanations to the perception of laymen, who feel that the monstrous nature of the Holocaust is only too real. I intend to take the "monster" perceptions seriously while exploring how exceptionally violent behavior can become routine and therefore be incorporated into the day-to-day workings of a bureaucratic apparatus. In other words, I want to put under my lens the processes that produce the routinization and bureaucra-tization of extremely violent behavior. What sort of social settings, and what sort of personal behavior in social settings, serve to implement the programs of an extremist movement?

Most bureaucracies have similarities that already have been studied and identified by behavioral scientists. These bureaucracies include government departments, large manufacturing concerns and, even, large not-for-profit organizations. All of these have a potential for operating with moral blinders. The bureaucrat's focus on a particular task and on the particular work context in which he or she operates often is accompanied by moral myopia. The exclusive focus on one's work-related task can obscure large moral issues, and moral consequences can be easily ignored. Considerations that go beyond the bureaucrat's immediate task are apt to be dismissed as irrelevant.[6] Thus, in focusing on the problems of transporting Jews and Gypsies to extermina-tion camps, or of the efficient use of wartime slave labor in munitions fac-tories in the German Ruhr, the morality of killing people is obscured. The bureaucrat claims that this issue is beyond one's particular responsibility and, most importantly, it stands in the way of accomplishing the tasks to which one has been assigned and for which one does have responsibility.

In trying to comprehend this phenomenon, this moral obtuseness to the suffering of individuals, one needs to bear in mind that a deliberate political campaign against the victims preceded and ran concurrent with it. They were portrayed as outcasts, as a species of lesser humans, as vermin. Doubtless this made an imprint on the bureaucrat's entire perspective, contributing to his or her moral myopia.

Yet one needs to go beyond looking at bureaucrats who have moral myopia because of their bureaucratic niche. One also needs to look at another crucial feature, namely, the incremental processes used to implement the annihilation of an entire people.

Some Characteristics of Nazism: Incremental Processes

There is every indication that the Nazis had no closely worked-out plans for the extermination of the Jews before they came to power in 1933. The extermination evolved in a step-by-step, incremental manner.

The first step, beginning in 1933, included a steady progression of repressive laws against Jews. These laws deprived Jews of a number of rights, with each law being more severe and more comprehensive than its predecessor. Every new law was an increment in a cumulative process that culminated in Jews being deprived of all rights of citizenship and the most elementary of human rights altogether.

For example, on 23 July 1938, a decree was issued that all Jews must apply for identification cards, to be carried at all times. A law passed on 17 August 1938 ordered Jews to adopt, as of 1 January 1939, Hebrew-sounding names—Sarah for women, Abraham for men. Such steps would serve to make Jews readily identifiable when it came time to round them up for transport to the death camps. Before that round-up came, these two laws made it easy to identify the Jews as targets for a variety of day-to-day harassments and persecution. Since the steps were taken legally they served to coopt, in an incremental manner, the legal machinery of the German state. In short, the existing legal machinery of Germany became an instrument whereby innocent citizens were systematically persecuted.

The gradual curtailment of citizenship rights became, in turn, a crucial step toward the 1942 secret order directing the physical annihilation of all Jews in Germany and the territories occupied by Germany. The piecemeal nature of the legislative sequence prior to that order deceived many, even many of the victims, into believing that the actual killing of Jews was unlikely to happen. The Nazi regime's series of ever more repressive laws built up into a course of action so extreme that it might have proven unacceptable to the German people—and perhaps impossible to carry out—if it had been attempted as one single action.

Could this happen only in Germany where, at the time, psychologists and anthropologists tell us there was a reigning "authoritarian personality"? (This personality, thanks to the authoritarian family structure in Germany, regarded obedience to authority as a major human virtue.) If so, then this would not happen in the United States, where individualism and a measure of resistance to blind obedience is a theme in the prevailing culture. As discussed in Chapter 5, Stanley Milgram, an American psychologist, set out to test this notion among Americans through a series of experiments in the 1960s.[7]

The participants in the Milgram experiments were asked to take part in a scientific experiment about "learning" that had been artificially contrived for a laboratory setting. The "learners" were to be jolted with an electric shock, administered by the program participants, if they made mistakes. In reality, the "learners" did not receive electric shocks. But the participants did not know this. They believed, and accepted, that the "learners" were to be electrically shocked, and that they, personally, needed to administer the shock.

The Milgram experiments found that people who are asked to follow instructions tend to do so, even if in the process innocent persons are cruelly hurt. Those charged with implementing instructions follow through, although the behavior may conflict with their own broader moral values. Apparently Americans were no different from Germans in their willingness to obey authority. Milgam's experiments were repeated in different settings, even in different countries, and the results were virtually the same in all of them.

It may be argued that the participants complied with the instructions because they respected a countervalue to their standard moral beliefs, namely the value of scientific research. But why accept this new value when it led to hurting innocent people in this context? Why could the value of scientific research here supercede humane values prohibiting cruelty? Presumably these implementers would not deliberately hurt innocent people in other contexts.

Although the Milgram experiments were highly creative and brilliantly conceived, I believe one needs to go beyond Milgram's own view that he was merely testing obedience to authority. It seems that Milgram's laboratory created a distinctive moral climate—a local moral world of its own, described in the previous chapter—where a particular set of values was created and enforced. Here "outside" values, on which the participants in the experiment were brought up, such as the value that you don't hurt innocent people, were declared to be irrelevant and out of bounds.

Apparently we humans are able to separate our behavior in one context from our behavior in other contexts. Sometimes this can mean an exclusive focus on an immediate problem by accepting the particular values of the present context and ignoring the values that prevail in other contexts. This can obliterate attention to significant consequences in one's current actions. Here persons solve problems one at a time, dealing with what confronts them immediately. Stated differently, an immediate context can embrace a specific set of values while shutting out other, possibly conflicting, values—values that might ordinarily govern one's actions. It creates the sort of Local Moral Universe I described in the previous chapter.

Restriction of the behavioral focus to the immediate context can have unexpected consequences. The behavior can expand incrementally in a cumulative process that develops truly monstrous results. Documented life histories of a number of the Nazi SS officials demonstrate this. Hannah Arendt's study of Adolf Eichmann, a study of SS officers by the British psychiatrist Henry Dicks, and the analysis of 581 biographies of early Nazis by Peter Merkl, all bear out the gradual nature of the immersion into the Nazi programs.[8]

Eichmann's evolution from a floundering youth to a grounded, dedicated Nazi is a good example of the process. The young Eichmann, upset by failures in his education and work, gave vent to his frustration by joining an organization of youths dedicated to pranks and totally unpolitical recreational activities. At that point, totally by chance, a friend asked him to join the Nazi party (the "National Socialist German Workers Party") instead. Eichmann did so, but evidently without commitment to, or even real knowledge of, the movement's ideology.

He advanced in the movement in a step-by-step sequence while retaining reservations about the murder of Jews. He had some Jewish relatives. He claimed, perhaps with sincerity, to retain loyalty to these persons. He even proposed different solutions to "the Jewish question," notably that European Jews be resettled in Madagascar.

These concerns did not keep Eichmann from complete adherence to the Nazi program of destroying the Jews, however. That adherence meant his becoming a highly significant and even innovative functionary in the mass murders. Much of Eichmann's activity was motivated by the urge to further his personal career, rather than with an ideological commitment to hating Jews. His career was carried out in the context of the Nazi state machinery. To live effectively, for Eichmann, meant contributing to that machinery.

Incremental processes are very common in the implementation of ad hoc political action. On the American national scene, for example, ad hoc action predominates in national policy making, in steering the economy, in reforming the welfare systems, in reorganizing bureaucratic procedures, and in adapting to international pressures. Ad hoc activity means, in each case, that one adapts to pressures by trying to find immediate, stopgap answers. One makes specific and direct responses to immediate issues, rather than developing long-term plans and carrying these out systematically.

When Abraham Lincoln was asked what sort of policy he would pursue after the end of the Civil War, he is reported to have stated: "The pilots on our Western rivers steer from *point* to *point* as they call it—setting the course of the boat no farther than they can see . . .and that is all I propose to myself in this great problem."[9]

I am not saying that ad hoc action is intrinsically bad or good. Ad hoc action can scarcely be avoided in a nation based on pluralistic politics. Where pressure groups are easily mobilized and where complex international alliances abound (including the necessity of some strange bedfellows), ad hoc responses are a necessary result.

It is not only the Eichmanns who develop their careers incrementally. Some years ago, a study I did with Harry Martin concluded that persons can enter into an occupational career by a series of localized, immediate decisions, and without any explicit commitment to that occupation at all.[10] A young woman may enter a nursing school because her closest friend is attending that school, and for no other reason. She may continue in nursing school because it would be costly to drop out and start afresh in another occupation. She may then continue on and enter nursing as a profession. In this sequence the student may not develop a special commitment to nursing, yet a career in nursing is very likely to result. There is no evidence to suggest that such a noncommitted nurse cannot carry out her profession fully. On the contrary, she can function as a full-fledged dedicated nurse even though her "dedication" is to something other than nursing.

In every occupation you can find persons who started out by an unplanned route. They incrementally carried out activities that eventually led to that particular occupation. They make decisions on an ad hoc basis, without ever having committed themselves to that occupation or to the ideals for which it stands.

It is often assumed that a person who goes through lengthy occupational training is bound to develop a commitment to that occupation during the course of training, if a definite commitment to the occupation did not exist beforehand. But this assumption should be regarded with skepticism. There are indications that persons can fully engage in an occupation without commitment to its core features. A particular teacher may not be committed to teaching, and yet be engaged in teaching.[11] A particular physician may not be committed to healing, and yet be engaged in healing. Each may come to the occupation via an incremental process whereby the commitment to the core feature is minimal, at best. The real commitment may be, for instance, to having a career. The career will, in turn, be embedded in a social context, to which the individual responds ongoingly, as career challenges arise.

Such an initially unplanned career may be carried out with great devotion. Robert McNeil, a very distinguished and devoted television journalist, was interviewed on the occasion of his retirement, after coanchoring a highly respected and innovative news program for twenty years. He stated that he had never planned to be a newsperson, let alone a television news reporter. He began his news career when he went to work for the Reuters news agency, where he had been hired because of his writing skills. Up to that time, he had never interested himself in the news or in news reporting. After that, he stated, he tried to respond to immediate news-reporting challenges as effectively as possible as they arose. His devotion, it seems, was to doing an excellent day-to-day job rather than a grand commitment to television journalism as such.

Eichmann and Heinrich Himmler, chief of the SS, also represent a devoted career focus, albeit careers with very different moral dimensions than Robert McNeil's. Both reached their career pinnacle through a series of un-planned, incremental decisions. Both occasionally expressed misgivings about their murderous work. But this did not keep them from enthusiastically and inventively embracing murderous deeds. On one occasion Himmler, in front of a group of *Einsatzgruppe* members ordered and observed the killing of a hundred persons as a demonstration of what the "liquidation" really looked like. During the killings he became visibly upset, yet decided to make a speech to the participants. He reminded them that they were "called upon to fulfill a repulsive duty . . . they were soldiers who had to carry out every order unconditionally." They surely noticed that he "hated this bloody business" but "he too was obeying the highest law of doing his duty" (cited from Raul Hilberg, *The Destruction of European Jews*, pp. 136–137).

Incremental processes lend themselves well to the practice of decep-tion. They do so by focusing attention on some aspects of the immediate situation rather than the larger picture. The Nazis tried at every step to ob-scure the direction of their actions toward mass murder. Deception even occurred at the decisive Wansee conference on 20 January 1942, where the mass killing of Jews was specifically decided upon and the methods for carrying this out chosen. Deception occurred in the transportation of Jews to the extermination camps, and in carrying it out (profitably!) with the victims even having to pay a fare for their "relocation."

In summary, the individual increments—such as the acts of individuals inventing and executing ever more efficient forms of murder—can be com-ponents of distinct personal careers. Yet these careers are apt to be embedded in a larger social context which, itself, consists of a composite package of values, programs, and actions. The nature of such packages, and the process of "packaging," need to, and can be, understood.

Some Characteristics of Nazism: Packaged Behavior

Nazism was a composite package of very diverse programs. This package included, somewhere near the top of its priorities, an official program of extreme anti-Semitism. It also included strong nationalism, entailing the ar-dent hope of recapturing all the land that Germany had lost as the result of World War I. It further included ethnicism (including the romantic master race theme), and economic development (including new career possibilities for many who had suffered in the crash of the 1920s).

All these components of Nazism were in a major way extensions of older, existing German values that were reformulated, resanctified, and revitalized to suit the Nazi purpose. The ideology of German nationalism, for example, was built upon the concept of an idyllic *Volk* already formulated by the philosopher Johann Gottfried von Herder, who lived from 1744 to 1803. In its early version, *Volk* referred to an organic, natural family, in contrast to the supposed artificiality of the nation-state. It was subsequently reinterpreted by the philosopher Johann Gottlieb Fichte, who lived from 1762 to 1814, to emphasize unique German individuality. Nazi ideologists gave added meanings to the *Volk* concept, particularly those of romanticism and idealized German superiority, postulating a German master race. The Nazis used these concepts extensively, starting with the indoctrination of children in the Hitler Youth groups.

Leading figures among the early Nazis were evidently attracted to different items in the Nazi package. It is likely that Julius Streicher, with his history of hatred for Jews, was primarily attracted by the anti-Semitism in the Nazi package.[12] Eichmann was initially attracted by, and committed to, the career possibilities for himself in that package. Hermann Goering was apparently also attracted by its career possibilities, but on a higher level of personal aggrandizement and power. Each of them saw at least one feature in the Nazi package that offered a link to something that was important to themselves.

Who was attracted to Nazism? Sociologists have shown that social movements recruit not only drifters and the unattached, but also people with definite social interests and links, to which the movement caters. The Nazi package attracted both. I suspect that in the beginning phase of Nazism—during its rise to power in the 1920s—the social misfits and unattached may have been the most important recruits. They became the foot soldiers that led to the movement's success and filled the ranks of the early storm troopers and ruffians. Later, when the Nazis were in power, the well-established, socially respectable people became more critically important to the success of Nazism. They supplied an educated staff with expertise in getting things done, as well as the economic resources needed to accomplish Nazi goals.

Fanatical anti-Semitism was a consistent component of the Nazi package, and it was linked to components of earlier German national life. In her book, *The War Against the Jews, 1933–1945*, Lucy Dawidowicz writes:

> Layer upon layer of anti-Semitism of all kinds—Christian church teachings about Jesus, Volkist anti-Semitism, doctrines of racial superiority, economic theories about the role of Jews in capitalism and commerce, and a half century of political anti-Semitism—were joined with the solder of German nationalism . . .[13]

Doubtless many adherents were attracted to Nazism because of its anti-Semitism, although the proportion of Nazis that fell into this category is not known. In addition, it is very likely that Nazism converted many members to anti-Semitism after they joined the Nazi party for any one of its additional component parts. Still others joined the Nazi Party and actively participated in anti-Semitism even though they did not have any personal commitment to anti-Semitism. Indeed, anti-Semitic actions could be carried out, with great zeal and persistence, by persons who may not have had any personal commitment to anti-Semitism whatsoever. Their commitment was to some other component of the Nazi package that led to the acceptance of the total Nazi package. Even so, deeds of noncommitted anti-Semites—those who were committed to, say, bureaucratic efficiency—were sometimes more anti-Semitic in practice than those of the ideologically committed anti-Semite.

As I already indicated, there is evidence that Eichmann had no pronounced hatred for Jews when he joined the Nazi party. Eichmann even publicly claimed that he was not anti-Semitic. He said it early, and he said it late. I tend to believe Eichmann's protestations, at least on his terms. But these protestations by no means absolve him of responsibility for his extremely anti-Semitic *actions*. (I shall discuss this further in the next section.)

Provided Eichmann's protestations are true, some powerful sociological conclusions suggest themselves about the nature of Nazism and, for that matter, other extremist movements: (1) People can be *zealous* participants in—and contributors to—a program of action to which they do not wholly subscribe; and (2) People can be indifferent or opposed to some components of a movement's program, which they are actually engaged in carrying out fully and unreservedly, but for which they hold their scruples in abeyance.

Anyone who has served in an army knows that these are not far-fetched ideas. Soldiers routinely disregard moral assessments of many aspects of their task of killing enemies. One should not be misled by the expressed revulsion against killing that emerged among some American soldiers in the Vietnam War. This was the exception rather than the rule. Usually military killings are carried out relatively unquestioningly, following severe indoctrination during "basic training."

The soldier's moral commitment against killing, however, remains intact in nonmilitary contexts. That is, in civilian life the soldier remains in a non-killing mode. Even while adhering to his total set of moral beliefs, a soldier in action may unhesitatingly kill the enemy. He just holds his "civilian morality" in abeyance. Participation in killing does not therefore mean a commitment to killing itself. People can be enthusiastic participants in programs to which they do not wholly subscribe, and can be committed to killing in one context but not in another.

Participation in the Nazi mass killings was largely unquestioned when the killings were routinized, as they were in the use of gas chambers. Earlier, when the method of killing was not routinized, many participants expressed revulsion; some are reported to have committed suicide. This occurred when German soldiers, stationed behind the Russian front lines in 1941, were ordered to kill civilians and prisoners indiscriminately.

To return to Eichmann's career as an SS officer, he evidently did not deeply support every item in the SS package. This was not atypical for SS officers. Eichmann repeatedly expressed fairly explicit reservations, but like the other SS officers, he carried out all aspects of the Nazi package. He expressed unhappiness about the decision to annihilate the Jews, but zealously pursued its implementation. He was accepting the entire Nazi package despite his linkage to just parts of this package.

A variant of this pattern was exhibited by Rudolf Hoess, the commandant of Auschwitz, under whose command millions of Jews were murdered. In his diary, Hoess[14] completely accepts the "need" to annihilate the Jews because he accepts the Nazi ideology that Jews are the ultimate enemies of Germany. Yet Hoess was able to maintain, to himself at least, that he did not hate Jews, and that he was appalled by the cruelty exhibited by some of the guards under his command. The Nazi overall ideology he accepted so dominated his behavior, however, that some of its components were largely ignored. Here, too, the entire package was accepted, even including components that were distasteful.

The acceptance of an entire package while having reservations about some of its components is a paradox. Yet it is a common enough paradox. In their daily occupational work, individuals may be highly committed to some aspects of that work and not at all committed to other aspects. Nonetheless, they usually carry on with their work, including those aspects to which they are not committed. The individual's real commitment is very likely to be to one or another item among the total number of items that constitute the occupation's total package of values, objectives, and expected activities. Yet the total package of behavior is carried out. I first encountered this phenomenon in my study of physicians for my doctoral dissertation.

Packages can also change. Individual items from one package can combine with items from another package to form a new package. And packages can be undone and the constituent parts "repackaged." An example of both is the case of Father Charles E. Coughlin, an American populist priest who, in the 1930s, enjoyed immense popularity, largely through a very successful radio program. (This was before the era of television. Radio was the chief medium of mass communication, other than newspapers.) The followers of Father Coughlin accepted his package calling for radical economic reforms to benefit the poor, rabid anti-Semitism, and support for the fascistic regimes of Hitler and Mussolini.

When the United States became drawn into alliance with the enemies of Mussolini and Hitler, notably Britain, the Coughlin package came into ever sharper conflict with official national policy. As war approached, a rival package emerged in full bloom in the United States. It emphasized loyalty to the country in time of emergency, along with increasing hostility for the country's potential enemies who, clearly, were Hitler's Germany, Mussolini's Italy and, possibly, Japan. The components of the new package included the honor of participating in military service, the need to provide active economic and military help for America's European allies, and considerable reorganization of the national economy to put the country on a war footing. This package included some of the same items as Coughlin's package, such as a high emphasis on nationalism. But the items were assembled differently. They were placed in conjunction with items that the Coughlin package did not include, and some of Coughlin's items were excluded altogether from the new package.

Many of Coughlin's followers could not resist the new package, especially its highlighting of nationalism in a state of emergency. They quite suddenly abandoned Coughlin—and they did so totally, as war seemed imminent. To be sure Coughlin's own package included a large amount of nationalism, but that package was very different from the new package being encouraged by the federal government. The repackaged version of highlighted nationalism—the govenment's package—won out.

Within Germany, in a similar vein, some of the early appeal of Nazism was based on repackaged long-existing themes of German national life, such as the themes of Germans as a pure *Volk*, and German national uniqueness and exclusiveness. High-level army officers, in particular, saw this fervent Nazi nationalism as something they could embrace. They also responded to other Nazi rearrangements of existing cultural ingredients, such as one's sense of high duty to country, to which many were already committed. The Nazis repackaged the sense of duty to country into duty to obey the Fuehrer, and both were treated as entirely sacred.

In short, repackaging can be seductive because it can make use of commitments that already exist and, then, bind them to new commitments within new contexts. Here the repackaging is regarded as a way to revitalize, to reenergize, already existing commitments.

Repackaging may operate in unexpected ways. For instance, when the Nazi youth movements were obviously winning a mass allegiance, some Catholic youth movements tried to repackage their own programs by including some of the Nazi items, such as paramilitary training and rifle practice, just to keep up with the competition. Thus the Nazi package contaminated its apparent rivals. It subtly and persuasively overflowed into its rivals.

In many ways the packaging of Nazism can be seen as a way of constraining the actions of individuals. Yet, to understand the real impact of packaging, we must also confront the ways in which individuals retain autonomy amid these social constraints.

Personal Autonomy within the Nazi System

"We were only following orders." "As officials, sworn to obey, we had no freedom to do anything different." These themes were frequently voiced by former Nazi officials when they faced trial after World War II. (A variant of these themes is what the villagers of Oberlauringen said, "We are just little people. What could we do?") Let us examine the validity of these claims.

It is true that Nazi officials were members of a state-organized bureaucracy. As bureaucrats they were subject to administrative regulations and controls. During the trials of Nazi war criminals the accused officials frequently referred to these controls and to their own lack of discretionary power in carrying out orders. Yet the focus on bureaucratic control leaves a crucial component out of consideration. Bureaucrats everywhere have considerable autonomy. Sociologists have shown that bureaucrats often carve out autonomy for themselves, so that they can innovate, make decisions on their own initiative, and even devise entirely new ways of doing things.[15] They have also shown that many forms of autonomy, as exercised by the individual bureaucrat, can be very useful for accomplishing the bureaucracy's goals. It can provide flexibility, and allows for problem solving. The autonomy of bureaucrats is part of the very fabric of bureaucracies. It is just as basic to the continuing operation of bureaucracies as are the controls.

When Nazi bureaucratic functionaries said they were merely following orders, they were hiding the fact that they had considerable autonomy. They demonstrated autonomy by their inventiveness in the course of their daily work and in their flexibility when they wanted to be flexible. (Rudolf Hoess, the commandant of Auschwitz, used to complain about having to be very innovative because the number of new prisoners arriving every day was so very unpredictable. He had sufficient autonomy to make the necessary adjustments in order to keep his organization on its murderous track.[16])

Eichmann displayed a great deal of ingenuity and adaptability in getting trainloads of victims to their final destination. He was successful even during the latter part of the war when there was a severe strain on the German railroad system. When it became difficult to obtain trains to transport people to the death camps, Eichmann made special trips to persuade regional officials to give him priority over troops. In his zeal, he even bypassed some of his own superiors.

Indeed, toward the end of the war, Himmler, who was Eichmann's over-all superior, ordered him to stop transporting Jews to the death camps. Himmler had not suddenly become a humanitarian. He just wanted to keep the advancing Allied armies from discovering the Nazi atrocities. He was also under pressure to yield facilities, such as trains and manpower, to the German army in its last-ditch effort to stop the Allied armies. Eichmann, however, sabotaged even Himmler's order and continued using transports to deliver the Jews to the camps. Here Eichmann was clearly demonstrating autonomy to accomplish what he regarded as the mission entrusted to him in his position within the Nazi bureaucracy. He was also demonstrating that the bureaucratic system allowed for considerable flexibility when it came to devising means of reaching objectives.

SS Major General Otto Ohlendorf similarly exhibited autonomy in implementing mass murders. At the Nuremberg trials he admitted to overseeing the killing of over ninety thousand men, women, and children on the Russian southern front. He prided himself, however, on the efficient and "humane" manner in which the killings under his command were carried out. He instigated methods whereby there was little delay once the victims knew what was in store for them. The killings were carried out with military precision and speed. Ohlendorf prided himself on thereby reducing mental strain, for both victims and executioners. He, using his own discretion, had lessened suffering in a context in which immense suffering was inevitable.[17]

Eichmann exhibited autonomy in his bureaucratic zeal even after his capture by Israeli secret agents. Using a bureaucrat's style, he collaborated to a degree that astonished the agents. For example, after his capture in Argentina, his captors asked him to sign a document acknowledging his willingness to be brought to Israel for trial. He insisted on composing a document himself, and in it, he expressed the intentions of his Israeli captors in far more formidable bureaucratic language than his captors had done.

Bureaucracies, the German sociologist Max Weber noted many years ago, are effective instruments for getting complicated work done.[18] They help coordinate the work of many different specialists. Priorities are arranged strictly so that objectives can be reached. Weber emphasized that bureaucracies were thereby engines of social control, geared to integrating and routinizing the work of many specialized functionaries.

He was well aware that bureaucracies could be established for diverse purposes, such as organizing military service, organizing political administration of a region, or organizing a business enterprise. However, he probably did not imagine that his own country would establish a bureaucracy to routinize mass murder. He also did not imagine that the autonomy of bureaucratic functionaries could provide a crucial component for reaching murderous objectives.

In granting functionaries a measure of autonomy in the interpretation of rules, bureaucracies provide a mechanism for rationalizing behavior. When functionaries need to acknowledge only adherence to rules, they can disregard their own independent contributions—even to murderous behavior. They can concentrate on "technical" problems, on the means rather than the end. By contrast, when recognizing the bureaucrat's autonomy—pointing out where he or she makes an independent contribution—one is clarifying where personal culpability exists.

When the Eichmanns invented ways of bringing victims to the death camps, they were operating within definite zones of autonomy. This autonomy was granted to them—and, to be sure, with ample encouragement to put it to use—by the Nazi regime of which they were members. Within their zones of autonomy Nazi officials enjoyed the exercise of much discretion. They could, and did, innovate, elaborate on, and amplify the instructions they received. Here, finally, lies their personal responsibility and culpability. In the folklore about bureaucracy the individual bureaucrat is merely part of the machinery. One bears no responsibility for one's actions. One merely follows rules; one does not make them. This is, of course, a very inadequate view of what actually goes on inside a bureaucracy. But it served as a shield behind which many Nazi officials tried to hide. And it may have served not only for public consumption, as the bureaucrat faced other people and tried to justify his or her activities. It may have been even more important as a framework for self-deception. Bureaucrats could justify their deeds to themselves on the grounds that these deeds, no matter how novel or resourceful, were merely the result of following orders. Those above oneself bore the responsibility. The bureaucrat could therefore continue to hold a conception of self that was completely at variance with their actual behavior within the bureaucracy. Thus Eichmann could say, with apparent sincerity, that he was not anti-Semitic. And Auschwitz commandant Hoess could say he did not hate Jews.

During the Nuremberg trials most of the Nazi officials, such as General Ohlendorf, claimed to have been overcome by an extreme version of the obedience-to-authority syndrome. (Even Stanley Milgram, that sophisticated psychologist, got seduced by the obedience-to-authority syndrome.) The accused murderers claimed that in carrying out the planning and execution of mass murders they were merely carrying out orders. Ohlendorf, for example, acknowledged during questioning by lawyers that he had had reservations about the morality of the killings. Why, then, did he carry them out? "Because to me it is inconceivable that a subordinate leader should not carry out orders given by the leaders of the state." When asked about questioning the legality of the orders, Ohlendorf answered (perplexed by such an unreasonable question) that when you had sworn to obey, the question of the legality of an order did not apply.[19] He was describing the Local Moral Universe in which he and his fellow officers were operating.

The interpretation of the court, and of many social analysts, was that statements such as Ohlendorf's were a denial of personal responsibility in the face of orders that *(a)* demanded much personal initiative and *(b)* were so extreme that they should have been disobeyed even if legally promulgated and delivered.

We need to go further in showing how Ohlendorf's autonomy was important to Ohlendorf. He clearly intimates that by obeying orders, most especially when obeying difficult orders, the officer is *making a morally justified contribution* to the honor of the position he occupies and to the larger system to which that position belongs. When he was inducted into his position he had sworn to carry out the orders he would receive. When would he be making the greatest independent—autonomous—contribution to the honor of his position and the organization to which it belongs: when carrying out orders that are easy or when carrying out orders that are difficult, even repugnant? I repeat, by obeying an order he knew to be horrendous he saw himself as contributing to the honor of the system to which he belonged.

The same theme was promoted by Himmler. In the speech to SS leaders cited earlier, he recognized the moral and emotional difficulties involved in mass killings. He emphasized that by participating in such abhorrent activities, Nazi officials were actually contributing to a "grand historic mission." Himmler said they should not dwell on the horrible things "I am doing." Instead, they should dwell on the horrible things "I have to witness while carrying out my sacred duty." They should regard themselves as persons who, while killing, were making a contribution to their own honor and to the honor of the great cause they were serving. They should take pride in that contribution. The morality of the overall system, that "great cause," is never questioned. Doing so would expose the Achilles heel of that cause.

The Nazi bureaucrats who say they were merely following orders ignore how they contributed their own originality while carrying out orders. They had considerable autonomy. It is easy to see that the people at the top of the bureaucracy had autonomy to make the big decisions. They formulated policies.

Their underlings also had considerable autonomy, even when they claim that they did not, that they were mere cogs in the machinery. It is true that, in general, bureaucratic underlings base their work on law, on existing rules, and on orders received from persons above them in the hierarchy of their work setting. But they can carry out orders with zeal or, figuratively, they can drag their feet. They can interpret orders in many ways. They can destroy the spirit of the law by insisting on adhering to the letter of the law. Or they can bend the letter of the law to achieve the spirit of the law. This behavior is common and "normal" in any bureaucracy.

Bureaucrats who deny their own contributions practice self-deception. This tendency does not make them into "monsters." Indeed, it is possible that many bureaucrats indulge in self-deception to some extent as part of the "ordinary" day-to-day activity of being a bureaucrat. Yet ordinary bureaucratic behavior, like ordinary incremental behavior and ordinary packaging of behavior, can become a key contributor to monstrous deeds.

Conclusion

Implementation of the Holocaust depended critically on behavior that is ordinary and mundane. Behavioral scientists start by examining ordinary human behavior, then try to show the transformation of ordinary behavior into monstrous and malignant behavior, even when this approaches the degree seen during the Holocaust. Through this knowledge one hopes that such transformation can be curbed. The starting point in this pursuit is the assumption that the behavior of Nazis during the Holocaust is typical of a genre of ordinary social behavior. It is crucial that we understand that genre and its possible transformations.

Studying "ordinary" behavior in the Holocaust phenomenon leads to the following conclusions:

1. Understanding where *autonomy* lies clarifies where inventiveness, for good or ill, can be practiced. Knowing where an individual's autonomy lies also clarifies where that person's culpability lies.

   The Nazis gave their functionaries considerable autonomy. These functionaries used it to tailor bureaucratic techniques to a task. The task could go so far as the attempt to annihilate an entire population on a scale that had not been attempted before.

   Autonomy often goes unrecognized, even one's own. This blindness can serve as a mechanism for obscuring, even to oneself, one's contributions to horrendous deeds.

2. A person's involvement in a social movement or a personal career may result from a series of *incremental decisions* that can solve immediate problems, one at a time, without the person's awareness of wider concerns. This limited outlook can result in a lack of response to moral issues involved in the total course of action.

   It is not known how many Nazi officials acted in such a fashion. But it is clear that Eichmann was not alone among the Nazi officials in the incremental way in which he became immersed in executing Nazi policies.

3. Nazism included a variety of political, economic, and racial programs which, together, formed a cohesive *package*, an amalgamated Nazi "morality" that attained an identity of its own. Because of this amalgamation, adherents to any one of the component programs were likely to

implement the entire package of programs, even those programs to which they had no strong personal commitment. This behavior dovetails with the incremental decision process. Both involve evaluating only selected components of a larger program in which one is, in fact, participating and to which one is actively contributing.

The Nazi package of programs contained some new items, but it was also a *repackaged* version of some previously existing themes of German national life. Therefore Nazism could gather followers by coopting their previous commitments rather than depending on entirely new ones. In this process the new items became acceptable. They formed part of a larger package that promised revitalization of the national honor and the economy. The extreme anti-Semitism of Nazism was, at the same time, an incremental increase of longstanding Western anti-Semitism and a repackaged form of early German anti-Semitism.

The combination of behavioral autonomy, incremental decision making, and packaging of behavior helps to explain how many German officials were able to participate in an extremist movement. Understanding these elements helps explain how these officials, ordinary humans all, could still devise and engage in routinized mass murder. The process of routinization of mass murder is what I shall explore more fully in the next chapter. It will give a larger sense of the workings of Nazism.

I arrived at this point through progress in my personal journey. After years of denial, I began to acknowledge that I am a Jewish survivor of the Nazi era, and that this has bearing not only on my personal sense of who and what I am. It also has bearing on my professional work. This realization enabled me to make progress as a scientist confronting that perverse moral universe known as Nazism. It enabled me to explore the moral world of Rudolf Hoess, the commandant of Auschwitz, and through it to try to gain greater insight into the mirrorings of the normal, the ordinary, and the benign within the most malignant of human behavior.

CHAPTER SEVEN

The Routinization of Evil

The Personal Journey Leads to Confronting the Holocaust

As I mentioned in the previous chapter, for many years after the Holocaust I denied to myself that it had anything to do with me personally. To be sure my parents, my brother, and many of my more distant relatives were murdered there. I escaped only by the skin of my teeth. Yet I could not confront Holocaust issues. Right after the Second World War ended I checked on the fate of my parents and my brother. Then, for about thirty years I refused to read anything about the Holocaust. I had been born into an orthodox Jewish family, and always considered myself a Jew. I stayed in contact with some of my surviving Jewish relatives. Yet during these thirty years I lived almost entirely in a gentile world. In my daily life, I dissociated myself from Jews and the practice of the Jewish religion. This was not a conscious decision. As I think about these thirty years, in retrospect, I realize that I was actually attempting to dissociate myself from my Jewish identity and heritage.

This showed up glaringly in my professional work as a sociologist. I shunned everything dealing with "Jewish" matters. The study of anti-Semitism and the status of Jews in contemporary Western life seemed unworthy of my attention. Of course I knew that some behavioral scientists did study these issues, but I could not see myself doing so. I had a fine set of rationalizations for not doing so. I told myself that such topics were, intellectually, second-rate issues, and they were attracting second-rate minds to address them. These judgments, I now realize, were both unfair and untrue. They were stories I made up to justify my turning away from a major self-challenge.

After my first semester of teaching sociology at a college in the American Bible Belt, a student said to me that as a result of my course she now knew what she wanted to do with her life. She would become a Christian missionary—in Israel! Is this what I was teaching? I suppose I conveyed ambivalence about being Jewish. I was deceiving myself, while belittling scholars who—I later grudgingly recognized—were doing serious and insightful research on issues bearing on the lives of Jews who were living in a non-Jewish world. But I did not realize this during my first decades as a professional sociologist. I simply could not imagine being interested in publishing in a "Jewish" journal.

Around the year 1982 I began coming to terms with myself and Judaism. It happened while I prepared an article about the Holocaust for *Modern Judaism*, a Jewish journal, which the editor had invited me to submit. (That article became the precursor to this chapter.) As I worked on the article I became aware that I was addressing myself to a Jewish audience. I realized that my message must take into account that Jews have a unique stake in the events of the Holocaust.

Yet it took several more years for me to realize that by writing for a Jewish journal I was also beginning to free myself from my self-imposed diaspora, that I was beginning to reconcile being Jewish and being a professional sociologist. I could be both. Perhaps more importantly, I was beginning to accept my survival from the Holocaust by, in a way, rejoining the Jewish community. I was overcoming my misdirected outrage at the Jewish community which, I had believed—in my lingering child's frame of reference—had failed to protect me from the Nazis and had, in fact, caused me and my family to be conspicuous and vulnerable targets for persecution. I had been blaming Jews for what the Nazis had done to Jews. I was a victim blaming my fellow victims.

I eventually found a more appropriate target for my outrage, namely our inadequate analyses of horrendous human behavior. We are repeatedly and invariably caught by surprise when massive horrors take place. Sensitive and humane individuals among us impotently point in quivering outrage at the inhumanity we humans inflict on ourselves. We point it out, but seem unable to do anything about it.

It is important to point out horrors when they occur, but that is not good enough. We need more than forthright, even eyewitness, descriptions of what is happening. We need more than outraged iteration of brutal facts. We need, desperately, far more coldly dispassionate but imaginative analysis of these events.

For me to accept this challenge as personal to myself—that I might be able to contribute some answers—meant that I must change direction in my professional and personal activities. Above all, I had to break down the wall between my "professional work" and my personal history. In the course of doing so, I realized that some of my earlier professional work was very applicable to Holocaust issues. And, perhaps more importantly for my own sense of well-being, I managed to shed some of the guilt about surviving when my parents and my brother had perished. In the manner proposed by Viktor Frankl,[1] I found meaning for my life by trying to wrestle with events of the Holocaust in new ways.

One consequence of my wrestlings is the following insight about anti-Semitism—and, further, insight about hatred directed at other categories of persons (this insight also formed part of our discussion in the previous chapter): The most dangerous anti-Semite, in terms of actual lethal anti-Semitic behavior, may not be the person who openly professes and preaches anti-Semitism. To be sure, professing anti-Semites do present a dangerous threat to Jews. But the most dangerous anti-Semite can appear in the form of a skilled bureaucrat who accepts anti-Semitism as a work-related task. That bureaucrat may have no deep personal commitment to anti-Semitism, but he can become frighteningly effective at implementing anti-Semitic programs because of his administrative expertise and moral myopia, a phenomenon so well demonstrated in the career of Adolf Eichmann.

Eichmann claimed he was not anti-Semitic. Despite this claim I strongly suspect that before he joined the Nazi movement, Eichmann had been exposed to the prevailing veiled anti-Semitism—such as the claim that Christianity has superseded Judaism—to which many Christians are exposed in the course of their religious upbringing. After he joined, such exposure to veiled but inactive anti-Semitism could have been enough for him to accept the engorged and active anti-Semitic mission assigned to him in the context of his SS career. It had vaccinated him against saying No to active anti-Semitism when it was first broached to him at the beginning of his SS career. From that moment on, his zealous career-enhancing activities, as a bureaucrat, were devoted to enacting the role assigned to him as a core functionary in the extermination of the Jews.

In practice, this pattern has implications for predicting outbursts of anti-Semitism (or other intergroup hatreds). Having overt and explicit anti-Semitic convictions, or "attitudes"—on which traditional sociological and psychological studies of anti-Semitism focus—may be a poor predictor of actual lethal anti-Semitic behavior. A better predictor might be the existence of sociocultural packages in which anti-Semitism is one of many veiled and inactive, but persisting, ingredients, combined with the tenacity with which an entire package is implemented. The most extreme perpetrator of anti-Semitism may be the most tenacious adherent to the entire package, and not necessarily the strongest personal believer in anti-Semitism.

During their rise to power, the Nazis offered an enticing package of programs that included the promise to improve the country's economy and provide jobs. At a time of high unemployment many people were drawn to the Nazi package because of these economic promises, not because of the accompanying credo of anti-Semitism. But once committed to the Nazi package, the new adherent was apt to be involved in implementing the entire package, including the portions to which he had no specific personal commitment.

As we saw in the last chapter, these "non-committed" anti-Semites performed some of the most horrendous anti-Semitic deeds. Their explicit and extreme anti-Semitic activities were obscured by their immersion in a package where non–anti-Semitic issues played a big part.

Conversely, yet similarly, the story of Oskar Schindler demonstrates that a wartime Nazi racketeer, womanizer, and profligate could perform some of the most wondrous rescues of endangered Jews. Schindler's swaggering, dissolute lifestyle—so conspicuous in his behavior package—obscured visibility (and detection) of his explicit actions to rescue about one thousand Jews from certain death. Here, too, a package obscured one of its major components.

The packaging of anti-Semitism in the Nazi movement is no different from packaging of other behavior by other social movements. The principles apply whether you are a potential persecutor of foreign nationals, of gypsies, of gay people or straight people, of poor people or rich people, of able people or disabled people, of white people or black people, of Tutsis or Hutus when you live in Rwanda, of Croats or Muslims or Serbs when you live in the Balkans. Your actions do not so much depend on whether you actually hate this particular category of persons. They depend, rather, on whether, within your culture's package of values and attitudes, that category of persons is already identified as somewhat different. Being "somewhat different" may be all it takes to identify a category of persons for future targeting.

The process which then transforms a friendly, though "somewhat different," neighbor into an "enemy" is based on repackaging. Components of the existing moral agenda are rearranged and different priorities are assigned to some components of the package. A particular component—such as a certain ethnic group—is now defined as immediately and pressingly dangerous. Once this redefinition is made, the component that was singled out can henceforth be defined—slowly and incrementally or suddenly and abruptly—as frighteningly dangerous, and something against which one must take up arms. It is declared a threat to the well-being and the very existence of the society. The adherents to the new moral outlook typically become very active contributors toward eliminating the perceived danger.

The process of zealous anti-Semitism emerging from a rearrangement of an existing, fairly benign package of values and attitudes can be seen at work even in the life of Martin Luther, who, at least among Protestants, is not known as a perpetrator of evil. In his early adult life, Luther was friendly to Jews, and said kind things about them. His attitude changed drastically when Jews refused to join his religious crusade, when they would not join his movement and become Christians in the particular mold he was proposing (indeed, they would not become Christians at all). He turned viciously anti-Semitic and issued the most malicious of diatribes against Jews.

In his pamphlet *About the Jews and Their Lies* (as cited by Raul Hilberg, in his book *The Destruction of European Jews*) Luther states:

> [The Jews] are thirsty bloodhounds and murderers of all Christen-dom . . . [they are] like a plague, pestilence, pure misfortune in our country. . . . They hold us Christians captive in our country. . . .[2]

These are the words of a man who used to like Jews.

Luther's additional themes included accusations that Jews "want to rule the world," and that Jews are "arch-criminals, killers of Christ and all Christendom" (Hilberg, p. 14–15). Such slurs have echoed down through the ages to later anti-Semites. Four hundred years after Luther formulated them, they were repeated by the Nazis. This time, in slightly repackaged form, Luther's dicta became part of a modern program of genocide.

For Luther personally, anti-Semitism involved a drastic repackaging of his own orientation. In his early years, as I mentioned, he had regarded Jews as potential allies to his own religious crusade. But when the Jews refused to convert to Christianity, especially to his particular version of Christianity, he saw them as total enemies, and a severe threat to his entire venture. In his later years he came to regard Jews as a major threat to much of what he stood for in his crusade for religious revitalization. In so doing, Luther was applying a new rider—a new overarching theme which stated that Jews were the terribly dangerous archenemy—to his package of values. Through this rider, Jews were drastically devalued and regarded as a source of contamination to much of what he wanted to accomplish.

The Luther example teaches us that violent anti-Semitism need not be the product of lifelong and publicly expressed anti-Semitic convictions. Rather, it can result from the rearrangement of the component parts of an existing package of morality or beliefs. It is quite possible that during his early, friendly-to-Jews phase, Luther may have had some anti-Semitic views within his package of personal beliefs, based on the religious teachings he imbibed as a child. But for many years these beliefs were held in abeyance. They were in a dormant state within his package, but available for activation and amplification in the future.

Closely parallelling this pattern is the sporadic nature of anti-Semitism and active persecution of Jews throughout history. Periods of tolerance are followed by periods of active and open persecution. These are then again followed by periods of deactivation of anti-Semitic invective, during which active and open persecution of Jews is not practiced. But, and this is crucial, in this inactive phase, anti-Semitism remains subtly alive as a dormant and veiled component of the culture, even though it is not actively practiced in explicit atrocities against Jews.

The recurrent pogroms in Eastern Europe are prime examples of such periodicity in the practice of anti-Jewish atrocities. During periods of quietude the anti-Semitic convictions are perpetuated, albeit in a dormant state, as components of the culture's package of values, beliefs, and folk mythology.

Any sociology of the Holocaust must take into account the fact that an outburst of massive human horror, such as the Holocaust, mobilizes components from within a cultural heritage, even if those components have lain dormant.[3] When we learn how malignant elements of a culture's package can be perpetuated in a dormant state, as well as how the activation and deactivation processes work, we may be able to forestall some potential social horrors before they actually happen. Intuition tells me that these processes are not random but, instead, contain orderly, law-like regularities. Furthermore, I believe the regularities can be discovered and indentified.

Surprisingly, modern sociologists have concentrated far more on anti-Semitism bearing on Jewish life in English-speaking countries than on the Nazi Holocaust. Given the large number of Jewish sociologists, this remains a riddle. Perhaps Hannah Arendt's quasi-sociological work on the banality of Eichmann's evil left a bitter aftertaste—particularly Arendt's claim, met by much outrage, that the Jewish victims of Nazi persecution contributed heavily to their own demise. Perhaps, too, the trauma of the Holocaust that affects all Jews, including Jewish sociologists, has substituted grief for intellectual inquiry, where dispassionate analysis is the last thing on anyone's mind. A prominent Jewish sociologist once told me that the most profound thing anyone could do about the Holocaust was to be silent. He then wished me luck in not being silent.

The upshot is that distinctive sociological contributions to the understanding of the Holocaust remain relatively untapped.[4] Such contributions would not duplicate historians' explanations of why and how the Holocaust happened. They would, instead, clarify ways in which the Holocaust is generalizable, in offering lessons in the production of social horrors, and, yet, retains unique specifics.

One of the ways the Holocaust can teach us about the production of horrors is its routinizing of monstrous behavior.

Routinizing Monstrous Behavior

By "routinizing monstrous behavior" I refer to how horrors, supported by a broad "moral" mandate, are actually carried out in an organized, planned, repetitive, mass-production format. When we consider mass production in industry, we think of machinery that is used to do much of the repetitive work that needs to get done. And we think of the social arrangements that go along with it—the jobs and careers in highly routine work, the ongoing duties of individuals, the allocation of responsibilities, the many kinds of administrative arrangements for having numerous people participate in producing a product. These, too, are core features in the mass-production process. They are the human side of mass production.

In the mass production of murder, as in the Nazi Holocaust, we also have a combination of machinery (such as the gas oven killing technology) and the social arrangements that go along with it. The latter ensure the active participation and contribution by individuals to producing the final horrifying product. This "human side" of the production of mass murder is what needs to be considered. Without it, no amount of machine technology would have worked.

∽

The Nazi regime engaged in episodes of mass killings almost from the start of the Second World War. There was, for example, the mass killings of noncombatants by the invading German troops on the Russian front. This was the direct, face-to-face slaughter of thousands of unarmed individuals. These killings were not routinized; they were not systematic repetitive actions that could be performed with considerable psychological distance between murderer and victim. This nonroutine format of killing led to some protest among German military personnel, who carried out these killings. I assume they were protesting against killing because they had to confront the fact they, personally, were killers; they did not have the luxury of social distance from their killings. The distress showed up in letters soldiers sent home. There were even some suicides among the German soldiers. Such responses were regarded as an embarrassment by the higher officials, something that required "corrective action." (It must be noted that these protests were only occasional, whereas many more mass killings were being carried out with nary the slightest murmer of protest by the military executioners. Most of them exhibited very little stress.[5])

The embarrassment was reduced when the murderous persecution of Jews became merely part of the "ordinary" day-to-day routines of the government's administrative machinery. There were few protests when participation in the Holocaust became part and parcel of "ordinary" career patterns of civil servants, of military personnel, and of many persons in the civilian, private sector of European nations. The routine relied, even, on a corps of specially trained staff of concentration camp administrators, persons who were human extermination specialists with bureaucratic careers. I shall dwell on one major exemplar of this species; Rudolf Hoess, the commandant of Auschwitz.

At the starting point for the discussion of Hoess, and as a vehicle for developing it, I make a harsh decision. Hoess will be heard to say that he had a "sensitive inner life" and that he "abhorred" the brutalities at Auschwitz. One is inclined to be utterly incredulous of such claims. To accept Hoess's claims seems tantamount to believing in the good intentions of the devil. Given Hoess's *actions*, one's mental world threatens to turn upside down when entertaining claims of this sort. Yet there is one reason, an overarching reason, for believing Hoess. It is that one might then learn something important. I shall attempt to do just that.

In my analysis, I am about to go beyond the conventional wisdom about bureaucrats, namely that bureaucrats are merely extreme examples of two common syndromes: (1) Obedience to authority; in which they personify obedient responses to rules which an authority imposes; and (2) Pursuit of specialization; in which each bureaucrat is fundamentally a specialist, doing his specialized task; within that specialty, there is little room for flexibility.

Once Again: *Incremental Processes*

As I have said earlier, the Nazi movement did not originate from a fully spelled out program to which it, then, adhered. Most notably, after the Nazis came to power in 1933, the extermination of the Jews was developed in a step-by-step incremental manner. Although the broad philosophy of hatred of Jews was indeed mentioned very early, the actual extermination process had not been spelled out in detail before its implementation began.

Before the systematic physical annihilation of Jews began in 1942, the Nazis harassed many individual Jews and conducted a highly orchestrated propaganda campaign of vilification against all Jews. At the same time, the Nazis started systematic persecution with a series of increasingly repressive laws depriving Jews of an ever larger number of civil rights. Hence, from the start, much of the persecution of Jews was done "legally," through the existing legal machinery of the German nation. No separate legal system was created; there was no separate system of courts and no separate judiciary staff. Systematic persecution of Jews (and others considered undesirable) was carried out with minimal attention to its novelty. After all, the existing state machinery was carrying it out.

For an individual German bureaucrat, accustomed to executing rather than initiating policy, the challenge of Nazism might not be fundamentally new. One was operating within the nation's administrative machinery, much of which was unchanged. The message had changed, but much of the general nature of one's job remained the same. One could engage in what developed into increasing persecution of Jews within an acceptable format, and one implemented Nazi policies in limited, incremental installments.

The incremental, step-by-step character of the repressive laws not only contributed to hiding its novelty. It also obscured the severity of persecution that was being carried out.

In the early and mid-1930s few people, even among Jewish citizens of Germany, could believe that total annihilation of European Jews was really going to happen. New legal requirements heaped on Jews during the early period of Nazidom, such as Jews having to obtain special identification cards or adopting a Jewish-sounding name, seemed isolated acts. They did not seem to presage wholesale murder.

Incrementalism camouflaged the process that culminated in the Final Solution, the mass murder of millions of innocent individuals. When, in 1942, the final secret decision was made to kill all Jews in German-occupied lands, this was but a further increment in what had become a gradually evolving, publicly known but curiously unchallenged course of action. It attracted a surprisingly low level of public response and negligible indignation. Incrementalism had anesthetized the public.

In other words, persecution of Jews had become routinized because its escalation was done incrementally. Bystanders as well as victims had become accustomed to ever more punitive measures. I am not saying that the victims got used to the brutalities. I am saying, only, that because of the continuing escalation of brutalities they had already experienced, they expected ever harsher measures to arrive. They did so with foreboding and dread, but with anticipation that escalation could, indeed, continue to happen. As the escalation of brutalities did continue, the victims concentrated entirely on each new immediacy—the new increment of horror—to which they must adapt.

I can speak for my own incremental reactions at the time. I was totally obsessed with the thought that I must leave home. I must get away from being beaten up every day while going to and from school. Neither my parents, nor anyone else was protecting me. I felt that my parents were as powerless as I against the ever darkening cloud of danger that was hanging over us. I was consumed by fear and increasing panic. These feelings obliterated all other concerns, such as, if I left Germany, who would take care of me? What does it mean to go to a place where you know no-one and do not speak the language? And, what would happen to my parents, if they stayed behind? I simply did not think of such things. As I see it now, I was thinking and acting incrementally, with concern only for one immediate issue, to escape the fearful situation. For many subsequent years I carried within myself the notion that I, entirely by myself, engineered my departure. I used to say to myself, "I badgered my parents until they let me go." And, disturbingly, I told myself that I abandoned my parents, knowing they would die, just to save myself. They call it "survivor guilt." It is very real. It is also the price of incremental thinking: That I blamed myself for failing to consider the fate of my parents when I, focused exclusively on my own immediacy, took the incremental step to save myself.

My parents' reactions showed they were aware of the severity of the Nazi actions. After they failed in their desperate efforts to escape as a family they, lifelong residents of a small isolated village, sent their last child away to live among strangers, in a strange country, speaking a strange language.[6] They surely suspected that they would never see me again. Perhaps they, too, acted incrementally, concentrating on the immediate issue of saving me and not confronting the unthinkable larger issues that they might not see me again and that they were handing me a highly unpredictable future. This gives me some comfort. Perhaps my parents were spared the dread of considering these issues by concentrating on immediacy, on one local, incremental decision.

The implementation of the Nazi program was doubtless facilitated by the fact that not only the victims, but the individual perpetrators of the horrors, acted incrementally. Their own incremental career processes, as noted in the previous chapter, enabled them to wholeheartedly participate in mass killings without having to do a larger moral accounting of their own immediate actions. Many could deny to themselves that they were anti-Semites while, in fact, performing monstrously anti-Semitic deeds. Through a route of small, localized decisions they participated in the entire Nazi package of programs, even things to which they had no great commitment. Yet they contributed to the package, including its totally evil features, in decisive ways. No-one personifies this more fully than Rudolf Hoess, whom I mentioned earlier.

Rudolf Hoess: A Closer Look at a Master Routinizer of Mass Murder

The career of Rudolf Hoess is highly instructive about the routinization of mass murder.[7] He may have the dubious distinction of having refined this process more than anyone in human history. His career deserves a close examination.

Hoess was the commander of the Auschwitz concentration camp when it was first established and, again, during the period of the mass exterminations. He oversaw the extermination of around two million Jews. Under him, at Auschwitz, the routinization of mass murder reached its zenith. What sort of a life can produce such a result?

Bertrand Russell, one of the leading philosophers of the twentieth century, described his amazement upon seeing Hoess at the court hearing after the Second World War, where Hoess was being tried. Russell says that here was this "very ordinary little man" who, nonetheless, was "perhaps the greatest executioner of all time." Russel reports:

He certainly never sought to hide anything he had done, and was more prone to exaggerate than understate, for he regarded it as a compliment to his zeal, capacity for work, and devotion to duty to have carried out his gruesome orders with such dispatch and efficiency."[8]

Hoess wrote his autobiography (titled *Commandant of Auschwitz*) while in prison awaiting his execution (the execution took place in April, 1947). On reading the book, one might question the veracity of Hoess's own descriptions, the possibility of self-serving biases, and efforts to rationalize his actions in order to gain favor from his captors. Given Hoess's ready acknowledgment of his guilt, however, there was no question that he knew he would be sentenced to death. And there is no indication that he used the autobiography to try to escape the death sentence or that he deliberately introduced falsifications. Of course, the autobiography may well contain falsifications, even if Hoess did not plant them deliberately. But it is more likely that Hoess saw the autobiography as the final element of a career that had a measure of internal consistency—indeed, in his view, a moral consistency—which Hoess felt should be known by the wider public.

Russell's description of Hoess as an *ordinary* little man—like Arendt's notion of the *banality* of evil in regard to Eichmann—diverts attention from a crucial matter. How is the ordinary (or the banal) transformed into the extraordinary? What is it in ordinary human nature, in ordinary social processes, that lends itself to the emergence of a profoundly extraordinary evil? And in ways that show up in routine, everyday activities? To find the answer, let us take a closer look at what made Hoess into the person who eventually had direct responsibility for the killing of millions of innocent persons.

Hoess was born in 1900, received a strict Catholic upbringing, volunteered for military service in the First World War, joined a reactionary organization after the war, met and joined Hitler in 1922, was imprisoned for a political murder in 1923, and, after discharge from prison in 1929, took up farming and married. Hoess had five children, two of whom were born during his service in concentration camps.

In 1934, Heinrich Himmler, the SS chief, persuaded Hoess to join the SS, which, from start to finish, involved Hoess in concentration camp administration. Hoess rose in the SS hierarchy and, in 1940, was ordered to establish a camp at Auschwitz. With the exception of some interim service at Berlin headquarters, he remained at Auschwitz, and was there for the period of greatest mass murder. His was a career in routinizing evil. Here the concentration camp was the delivery system. Here a specially trained staff, headed by Hoess, made the day-to-day decisions that routinized brutality and killing. For those who served under him, Hoess reigned as the master and model for carrying out the routinized brutality and killing.

Hoess describes his childhood love for animals, trees, and solitary activities leading to a lifelong "passion" for farming. This externally muted man described himself as leading a "sensitive inner life." From his devoutly Catholic parents he learned to value absolute adherence to authority. "I had been taught since childhood to be absolutely obedient and meticulously tidy and clean . . . ," Hoess wrote.[9]

Hoess was imprisoned for participating in a political murder in the 1920s, and found that obedience to authority served him well there. "I did not find it difficult to conform to the strict discipline in prison," he wrote. "I conscientiously carried out all my well-defined duties. I completed the work allotted to me, and usually more . . . [!]—my cell was a model of neatness and cleanliness."[10]

Here one must note the sense of honor and gratification derived from obedience, even if it means obedience to a harsh authority, that so typified Hoess. He showed by his example that obedience to authority is not something one accepts grudgingly or alienatedly. On the contrary. His autobiography glorifies and sanctifies the act of obedience; he proudly proclaims that he did even more than was demanded by prison authorities. He sees himself producing honor through his obedience to authority. Doing even more than is demanded means contributing honor not only for himself but for the larger system—the Nazi moral crusade—in which he has a meaningful place.[11]

Hoess's writing suggests that, at any one time, he was personally committed only to some items in the larger cause to which his obedience was then directed. At one extreme, I repeat, he was in prison and, nonetheless, zealously obeyed the prison authorities. He did so while he was fighting against the government that was behind his imprisonment. By his action he was contributing to the routines of a hostile prison's management while, at the same time, contributing to the honor of the Nazi cause he had embraced.

Hoess's case has some elements in common with the reaction of British prisoners in a Japanese prisoner of war camp during the Second World War, fictionalized in Pierre Boulle's book, *The Bridge on the River Kwai*, and the subsequent motion picture.[12] The prisoners cooperated marvellously in building a bridge for the Japanese, despite hardships and danger, despite hatred for the Japanese, and despite the possibility that the bridge might aid the Japanese war effort against their own British countrymen.

As the leader of the British prisoners saw it, they were living up to a grand element in that British character. They were showing the Japanese the British character's moral superiority. The prisoners could hold their heads high, even while contributing to the enemy's war effort, knowing that they were contributing honor to their distinctive British character. That character meant accepting a very difficult moral challenge and, once accepted, one performed one's task superbly.

The prisoners were thus living in a special, locally formulated moral system. Within that system, building a bridge for the enemy was regarded as a contribution to the honor of one's own country. This system had its own focus, its own interpretation of a larger morality, its own directives for living up to one's moral obligation. It was a Local Moral Universe.

In his autobiography, Hoess states that the order to prepare the extermination process, given to him by Himmler, "certainly was an extraordinary and monstrous order" (Rufolf Hoess, *Commandment of Auschwitz,* op. cit.). Yet it was totally inconceivable to disobey even such an order. He reports that since his arrest at the end of the war, a number of persons had asked him why he did not disobey the order or, even, assassinate Himmler. He finds this totally incomprehensible. Not a single SS officer, says Hoess, could even entertain such a thought. One might complain about harsh orders, but one carried them out. It was a moral obligation.

To be sure, there was some element of fear. The SS brooked no disobedience in its ranks. But even more than the existence of fear, there was the idealization of obedience, especially of harsh orders, as a source of great moral satisfaction. By obeying a monstrous order one was actively contributing to the honor accruing to oneself and to the large cause one was serving. Obedience, itself, was a crucial component of the moral universe in which the Hoesses lived.

In practice, in this universe obedience did not mean grudgingly doing the minimum of what one was ordered to do. It meant actively making a contribution to authority by supporting the *spirit* of an order rather than minimally accepting the letter of an order. All this is most magnificently accomplished when, in the eyes of a Hoess, obedience is applied to a task that is difficult, even horrible, from an objective standpoint.

The incremental character of Hoess's involvement in Nazism includes his claim that when he was ordered to establish extermination installations at Auschwitz, in the summer of 1941, he "did not have the slightest idea of their scale or consequences" (Hoess, *Commandment of Auschwitz,* ibid., p. 88). He notes that he simply did not reflect on such matters. Nor did he reflect on whether mass extermination of the Jews was necessary. Such broad issues were beyond his purview.

His obligation, as he saw it, was a more limited one: to carry out the orders he received. He would single-mindedly concentrate on them without allowing himself to be distracted by other issues. His concern was with a particular segment of the Nazi package, not with all of it. Yet by concentrating on that segment he was contributing to the total package.

Hoess maintained the same pattern of incremental involvement without addressing larger issues throughout his career in the SS. When he began his duties as a guard in a concentration camp, he notes, he gave no consideration to its being a "concentration camp"; or, one might add, to the larger issue of what concentration camps were doing to the German nation.

"To me it was just a question of being an active soldier once again, of resuming my military career," Hoess wrote in his autobiography, thereby fusing his previous military career with being an SS guard in a concentration camp.[13] Both involve life in uniform, military discipline, and service to the nation. Hoess saw his SS service as a continuation of a military career, a viewpoint that makes the Nazi package of programs practicable and acceptable. It was a repackaged version of his previous military career. That "military career" is his point of attachment to the new package, as he sees it.

Hoess claims that, during his early days as a guard at Dachau, he was greatly upset when he saw other guards flogging prisoners. He claims that he deliberately absented himself when he knew that floggings would occur; that he deplored that some SS men enjoyed the spectacle of public flogging of prisoners; that due to his own experience as a prisoner, he could identify with prisoners; and that, finally, he resented being placed in charge of a group of prisoners—he would have preferred to be simply a soldier in a unit of soldiers.

In the role of guard, Hoess points out, there is considerable autonomy: The guard "can make life hell for prisoners, but [he] can also make his wretched experience easier and even tolerable."[14] He obviously devoted considerable thought to this matter. During his years of imprisonment he had much time to do so. He claims it is not physical hardship that makes the prisoner's life horrible, it is mental suffering "caused by the tyranny and meanness" of individual guards or superiors. As commandant, Hoess could not stop the guards' misdeeds. Although he was in charge of the camp, his own autonomy was severely limited, at least as he saw it.

Hoess's own scruples disappeared early in his SS career under the tutelage of a severe taskmaster, the commandant of the Dachau concentration camp, Theodore Eicke. (Dachau was the concentration camp nearest to my village. Our neighbor, Margot's father, was sent there.) In his autobiography, Hoess describes how he became accustomed to doing brutal things in a step-by-step, incremental manner. He recalls how, rather soon after becoming an SS officer, he had to supervise the execution of a close colleague, a man who had the misfortune of having a prisoner under his control escape.

"I cannot understand to this day how I was able, quite calmly, to give the order [to the firing squad] to fire." He recalls how he, along with the other officers, was deeply upset after the execution. When they gathered afterwards, no one talked.[15]

After this event, further executions, particularly those of prisoners, came far more easily to him. Obviously the critical threshold had been crossed. A precedent existed. And the existence of the precedent made similar acts acceptable options for the future.

One way of understanding the incremental process of escalating cruelty is as follows: When a person's career is seen as a sequence of events, a single event may leave an imprint upon subsequent events. It becomes a permanent rider to all future activities by that individual. Indeed, one event can be a critical increment, one that hovers over all subsequent events. Hoess provides us an example when he states, "This event [the execution of the fellow officer] was always before my eyes to remind me of the demand that had been made upon us to exercise perpetual self-mastery and unbending severity."[16]

Hoess reports another critical increment from early in his career as a concentration camp officer. At one point he felt that he was totally unsuited for such work. He felt that, given his own background as a prisoner, he had far too much sympathy for prisoners. But he lacked the courage to resign, to face the shame of being discharged from the SS. That event—the recognition that it would be shameful to resign—became a critical increment that would hover over the rest of his SS career. From that moment on he was hooked, becoming an unflinching and enthusiastic concentration camp officer. From that moment, too, he says, "my guilt begins" (Ibid., p. 88).

Hoess frequently reports grisly scenes under his command: how children were thrown into the gas chambers together with their mothers, how a member of the Jewish Sonderkommando, busy dragging corpses out of a gas chamber, abruptly stopped in his tracks when he recognized that he was dragging the corpse of his own wife.

Hoess, who witnessed this event, was himself horrified. But his feelings of horror had to be "ruthlessly suppressed." He reports that his SS men occasionally expressed horror about their task to him in private. He always told them they must continue their noble work and not be sidetracked by feelings of horror.

This makes it doubly astounding that Hoess and the SS people under him continued on course, carrying on their grisly activities. If Hoess and his underlings had expressed no horror, if they expressed only ghoulish satisfaction about their activities (and some did), then one could write them off as sadists or psychopaths. But this was not the case. Hoess and some of his subordinate SS men occasionally expressed precisely those sentiments one would expect from a normal, decent human being, people like ourselves, who have utter revulsion for the horrors of Auschwitz. Yet these very same individuals continued to participate—actively and exuberantly—in the murderous course.

Some people dismiss Hoess's professed horror as lies, manufactured to curry favor from Allied authorities. This view cannot be completely ruled out. However, if it is correct that Hoess and the other SS men did experience a sense of horror, this raises far more profound questions than considering him and other SS officials mere sadists or psychopaths. From a moral standpoint, it raises the question of how persons may carry out, indeed enthusiastically embrace, "radical evil" while their faculties are intact. While they are able to distinguish good from evil, how can they engage in evil on a level that wholly violates ordinary canons of moral conduct?

The answer to the astounding issue that SS people feel and express horror and yet continue their ghastly deeds, seems to include: (1) the honor-derived-from-obedience syndrome, which I have already begun to discuss; and (2) the packaging and contextualizing of events, resulting in a Local Moral Universe that supplants the morality on which the participating individuals were brought up. Let us consider each of these in turn.

Hoess reports that he was always at great pains to emphasize to his staff that orders from above must be obeyed, that there could be no question of disobedience, that the existing authority system (including his own) was fully justified, and that it was especially honorable to obey difficult orders. To be "hard" is good, he said.

He states that there was no doubt in any officer's mind that Hitler's orders must be obeyed, even though all of them were touched by severe doubts. In order to encourage his subordinates to continue to function he, himself, must never admit having doubts or allow his feelings to come out into the open:

> I had to appear cold and indifferent to events that must have wrung the heart of anyone possessed of human feeling. . . . I might not even look away [when horrors were performed] . . . afraid lest my emotions got the upper hand.[17]

In another context he states he was aware of the impending horror of having to exterminate the Gypsies, yet "nothing surely is harder than to grit one's teeth and go through with such a thing, coldly, pitilessly, and without mercy."[18]

One cannot escape the interpretation that Hoess derives a sense of honor from carrying out orders even when, or perhaps *because*, they are horribly difficult. He is thereby making a distinctive contribution to his own honor and the honor of the Nazi cause. That Nazi cause constitutes the large moral mantle under which individual acts of horror are being justifed. Thereby they are "moral" acts, as Hoess sees them.

This leads us into the concept of contextualizing gruesome actions through packaging and acceptance of a Local Moral Universe. In our society, when a soldier kills an enemy soldier in the course of a battle, this is regarded as heroic and desirable. Killing in war is "packaged" and, thereby, placed in a distinctive context which gives killing societal sanction. This packaged contextualizing of killing is spelled out in the rules of warfare, including when and how killing is permitted and encouraged.

The packaged contextualizing of killing includes the soldier's separation from home, the official declaration of a state of war, the abandonment of certain peacetime prohibitions against killing and other forms of violence, and the legitimization of violent acts against the enemy. Killing is separated from civilian, peacetime pursuits. It is also not carried out as a starkly isolated activity. On the contrary, it is part of a behavior package that has a degree of internal consistency, logic, and a culture of its own. It also contains a purported morality. Traditionally, for example, soldiers are not supposed to kill unarmed civilians. And on occasion certain weapons—such as poison gas and explosive bullets—have been ruled out as illegitimate weapons. Indeed, killing is usually carried out in the confines of a particular Local Moral Universe.

At Auschwitz, too, there prevailed a Local Moral Universe. Its core was the moral blessing conferred upon mass murder. Rudolf Hoess, perhaps more than anyone else, helped to design this Local Moral Universe and oversee its actual implementation. Hoess contributed significantly to the "moral" packaging of mass killing and the practice of unmatched brutality.

One component of that package, as Hoess sees it, was the "need" to exterminate the Jews. He tells himself that he was not anti-Semitic, that he did not personally hate Jews but believed the Nazi credo that Jews were the "enemy of our people." (Similarly, from Eichmann we heard the claim that he was not anti-Semitic, but that the extermination of Jews was necessary in order to "preserve the German people.") In short, personal hatred of Jews was not, in Hoess's mind, a factor. But accepting the anti-Jewish credo most definitely was a factor. This credo was transformed, through the process of packaging, into the moral imperative of personal killing—"personal" in two senses: that individual Jewish *persons* were to be killed; and the SS man's *personal* participation in carrying out the killings was absolutely necessary and justified on high moral grounds. Hoess spells this out in his autobiography, written while awaiting his own execution. He reports that when SS men occasionally came to him complaining about the bloody deeds they were doing, he told them that he understood their misgivings but that it was absolutely imperative—in contributing to realizing the grand vision of a better Germany—that they continue to do what they were doing.

Another component of the Hoess package was that at Auschwitz he attempted to prescribe moral standards. He objected to guards stealing from prisoners and raping the women. Due to acute shortage of personnel, he had to accept very "low-level" personnel. For example, among female Capos (inmates turned supervisors), in charge of female prisoners, he says: "I find it incredible that human beings could ever turn into such beasts . . . tearing [Jewish women] to pieces, killing them with axes, and throttling them—it was simply gruesome."[19] He claims that he could not get better personnel and, what is more, could not prevent brutal behavior by the guards.

A third component of the Hoess package was the use of modern technology to—as he claims—minimize suffering. Hoess takes great satsifaction in the marvel of gas chamber technology. This lessened the need for massive bloodbaths.

> I always shuddered at the prospect of carrying out extermination by shooting when I thought of the vast numbers concerned, and the women and children. . . . I was therefore relieved to think that we spared all these bloodbaths and the victims would also be spared suffering until their last moment came.[20]

This "caring" method of killing would also prevent what happened during previous mass killings by means of shooting.

> Many gruesome scenes are said to have taken place. . . . Many members of the *Einsatzkommandos* [who carried out mass killings after the German army invaded Poland and the Soviet Union; this was before the mass killing technology had been developed and they had to do the killing in a more "personal" way], unable to endure wading through blood any longer, had committed suicide. Some had even gone mad."[21]

He tells himself that the new form of killing, packaged in mass-production technology, was infinitely preferable. Hoess reports that members of his staff repeatedly asked him whether the mass killings were really necessary. Despite his own qualms he would reassure them that it was done on Hitler's orders and that it was necessary to safeguard the German people. In short, the killing was packaged with high-sounding ideals and the honor derived from obeying orders. What is deliberately left out of the package are many of the values and ethical standards with which most Germans grew up.

To an incredible degree, the killing and brutality was contextualized. So thoroughly separated was life at Auschwitz from other moral contexts, that it was largely immune from influence by other contexts. In addition, contextualization inside the camps contributed to ever increasing escalation of evil, where evil would contribute its own momentum to ever growing evil. The career of Hoess, and life at Auschwitz altogether, contained many such contextualizing processes. When Hoess brooked no sign of mercy, the guards under his command would brook no mercy. This, in turn, meant that Capos would brook no mercy. Hoess could then complain about brutality among the Capos and the guards, and justify further brutality by himself. It was a context where evil begot ever more evil. It was a Local Moral Universe feeding on itself.

Hoess's Autonomy and Life in Two Moral Worlds

Much of Hoess's autobiography emphasizes his claim that he had little autonomy while he was the commandant of Auschwitz. He claims that he had little influence over the day-to-day execution of policy in the face of relatively great autonomy by those under him. This, in turn, prevented him from controlling some of the brutality in the camp.

Whether this is true is simply not known. Hoess's claim that he wished to lessen brutality at Auschwitz but was unable to do so certainly appears absurd on its face. Surely, if anyone could, he could. Perhaps Hoess had subtle ways of encouraging brutality while saying to himself that he opposed brutality. At any rate, the fact that he himself appears to *believe* that he opposed brutality, but could not prevent it, is worth examining. His statements about limitations to his autonomy should not be dismissed arbitrarily.

All persons in leadership positions, be they executives of business firms, high government officials or heads of prisons, have limitations on their freedom of action—and not only in a democratic society but also in totalitarian societies. For example, and contrary to popular thinking, the distinguishing thing about American business executives is not that they have more autonomy than those under them; they have *different sorts* of autonomy. Executives of a business can make decisions affecting the firm, which underlings cannot make. Most notably, they have autonomy to establish and set in motion company policy. By contrast, blue-collar workers have virtually no autonomy in respect to establishing company policy. They ordinarily do not participate in policy decisions.

However, there are areas of behavior where executives do not have autonomy but where those under them, notably blue-collar workers, do have autonomy. While on the job, blue-collar workers can, and do, spend time talking about their life outside the factory. But it is more than mere talk. Some decades ago, sociologists did much to illustrate the "informal culture" of the workplace, showing it to be a culturally rich and innovative system of behavior. Newcomers are carefully initiated, and the work group has its own code of behavior created by the workers, using considerable autonomy. (I shall elaborate on this theme later, in Chapter 10, in the section on "cultures of cruelty.")

The blue-collar workers' informal culture can affect production and influence the quality of the work done. In the automobile industry, thanks to Japanese competition after the mid-twentieth century, the workers' informal culture has come to be recognized as extremely relevant to the quality of goods being produced.

Yet much of this informal culture is entirely separate from the ethos and culture of executive personnel. Indeed executives are excluded from this sphere of life in the factory. From this perspective, Hoess's statement that the guards under him had a great deal of autonomy comes as no great surprise.

It is also important to recognize that, in comparison to the blue-collar worker, the executive's role travels with him beyond the factory gates. That is, when a Vice President of Personnel takes part in a community fund-raising campaign to support the community's Little League baseball team, he remains labelled as a company official. He cannot shed that role very easily when he leaves the office.

Hoess had similar problems. He noted that if he was "deeply affected" by an event at the camp, he found it impossible to go home right away. He would instead seek solace among his beloved animals. He would take a ride on his horse, or walk through the stables, anything at all to stay away from his family until the feelings disappeared. This was important to him because he regarded his family life at Auschwitz to be exceedingly happy—a "paradise," he called it. Only occasionally was his family compound visited by the realities of his monstrous work. He attempted to keep family and work thoroughly separate.

Much of the time, Hoess evidently succeeded. He and his family appear to have led a life of comfortable German burgherhood. There were bucolic joys of quiet walks in the woods, not far from the electric fences and the chimneys. There were the privileges of the high executive combined with a virtual feudal lord's unlimited access to human services for personal pleasure and comfort. Paradise indeed!

The juxtaposition of bucolic family life and the demonic work life is incredibly extreme in Hoess's case, but Hoess was able to maintain considerable autonomy of each to the other. Although he travelled between them and they were linked, they were two distinctive contexts. They were utterly different in moral tone and behavior content. Evidently there was no brutality—certainly no physical brutality—in the Hoess household. There appeared to be a measure of German familial kindness, emanating especially from Mrs. Hoess. Interestingly, Mrs. Hoess acted kindly not only to family members but also to camp inmates who worked in the Hoess household. The Hoess household, with its children at play, its wife and mother devoted to household maintenance, and its docile servants (drawn from the camp inmate population) represented some measure of tranquility and "ordinary" German family life for the Hoesses. So, despite Rudolf Hoess's complaint that his camp experiences occasionally intruded on his home life, his family enjoyed considerable insulation from the camp's mode of life as it maintained a substantially autonomous way of life. Hoess, as head-of-household, evidently exhibited none of the cold and limitless severity that was so typical of his behavior in the camp.

Hoess personifies not only the reality of both modes of life. He also personifies, *in extremis*, man's capacity to coexist in two different moral worlds. The easiest thing would be to dismiss Hoess, the individual, as some peculiar psychopath who could operate in two worlds by being a master of the art of cognitive denial, or one who did not understand the difference between the two worlds. I do not dismiss Hoess this way, and I invite you, the reader, to also avoid this type of analysis. It would amount to abdicating one's responsibility for trying to understand how bucolic and demonic modes of life can coexist, as they did, on a large scale, in much of Germany in the Nazi era.

In a sense the two worlds represent a version of life one might find near a U.S. army base. There, too, families of soldiers, living in compounds adjacent to field-training areas, lead a relatively mundane, family-centered life. In the morning the husband-father leaves for "work," to practice the highly refined art of modernized killing so that he will be ready when the next war comes. He returns at night, as though nothing had happened, to concern himself with his wife's needs for conjugal affection, his children's need for help with their schoolwork, and the need to do various sundry household chores.

Of course, the Auschwitz context is far more extreme. In this camp, one was not merely preparing to kill. Actual killing was everyday business. Some of it was relatively routinized. Some of it was sporadic. All of it was bestial by any standard of human morality, *even by the standards in place within the family context of the Hoess household.* But despite the difference in scope and proximity to actual killings, Auschwitz and army camp life share a common thread. There is routinization of violence in both made possible by contextualization.

The question remains how could the demonic and the bucolic worlds coexist at Auschwitz? The town and the camp were in close proximity. So close, in fact, that townspeople could not possibly be oblivious to the camp in the course of their day-to-day lives. What is more, some townspeople existed and participated in both worlds. Hoess himself and some of the inmates who worked in the Hoess household as servants traveled back and forth daily.

The answer to this apparent anomaly is that the true measure of the "separateness" of a social structure is not its physical separation from other structures or, even, its separation of participants who may have roles in both. The critical factor is the degree of autonomy, of independence of action, that exists in each structure. The bucolic Hoess household and the demonic world of the Auschwitz camp were separate contexts that had great independence from each other. Each contained a separate package of items that cohered, packages in which the items mutually reinforced one another.

The Hoess household had a package of relative affluence. There was ample food, comfortable shelter, and adequate clothing. Daily family routines

took place in a benign country setting. Every one of these items contributed
to the bucolic atmosphere. Each item also reinforced the other items. Thus,
economic affluence contributed to relatively nurturant family activities, and
nurturant family activities, in turn, contributed to the enjoyment of affluence.

In the camp, the local package included various interrelated items in the
cycle of violence: the starvation diet, the supremely arbitrary power of guards
over inmates, and deliberate administrative brutalities. These items contributed
independently to the totality of violence, and, in turn, each item was influenced
by all the other items. The starvation diet, for example, contributed to illness
and death and augmented administrative brutality by debilitating the victims,
lowering their capacity to resist or evade brutal measures. In turn, the administrative brutalities, even when they did not directly include depriving inmates
of food, contributed to inmates' susceptibility to starvation. Sometimes, indeed,
succumbing to starvation was embraced as the lesser evil (as happened among
the Musselmänner, the individuals who had given up on life).

In short, the camp and the Hoess household were each maintained by
composite and distinct packages that contained mutually reinforcing parts. This
contributed to maintaining two separate and distinct worlds, each largely independent of the other, despite their propinquity. Each world had a distinctive moral
climate. In each the component parts sustained and reinforced that climate.

Hoess apparently made every effort to insulate the autonomy of the
camp from the autonomy of his home, so that each would retain its own,
distinctive way of living. When, while at home, thoughts about the day's
executions troubled him, he would go for a solitary walk or ride one of his
horses. He would not discuss the problem with his wife. This way of sepa-
rating his two lives appears to have succeeded to a considerable extent. It
helped Hoess nurture the separation, the coexistence, and the routinization of
a demonic and a bucolic world.

Doubtless the life of Hoess contains aspects that are unique and idio-
syncratic to Hoess, the individual. I have deliberately not dwelt on these.
Instead, I have concentrated on aspects of Hoess' life that can be generalized.
His life suggests how drastically different worlds can coexist: how a measure
of human concern for others can exist alongside unparalleled evil; how blind
submersion in one's place of work and career can be harnessed to the service
of limitless savagery; and how both can contribute to the routinization of
monstrous behavior.

CHAPTER EIGHT

A Career in Doing Evil:
The Case of a Sensitive Physician

Can individuals who are not necessarily morally depraved to begin with come to devote their careers to doing evil? It seems that this is not only possible, at times it actually happens. It can be explained, without being forgiven.

Concomitantly, promoters of evil can often rely on individuals who are not committed to evil to become major contributors to evil—not only as implementers of existing evil plans but also as designers of evil programs, and as creators of new evil. It happens when these individuals accept clear evil, even from their own point of view, as a necessary part of a larger moral cause to which their evil deeds make a vital contribution.

The most surprising thing about the Nazi era may not be that someone, a Hitler, could dream a dream that required exterminating entire categories of persons, but that this dream was taken so seriously, and that efforts were undertaken to actually implement it. Hitler's dream was to create a pure Nordic master race that would populate Germany and make her once again into a world-class power—or even *the* dominant world power. Hitler proclaimed that, to achieve this grand German destiny, it was critically important to eliminate the influence of racially inferior people. He proclaimed that they were ready to contaminate Germany's people and would prevent them from reaching the grandeur that rightfully was theirs.

The dream itself is unusual mainly in its grandiosity. On a far smaller scale, many of us occasionally dream of exterminating enemies in order to purify the world in which we live. If we are convinced that the easy availability of guns is the major source of violence in America, we might dream of exterminating all members of the National Rifle Association in order to rid America of its horrendous violence. Or, we might want to do away with all persons who habitually drive while under the influence of alcohol and thereby constitute a mortal danger to innocent drivers on the public highways. Or we might want to kill off political extremists who are poisoning the nation's social atmosphere through their inciting speeches. But our ruminations and anger do not usually go beyond the state of dreaming; they remain imaginary games.

In the case of the Nazi era, the profound surprise was that systematic and sustained efforts were made to actually implement Hitler's crazy dreams. Ordinary, sane people neither laughed at Hitler and his grandiose hallucinations nor did they immediately dismiss his message as the product of a disturbed mind. Some people reacted in just these ways, but they were a minority. A majority of Germany's citizens apparently accepted Hitler's dream as a blueprint for achieving the highest moral goals for their country. Eventually millions of people joined the Nazi cause and participated, openly and enthusiastically, to transform Hitler's dream into reality. In doing so many contributed their personal careers—their knowledge, their skills, their energy, their commitment—to devising and carrying out a diabolical system for realizing Hitler's dream.

Hitler's dream could not possibly have been implemented without broad support. He required and received the help of citizens of every kind: lawyers, physicians, engineers, architects, economists, teachers, and writers; scientists and artists; administrative managers and skilled and unskilled laborers; members of humanistic professions and members of the military professions. Many of these contributed their particular expertise, their abilities, and their very lives. They donated their careers to an evil cause, often participating personally and directly in the practice and promotion of evil.

Lawyers, for example, helped design the legal mechanisms for an increasingly restrictive series of laws that deprived Jews of their citizenship rights. Meticulously crafted laws made it possible for the Nazis to implement the persecutions "legally." It was not a matter of lawyers, perhaps inadvertently or under duress, drafting one new law. Lawyers continued their work of crafting a distinctive legal strategy for implementing the Nazi dream over the entire twelve years of the regime's existence. These were not specially trained Nazi lawyers; they were lawyers trained under the traditional system of German legal education.

In the same way, physicians were recruited to help design and implement the initial phase of genocide, which was the murder of thousands of mentally defective individuals. Later, at Auschwitz, physicians carried out the "selections," deciding who would live a little longer and who would die immediately. They contributed their professional expertise to an evil cause. They were professionals who believed, while doing the work of Nazis, that they remained professionals.

What is a professional? Above all, a professional is the moral guardian of a body of knowledge. In the case of the physician, this means that he or she is the guardian of medical knowledge. The society has entrusted that person with the responsibility of using and safeguarding medical knowledge in ways that promote healing the sick and, under no circumstances, using it to harm people. The physicians who collaborated with the Nazi system by donating their medical expertise to realizing its demented dream betrayed their guardianship; they betrayed the trust society had placed in them to safeguard medical knowledge.

To realize the Nazi dream, other citizens contributed their material resources. Still others merely contributed their enthusiasm. Not a few willingly donated their lives. Most of them were not reluctant, or recalcitrant followers of the Nazi dream. On the contrary, they contributed with zeal, often with imagination and creativity.

Given the vast quantity of people who were engaged in actively carrying out the Nazi program, one must assume that the majority began as ordinary sorts of people, not as people who, to begin with, were singularly demented and murderous. (An alternative to my view is Daniel Goldhagen's thesis that a majority of Nazi era Germans were under the sway of a particular "eliminationist" form of anti-Semitism. Daniel Goldhagen, *Hitler's Willing Executioners: Ordinary Germans and the Holocaust.* New York: Knopf, 1996.)

How is it that people could join a course of action which surely most could easily identify as being thoroughly inhumane and evil? How does it work? What are the mechanisms?

Some may answer that a kernel of morally depraved people, who are ordinarily submerged within civilized society, can, under the right conditions, come to the surface to practice and promote the evil that already lurked in their makeup. This "monster" theory does not deserve much credibility. There were so many participants, and the participants were so diverse, so variegated, that one simply cannot accept the idea that one is dealing with only some, identifiable, monsters.

Once we modify the monster theory to say that all humans carry monster potentials within themselves, we might be getting a little closer to the truth. But we are still stuck with the sterile notion that our monstrous nature gets us to do monstrous things. We must dig deeper. We must try to understand how *ordinary* people can be recruited for participation in horrendous activities, and how this can be done fairly effectively. To help us understand how this works, let us review the career of Dr. Eduard Wirths, whose career was studied in depth by Robert Jay Lifton, a distinguished psychiatrist. I am basing my analysis on information presented in Dr. Lifton's work, *The Nazi Doctors: Medical Killing and the Psychology of Genocide.*[1]

Dr. Wirths, a Christian, started out as a dedicated, humane country doctor in his native Germany. After the Nazis came to power, Jewish doctors were increasingly prevented from practicing medicine, and non-Jewish doctors were increasingly reluctant to treat Jewish patients. The result was that, in the 1930s, Germany's Jews were increasingly deprived of access to medical care.

Dr. Wirths was an exception. He responded to his Jewish neighbors with an open heart. He set up a system allowing Jews to come to him in secret, at night, for medical treatment. Sometimes he treated them for injuries received at the hands of Nazis. Dr. Wirths was humane, morally upstanding, and courageous; he was a physician in the best medical tradition. By treating Jews during the height of the anti-Jewish hysteria, Dr. Wirths placed himself and his family at considerable risk. He accepted that risk, and continued to treat Jews.

As we look at the career of Dr. Wirths, there is a surprise in store for us. At Auschwitz, in 1942 and 1943, the "selections"—the decision as to who would be killed immediately and who would work in the forced labor projects until they died or were later transferred to the gas chambers—were made by doctors. Many of us will immediately think of the infamous Dr. Josef Mengele, standing on the ramp at Auschwitz, dressed in his elegant SS uniform, and flamboyantly making life and death decisions by directing the prisoner facing him to go to the right or to the left: "right," "left," "right," "left," . . . One of these meant immediate death, the other meant death a little later.

Who was the doctor over Dr. Mengele? Dr. Wirths. Who was the doctor in charge of all Auschwitz doctors who carried out the selections? Dr. Wirths. Who designed the "selection" process as it was performed by physicians? None other than Dr. Eduard Wirths. This decent, humane man had joined the murderers. Not only had he joined them, he participated in their program in a highly influential, administrative, and "professional" capacity. He was donating much of his expertise to the murderous cause.

To be accurate, Dr. Wirths had joined the Nazi party quite early in the Nazi regime. Even while he was treating Jews medically, he was already a member of the Nazi party. He believed much of the Nazi ideology, including that the Jews were a danger to Germany. Here is an anachronism.

At Auschwitz, while actively participating in murder, he was fully aware of engaging in horrifying, inhumane acts. He said so many times. Here is another anachronism.

Finally, Dr. Wirths did commit suicide. But only after the war was over, and after he was captured from his hiding place. He did so a few hours after a British officer said to him that, in Dr. Wirths, he had now met a man who was personally responsible for millions of deaths. Here is yet another, a final, anachronism.

Dr. Wirths's case forces us to go beyond the simplistic notion that only bad people do bad things. He forces us to examine what it is in the workings of human nature—*our common human nature*—and in the operation of social contexts, that lets people take part in evil.

It is very tempting, and far too easy, to look for the answer by claiming that there must be a preexisting sickness in the makeup of the likes of Dr. Wirths. He can teach us far more if we accept, as a starting point, that he was an ordinary human being who, in his route to personally and actively contributing to horrendous evil, followed ordinary human ways. If we have the courage to look at the actions of such a man as ordinary actions, we may yet discover tools for attacking extraordinary evil. So, let us return to Dr. Wirths.

In the 1930s Dr. Wirths treated Jews, at great risk to himself, because he believed it was the moral thing to do as a physician. At that time he also already believed the Nazi view that Jews were a danger to Germany. In the 1940s, he participated, actively and innovatively, in the massive process of murdering Jews, even though he believed that these murders were a horrible and ghastly thing to do.

In each period he accepted a package of moral commands. In the 1930s, the traditional medical package prevailed. In the 1940s, the Nazi package prevailed. From Wirths's perspective, each package included distasteful components. Yet each time Dr. Wirths was able to live with himself, despite the distasteful elements in what he was doing.[2] Each time he accepted a total package, even when he knew it contained distasteful items. And the distasteful items—such as the "need" to murder Jews—were not to be avoided. They were to be implemented fully, with imagination and tenacity.

The existence of distasteful elements in the package of physicians is something I first encountered in my research on the careers of American physicians who were entirely decent and humane.[3] They were not engaged in the pursuit of evil, as the SS doctors were, but they often saw themselves doing tasks, in the course of their professional work, which they found distasteful. They did not shirk these tasks. They carried them out fully and energetically. In short, their work setting typically contained a package of obligations, and they accepted the entire package, even those they found distasteful.

What holds for medical careers probably holds for many other careers. We frequently do things we do not like to do, or even things we know to be wrong. Still we do them. We live with compromises. This is surely rather "ordinary" and commonplace. Dr. Wirths is noteworthy because he presents us with an example of the extreme consequences that can follow from such "ordinariness" as accepting distasteful compromises. These can, incrementally and cumulatively, become ever more monstrous.

∼

My earlier studies on how people make career decisions led me to realize that some people—I do not know how many—enter a career through a series of small, localized decisions, without ever making an advance commitment to the career. Instead, in their current life situation they solved one problem at a time, dealing with each immediacy as it came up. The small, localized decisions accumulated, so that it is hard to say when a person actually embarked on a career with particular life attributes and particular consequences. (This is also discussed in Chapter 6 of this book.)

Some Nazis joined the party early on, during difficult economic times, and did so mainly to obtain a job, to earn a living, or, possibly, to embark on a long-range occupational career. Additionally, some professionals who were already well established joined the Nazi party to avoid losing clients. Such economic decisions could be made without commitment to the Nazi racist dreams, anti-Semitism, or political yearnings of greater glory for the German nation.

Let us look at a composite of a person, call him Heinz, who, hypothetically, joins the Nazis merely to qualify for a job as a lawyer at the Nazi party headquarters. At the time it was the only job he was able to obtain. After a few years, Heinz's wife reminds him that they now have two children, and she wishes they were not so financially strapped. Could he not find a way to earn a bit more? He realizes that yes, he could. He could be more diligent in his work—in his work as a Nazi functionary! With this urging he begins to be more creative, more forthcoming, more active in making the Nazi dreams come true. He designs ever harsher legal measures directed against Jews.

Heinz could honestly say he did not join the Nazi party in order to embrace its anti-Semitism. However, this did not keep him from contributing mightily to its anti-Semitism while seeking to further his personal career and meet his family obligations.

The converse side of this picture is that the Nazi package of programs consisted of a variety of different items, as I mentioned earlier. There was the promise to revitalize the German economy, to stop the nation's economic bleeding induced by war reparations, and to recapture vital industrial resources in the Ruhr district. There was the promise to restore Germany's political glory, to restore its place in the sun among the great nations, and to wash away the shame of losing the World War of 1914 to 1918. And there was the promise to purify Germany racially to enable it to achieve its maximum biological destiny by eradicating inferior races, notably the Jews.

Any reason bearing on any one of these elements could convince an individual to join the Nazi party. Dr. Wirths's reason apparently was the opportunity to continue to take part in genetic research fostered by the Nazi racial dreams. During the 1930s, even while he was practicing clinical medicine, Dr. Wirths engaged in race-focused genetic research, in the tradition of Darwinian theory. For this work he received financial and other tangible support from the Nazi regime. This was in the aftermath of the triumph of Darwinian evolutionary theory in biology. The fittest species were shown to survive. They do so because they are superior to other species. Some quite respectable scientists tried to apply Darwinism to human populations. They equated human races with biological species, where some races were surely "superior" to other races. Dr. Wirths was among these. Alongside his clinical work of treating patients he did research on human racial populations, in the hope of discovering genetic attributes that differentiate among human races.

Dr. Wirth joined the Nazi movement because he received support from it for his genetic research. He did so even though he had no commitment to every element in the package of Nazi programs. But the different Nazi programs were amalgamated. They were linked. As a result, Dr. Wirths, the hypothetical Heinz, and thousands like them, were very likely to become involved in carrying out the entire package of programs, even supporting, through their actions, those items to which they personally had no great commitment.

In my previous research on physicians I had found that any one doctor was apt to have a strong initial commitment to some specific element of medical practice. However, when he found himself in a situation where he had to implement other elements, even those he actually resented, he tended to carry out those elements as fully and vigorously as he carried out the elements to which he was committed initially. He did so because of the linkage between new assignments and the work to which he originally was committed, and because he was committed to the medical package as a totality. He usually had a convincing rationale for why he needed to do what he disliked doing—how he could live with himself despite the disagreeable components in his career.

How did Dr. Wirths come to be at Auschwitz? Following an outbreak of typhoid among the guards at Auschwitz, Dr. Wirths was ordered, as an active member of the Nazi party and as a practicing physician, to go to Auschwitz to stop the outbreak of typhoid. He went there and, by adopting appropriate public health measures, succeeded in stopping the typhoid epidemic.

While serving at Auschwitz, Dr. Wirths expressed his disgust that the "selections" among newly arriving prisoners were being carried out in such a haphazardous manner by totally untrained persons. Surely, he proclaimed, these decisions ought to be made by medical persons, who are far better trained to make these judgments. He succeeded in establishing a "medically supervised" program of selection among the newly arriving victims. He was, in his own mind, making a professional medical contribution to an existing system. It was a murderous system, but even here one could make a professional medical contribution.

Dr. Wirths told himself two stories that enabled him to live with his evil deeds at Auschwitz: One, by having physicians supervise the selection process at Auschwitz he was able to save some lives, or at least postpone death. Formerly, as I mentioned, the selections had been carried out by nonmedical SS men, including the camp commandant. Dr. Wirths fought to have physicians take over this task. He told himself that some individuals whom nonmedical personnel would immediately have sent to the gas chambers were really capable of serving on work details, and therefore be saved from immediate execution. Above all, it would make the system operate far more efficiently; it would make use of people who were still capable of working. He proclaimed that only a physician could make a really informed decision, and thereby contribute to the greater efficiency of the system.

Wirths's second story came out in his passionate love letters to his wife during his time at Auschwitz. He told her that he was involved in horrible activities, but it was all worth it so long as he had her love. He was doing all of it for the sake of her, their children, and their joint future. In the interest of contributing to their country's, and thereby their family's, better future, he would go through with the horrors.

In short, Dr. Wirths demonstrates that ordinary, even morally sensitive, persons can invent justifications for taking part in the greatest of horrors. Such self-justification produced a breed of functionaries who created careers in manufacturing evil and who were able to live with themselves, with their own conscience, while doing evil. These functionaries were then free to dedicate their knowledge, their skills, and their energy to making mass murder into a banal, everyday reality. They did so by following very conventional ways of living that, if not carefully scrutinized, periodically reassessed and interrupted, can constitute the pathway to moral monstrocity.

In this chapter I focused on individual careers, a hypothetical one and a real one. However, there is a larger picture into which individual careers fit, especially when it comes to careers in science in Nazi Germany. It turns out that some serious and significant scientific work continued to thrive in Nazi Germany. It turns out that in the Nazi confines, German scientists did highly advanced work, notably in cancer research. Only many years later this level of work is being reached and replicated in the West.[4] In short, some scientists were able to do serious and significant research under the Nazis. As suggested in the case of Dr. Wirths, this could happen because the Nazi package included support for science, even while that package also contained the most horrifying components. The support-for-science item was the node on which the scientist might be attached to the Nazi package, making Nazism a beguiling system for many serious scientists. The fact that all of the items of the Nazi package were fused into one amalgamated entity meant that the serious scientist might also become a major contributor to horrors—as was Dr. Wirths, this initially sensitive physician.

CHAPTER NINE

A Sponsorship of Evil:
The Nazi Package as a Moral Mantle

Can a society actively sponsor the practice of evil by its citizenry? Are there explicit processes for bringing this about?

The Nazi regime that prevailed in Germany from 1933 to 1945 provides an illustrative and instructive example of such processes.

In the previous chapter, we discussed a kind of career development whereby an individual can engage, even zealously, in activities in which that individual does not believe. The individual can do so without ever confronting the real nature of the career in which one is, in fact, engaging and, through it, carrying out activities that can be entirely horrendous—even from the point of view of the individual's own morality.

A basic feature behind these phenomena is that a society's packages, such as its package of values, or its package of political programs, are not mere passive background factors. They can be powerful, dynamic, and decisive social processes in their own right. In the case of Nazism, such a package constituted a moral mantle for the sponsorship of active evil that would be perpetrated through the personal life of individuals.

The Nazi political package consisted of a variety of programs, each of which appealed to some sector of the German population. The package gained a wide following among the Germans precisely because it offered something to virtually everybody. The themes were that Germany must regain the territories she had been forced to give up in 1918; Germany must revitalize her economy; Germany must rebuild her military strength (the peace treaty had placed severe limits on Germany's army); Germany must restore its national glory; and Germany must purify itself racially, particularly of the Jews.

Hitler promoted these themes in his fiery speeches in the 1920s before he came to power, and in the massive propaganda campaign after he came to

137

power in 1933. To achieve its grand objectives, he proclaimed, Germany needed a strong government, under a strong leader and a unified program. His leadership and the Nazi cause were the answer. He personally would see to it that the nation's ills would be confronted. He would do so effectively, courageously, and totally. Under him, after so much confusion and national pain, there would be a unified course of action.

In order to be successful, the Nazi package must be accepted in its entirety, with "the leader" as the final arbiter of priorities. That Nazi package—Nazism, in short—must be regarded as the overarching moral system for the German nation. Under it alone all national goals would be identified and addressed. And under it alone all individual Germans would discover their own sacred mission in life. The total Nazi package became sacrosanct, where any personal misgivings and doubts must be ruled out—on the highest moral grounds. Any deviation from Nazism was unthinkable.

The power and effectiveness of this outlook was glaringly demonstrated at the Nuremberg trials of Nazi mass murderers. At these trials it was common to hear the accused persons state that, while doing murderous deeds, they were "following orders." Western judges, speaking with understandable outrage, then proclaimed that some orders are so horrendous they ought not to be obeyed.

These judges usually failed to understand the murderers' next statement: "It was unthinkable" not to obey. In their own view the murderers were taking a moral stance. We may find this "morality" abhorrent, as did some of the perpetrators themselves. But the Nazi murderers believed they were acting on a moral basis. (Would not the biblical Abraham have found it abhorrent to sacrifice his own son? But, in "obedience to a divine voice," he was prepared to do so. Here the specific act—the sacrifice of one's own son—became secondary to a more fundamental issue, one's willingness to obey a higher calling.) In the courtroom at Nuremberg, the Nazi murderers declared with unshaken conviction that obedience to Nazi orders—even to horrendous orders—was a supremely *moral* imperative. It was obedience to a higher calling. They had sworn an oath, a sacred oath, to do so. It was the Nazi package at work.

That Nazi package operated as one entity. One could not pick and choose among its component parts, obeying some of its orders and not others. That would be sacrilege. The Nazi package had become the greatest moral imperative in the lives of these Nazi functionaries, and the Nuremberg trials showed its workings through the testimony of the accused murderers.

That Nazi package created new priorities for the German people. At the onset of the Nazi regime, anti-Semitism was probably not the most pressing daily concern for most Germans. Yet the Nazis made it an active component of their agenda, and they publicly and frequently promoted it as vital to Germany's very survival. It eventually became a prominent, national obsession.

Over time, the Nazi package itself underwent change. At first the focus was on the national shame. In the Germany of the 1920s there was considerable national shame about the loss of the recent war and Germany's subsequent treatment by the Allies. Hitler would not let the Germans forget it. In speech after speech he addressed the theme of the nation's shame at being treated so badly by the victorious Allied powers. He said it was the national imperative to regain Germany's rightful grandeur. Germany must recover its historical destiny which had been so unjustly denied. Hitler also offered solutions to many immediate problems, most notably the economic ones. And he promised to provide a strongly assertive government, in contrast to the weak government then ruling Germany.

Germany's unjust national shame was the overarching theme to Hitler's early package. The various promises were being offered as one total entity, in one amalgamated package that utilized Germany's national shame. It became the glue that held the Nazi package together on Hitler's road to power. The Nazi amalgam was the way to wash away the shame unjustly inflicted on Germany by the Allies. It alone would enable Germans to hold up their heads once again, doing so with honor and dignity. It would be accomplished by a forceful government, one that must be permitted to push through its entire agenda, its total package, even though some of the new measures and initiatives might entail sacrifices and difficult decisions. The German people could be counted on to make the sacrifices, the difficult decisions, and to do so proudly and dutifully. There was great emphasis on carrying out the entire package, even those items to which the individual had no prior commitment.

During the era of Nazism, this intial glue, the national shame based on the hostile world environment, was eventually replaced by a different glue, anti-Semitism. It was addressing the supposed internal enemy, the defiling Jew who was the enemy within Germany, against whom the German nation must purify itself on its road to rightful grandeur. Again, there had to be adherence to the total Nazi package, although now the danger was portrayed as coming from pollutants within the nation. In the eyes, ears, and hearts of the faithful, that danger served to emphasize the threat to the sacred cause in which Nazism was engaged. Vigilance must not only be maintained, it must constantly be amplified, for the dangers were increasing. Moral fervor was thereby kept at a high pitch.

Emphasis on the glue that held the Nazi package together is important, because initially the individual citizen was likely to be attached to the Nazi package at a particular point, such as the economy. Similarly, whole sectors of the German population—military veterans of wars, the medical profession, the legal profession, academic disciplines and members of religious faiths

(such as Catholics)—were likely to have a particular point of initial attachment to the Nazi package. It was critically important to the Nazi movement
that there be a convincing glue that held it all together. Its primary symbolic
glue, of course, was the person of Hitler. To him was attributed total infalli-
bility and saintly stature. He personified Nazism—its entire program, its
mission, its destiny. And he, in turn, was continually emphasizing the unitary
nature of the Nazi cause—the cohesion and interdependence of its component
parts in the pursuit of the sacred cause. There could be no deviation, no
slackening of effort to bring to fruition Germany's destiny through *total*
adherence to the *total* Nazi program.

Hitler's package did not just remain rhetoric. Over a period of twelve
years the Nazis succeeded to a considerable extent, not only to amalgamate
the component parts of their package conceptually, but to actually implement
many of these component parts in practice. The Nazi regime did revitalize
Germany's economy; it did develop an awesome military machine; it did
recapture the territories Germany had to give up after the First World War;
and it did virtually destroy all the Jews in Germany's midst.

In addition, under Propaganda Minister Joseph Goebbels the Nazis made
sure that their agenda was seen as one gloriously coherent entity. The German
people, Goebbels told them, must accept the entire Nazi agenda because it
meant that each person was participating, under Hitler's uniquely inspired
leadership, in a noble crusade for the German fatherland. He saw to it that
moral fervor for the entire Nazi cause was kept at a high pitch. In terms of
personal skill, Goebbels was perhaps the world's foremost practitioner of
political propaganda. Goebbels was also the master packager. He made adherence to the entire package amount to a moral crusade. Perversely, that moral
crusade formed a moral mantle under which the individual citizen acted.

That crusade relied more and more on the theme of racial purification—
in the form of increasingly lethal anti-Semitism—as the glue that would hold
the Nazi package together. It would keep the Nazi dream on its sublime
course. It would help keep the entire Nazi vision intact. It would help
Germany reach its destiny.

An individual might accept the Nazi package of programs because one
was attracted to one or more of its specific programs, but the process of
actually implementing the Nazi package relied on the individual's contributions. In accepting Nazism—particularly in joining the Nazi party—one was
accepting the entire package of Nazi programs; one's contributions could
therefore include implementing programs to which one did not have a great
personal commitment. As we discussed earlier, the Hoesses and Eichmanns
teach us that one can be recruited into contributing to murderous deeds even
if one is not initially committed to such deeds. One merely needs to accept
the Nazi package as an entirely sacrosanct entity.

Thus one can become a killer, even a grotesque mass killer, without being committed to being a killer. Hence many different sorts of persons can be recruited to kill. Once recruited, they may become very effective killers, even when they retain a sense of revulsion about the killings. In Nazi Germany, they did so because the total Nazi package became a moral mantle, an overall assurance that whatever Nazi-directed horror an individual was committing was forgiven. Indeed, it was honored, because it was a contribution to a large noble cause.

The Nazis knew that this was an appeal to ordinary, relatively healthy people. They attempted to weed out psychopaths and other emotionally disturbed persons from the ranks of concentration camp officers. They found that "ordinary" sane people were more dependable killers.

Anyone who has served in a military service knows how it feels when, upon arriving with a civilian's mentality, you find yourself in a situation where killing of designated enemies is regarded as an entirely acceptable and necessary task. You may start by being appalled, feeling shaken. But most persons get used to the task of killing. To be sure, a person who joins a military service—especially one who is drafted, against one's will—does not suddenly feel committed to being a killer, not even a killer of the nation's enemies.

Some people (I am one of them), join the American military not merely because of a commitment to serve the country but, also, out of concern for a more immediate issue, namely, to obtain funds for a college education. I, fortunately, was never called upon to serve in a killing situation, but many soldiers are not so fortunate. They learn, in the most practical way, that they really have the task of killing, that the human species is a killer species, and they, individually and personally, are expected to live up to that attribute. Further, they are to do so out of a sense of loyalty to that larger moral entity, their country.

Since the arrival of instant television things have changed in the reporting of military actions and, thereby, our awareness of some items in the moral package to which our country is committed. With the televised reporting during the Vietnam War, military killings were no longer so effectively segregated from the civilian world. People saw the convergence of both of these worlds while they watched television at dinnertime. In short, no longer are the military services a totally segregated Local Moral Universe, where killing is required and encouraged in a context that is insulated from the Moral Universe of civilian life.

Yet, as the carefully contrived television coverage of the Gulf War showed us, in the early 1990s, and in the Afghanistan and Iraq wars a decade later, there still is no fully complete access between the civilian world and the military world. The "morality" of wartime killing remains intact or, at least, so obfuscated that the civilian Moral Universe remains distant and very unchallenged by the human horrors our own kinspeople are occasionally encouraged to perform under a local moral mantle.

One might argue that taking part in killings as part of one's military service obligation in time of war is very different from taking part in killings as part of one's service as a guard in a concentration camp. My review of the material on concentration camp guards suggests that many of them, perhaps the majority, did not start out as enjoying murder. Some were previously members of respectable professions; some had families to which they remained attached and loyal; some, including Hoess, seemed to retain some sensitivity to human concerns—all this while they were doing the most horrendous deeds one can imagine.

Among the *Einsatzkommandos*, the SS men who carried out some of the most gruesome killings on the Eastern Front (the area of the German invasion of Poland and Russia during the early stages of World War II), there were many who had higher education, even doctorates. Perhaps the advanced professional education of such people had taught them that in the course of one's professional work one must be prepared to do things one finds emotionally upsetting, or things one finds morally abhorrent. For example, a physician must be prepared to deal with the death of persons one has struggled to keep alive, and to whom one has developed some attachment; a lawyer must be prepared to defend persons one knows to be criminal, and whose actions one finds repugnant, going entirely against the grain of one's own moral beliefs. In short, many professionals are trained to accept ambiguity and dissonance as part of their professional work. Yet few could have been prepared to encounter the level of brutality they were expected to perform under the Naxi regime. Some, a majority, did carry out the rawest brutalities. Others, a minority, committed suicide rather than participate.

The Nazi package certainly contained component parts that were murderous and inhumane. But it also illustrates something very mundane and "normal" in our lives as citizens under political government. The political programs of a government are likely to be a composite package containing very diverse content. We, the citizens, are likely to carry out the entire package promulgated by our government, even items we do not like, because we are locked into accepting the entire package. We accept this as the price of citizenship. As a member of a human community we accept the programs of the political community, even when we do not like some particular programs. This surely is part and parcel of being a member of a society, where we do not, each one of us, go our own way, alone, by and for ourself. The Nazi picture illustrates, however, the moral pathology that can arise from uncritically accepting such a "normal" process of social existence.

Now let us turn to another fact about a society's packages: Particular component parts of a package may stubbornly persist, long after we thought that they had disappeared. They can persist in a dormant state, available for reactivation when new conditions arise. They can be moral contaminants that are hidden, but may return to public and active status, haunting those who had blissfully thought these contaminants had been eliminated. We discussed this briefly earlier.

The resurgence of ethnic loyalties and ethnic hatreds that erupted in the former Yugoslavia, starting in 1993, is a poignant example. In the forty years following World War II, Yugoslavia seemed to have eliminated the various ethnic cleavages that had formerly existed. Serbs, Croats, and Muslims had seemed to coexist in peace, loyal to the larger nation-state of Yugoslavia and not displaying ethnic separatisms and antagonisms. Ancient, centuries-old schisms seemed to have been eliminated and forgotten.

But it was not so. Once the unifying central government dissolved, local ethnic groups embarked upon unthinkable, atavistic atrocities against one another, who had been getting along with one another, who had an intermarriage rate of thirty percent, who, for decades, were friendly and neighborly with one another, started self-righteously slaughtering one another.

Shortly before the events in the former Yugoslavia there was the breakup of the former Soviet Union. There, too, we saw a sudden reemergence of ethnic separatisms among groups of people who had been coexisting peacefully within the Soviet nation-state. They had done so for seventy years. Suddenly ethnic loyalties, ethnic suspicions and fears were reasserted, sometimes in violent ways. Killings became commonplace. There was also a reemergence of Orthodox Christianity, after formal Christianity had been discarded by the Soviet government and the Communist party, and after atheism prevailed officially for seventy years.

Some twenty years earlier, we saw new ethnic tribalisms erupt in Africa. There, after the European colonial powers were forced to move out, it was thought that former colonies would form modern "European-type" nations. Instead, they tended to break up into small, fractious ethnic tribal entities. Many were quite willing to rekindle ancient hatreds against their neighboring tribes, which resulted in brutal tortures and killings.

In the United States of America, many thought that the Civil Rights movement of the 1960s and 1970s would give Afro-Americans full equality in America. But as Afro-Americans have painfully learned, old racial prejudices have proved hard to eradicate. They are very stubborn. They seem to remain as part of the package of being American, even after the legal system outlawed overt racial discrimination.

Like other ancient hatreds, anti-Semitism has sometimes been active, sometimes inactive. But always, it seems, it persists. In various countries, particularly in Eastern Europe, it has been reactivated periodically in brutal actions against the Jewish population. Consider the periodic pogroms in Poland

and Russia. For a time, the anti-Semitism is apt to subside and seemingly disappear altogether. Yet it reappears later, sometimes many years later, whenever social stresses take place.

During the first part of the twentieth century most German Jews thought that German anti-Semitism was a thing of the past. At the time, Jews of Germany were more assimilated into the mainstream than in any modern gentile country. It was thought that in Germany, with its highly sophisticated modern culture, surely ancient tribalistic provincialisms were a thing of the past. Yet it was precisely there that we saw the most gruesome programs of mass hatred, fueled by the rekindling of ancient fears and hatreds. Apparently anti-Semitism had persisted underground, even in Germany, hidden in its cultural package.

A lesson in all this is that when a culture's packages are composites, then particular items, such as ethnic fears and hatreds, can remain within a package in dormant form. While not seen nor heard from for periods of time, they can remain as ingredients in that package nonetheless. They are available for reactivation.

Presumably there are definite mechanisms for activating dormant items. The mechanisms of activation may conform to some sort of law of social nature. But at this point we know neither the precise activation/deactivation mechanisms nor the precise laws that might govern these mechanisms. We know only that components of packages seem to appear, disappear, and remain in storage, then reappear from storage. Once out of storage, they still contain the potential for enormous violence. Furthermore, latent gruesome violence seems to continue to grow during the dormant state even if the civilizing powers of an ongoing society curtail such violence, regarding it as total anathema to the prevailing ethos. Alas, it seems, expression of violence is often only temporarily suppressed while, at the same time, the potential for extreme violence might actually continue to grow, albeit in subterranean fashion. Being subterranean, its growth may be uninhibited by the overt, prevailing constraints against extremism.

Here is an example. In the book *Immediacy* I discuss Benzion Netanyahu's study of the Spanish Inquisition, and its persecution of Jews.[1] It turns out that over a period of a half-century there were repeated efforts to overthrow the Spanish king's retinue of a powerful ruling class. Each time, anti-Semitism was used as a vehicle because the king's retinue contained a number of prominent *conversos*, former Jews. Each failed effort to overthrow the king's retinue led to an increasingly virulent version of anti-Semitism being placed into storage. While in storage the anti-Semitism was outwardly dormant, but actually it became increasingly virulent. Eventually it all erupted with lethal force.

The persistence of items in dormant form, within a package, contradicts much of what we believe. In America we assume that what do not see, what is not active, does not exist. We have great faith in education as a way to eradicate prejudice. We tell ourselves that if we get to know people who are different from ourselves, then we will surely drop our prejudices and free ourselves of narrow distrust and meanness directed against people who differ from ourselves. But even in America the unwelcome reality seems to be that, as we learn to live with people who are different from ourselves, many of our prejudices are merely repackaged. They are placed in a dormant mode, rather than being eliminated from our package. They can, on suitable occasions, be reactivated.

I am not saying that people can never change, that ethnic prejudices and hatreds can never be eliminated from a package. I am saying that much of what appears as change is really a case of repackaging. The discordant and socially obnoxious items are sometimes, in fact, hidden from view in a dormant mode and persist unseen within a package.

This conclusion leads to new and unanswered questions. For instance, are there rules, or laws of sociology, that govern how elements from a package are transformed from an active mode into a dormant mode? How can we differentiate an element that is really eliminated from a package from one merely placed in a dormant mode? What governs the process that activates dormant ingredients into active ingredients? How are dormant ingredients passed on from generation to generation?

I am not upset about not having the answers to these questions. New questions are a sign of progress in one's thinking. Perhaps some readers of these words will help find answers to these questions, and I intend to keep working on them, too. A reasonable starting point seems to be that ethnic tribalisms can be perpetuated in dormant form through our religious education, through family-based experiences, and through any one of many other intimate learning experiences in the course of our personal and communal living. They thereby provide a distinctive moral mantle for activities that are not quite acceptable under current circumstances, but which might be acceptable in the future. They are a mantle for a virus.

There is yet another lesson to be learned from the Hoesses and Eichmanns and the way their packages worked through them. When these individuals told us that they were not anti-Semites, they were being only partially honest with themselves. They may not have been openly raving anti-Semites. But, I suspect, they had enough anti-Semitism in a *dormant mode* within their packages—derived, perhaps, from their religious upbringing—to neutralize any moral qualms about singling out Jews for persecution, especially when, at first, it is presented to them in small, incremental ways. A little bit of anti-Semitism can go a long way! Indeed, *a little bit of prejudice of any sort can go a long way.* It can act as innoculation against saying, "No, I won't take part in such inhumane activities as are now being urged upon me." In preventing disease, we have found that "a little bit of a disease," in the form of a vaccine, can get our body to say no to an invading disease. The vaccine produces antibodies that are activated when a full-fledged version of the disease attacks the body. By contrast, a dormant prejudice, existing in a subsurface reservoir as "a little bit of a disease," may actually permit more of that disease to take root in ourselves. The reservoir enables larger, more virulent versions to enter and flourish. The "little bit of the disease" seems to disrupt the body's immune system against that disease by producing antibodies against the body's *police* which combat that disease. It has produced antibodies against the body's own defense system and keeps it from operating effectively when the major threat from an outside intruder comes on the scene.

~

I have been discussing packages as potentials for evil, particularly how the Nazi package actually sponsored evil. Packages are not, in themselves, evil. They are ordinary ways of organizing human behavior. Every government creates packages of programs for its citizens. Every family creates packages of programs for its members. Every organized enterprise—every business, every voluntary association—creates packages that define its mission and objectives. In each case, the package is apt to be treated with a measure of respect and, even, sanctity which ensures that its adherents have a sense of cohesion and common destiny. And every package contains priorities establishing which elements can be actively pursued at any particular time and which must be kept dormant until an appropriate moment arrives for its activation.

Packages are a necessary part of our social existence, of how we manage to live with one another. By amalgamating different social programs into packages, by attributing some sanctity to such packages, and by having some items be active and others dormant, we are doing normal and necessary things. They are part of our everyday life, just as careers based on an accumulation of small incremental decisions (discussed in the previous chapter), are part of everyday life.

What must be understood, however, is how such normal, ordinary processes can be used for creating entirely horrific actions. This can lead us to an understanding of evil that goes beyond assuming that its causes are mysterious forces, monsters, and devils. We can then move forward and exercise more control over the production of horrific actions.

Stated in less moralistic terms, societal packages, such as packages of political programs, are structures that operate in predictable and knowable ways. In this chapter I have given illustrative examples of packages and packaging processes that affect moral behavior. These, surely, touch only the surface of such phenomena. We need far more precise knowledge of the rules, the orderliness, that govern the workings of packages. I am convinced that we can indeed discover these rules, and from that gain a greater measure of control over our human social existence. As a start, however, let me summarize the findings of this and the previous chapter.

From the previous chapter we found:

- Nazism was a package of different programs that, together, formed a composite.

- The individual is ordinarily, to begin with, attached to one node of such a package.

- But the content of the package is fused; its content of different programs is amalgamated. Therefore the individual can contribute to implementing its entire content, even though lacking an initial commitment to some of its parts.

From the present chapter we found:

- The Nazi package was promoted as a comprehensive and definitive formulation of the German society's very foundation and destiny.

- It was proclaimed that the Nazi package must be carried out fully, in its indivisible entirety.

- The individual citizen was encouraged to perceive, through the most intensive propaganda campaign ever devised, that from the Nazi package emanated one's personal cause, the mandate for one's own life. This gave one a sense of moral incentive, a focus, and a life-transcending mission to help implement the programs of the Nazi package.

- At any one time some components of a package may be hidden from public scrutiny because they are *dormant*. Dormant components—such as ethnic hatreds in pre-1990 Yugoslavia and anti-Semitism in pre-Nazi Germany—may continue to develop and grow despite being publicly unmentionable or discredited. Such dormant components may therefore become available for activation in a most unexpectedly lethal form.

CHAPTER TEN

Enjoyment of Evil:
Cultures of Cruelty

A troubling question arises when we confront evil: Can deliberate cruelty be enjoyable? Even more troubling are these follow-up questions: Do only sick sadists enjoy behaving cruelly? Are people who enjoy acting cruelly at least morally depraved, if not sick?

The answer to all these questions is discomfiting. There is every indication that cruelty can be so organized that it is enjoyable, and that cruelty can be made attractive to persons who are not necessarily sadistic or otherwise emotionally or morally obtuse. Indeed, it can appeal to persons who are morally sensitive. Cruelty can, in fact, be the rallying point for a localized moral system, a Local Moral Universe that highlights and celebrates cruelty.

There are contexts that so engage people that, even though they know the difference between humane behavior and cruel behavior, they will, in these contexts, deliberately choose cruel behavior—behavior they know is evil, behavior they know violates the moral values they were taught. They do so when they perceive that they have an entirely persuasive local moral mandate.

By this I do not mean that people do evil only when they are coerced by something in the context in which they find themselves, and are therefore forced into doing things they would not ordinarily do. Quite the contrary. Within the right "contexts," in the proper places and at proper occasions, participating individuals can experience a sense of great creative freedom and real joy while engaging in recognizable evil.

The context of which I speak can arise from something altogether commonplace: the culture within groups. Such a culture consists of the set of customs, beliefs, and ways of behaving that are shared by the members of the group. They provide these individuals with a distinctive identity. Every youth gang has a culture, every baseball team has a culture, the U. S. Congress has a culture, and so does every stable family. In each case the particular culture creates a moral community among the members. There are many sorts of cultures.

Culture of Cruelty

I want to draw attention to one particular culture: a culture of cruelty. Here cruelty is created precisely because it is cruel. Here, among a group of persons, cruel deeds toward selected victims can form the basis for their interactions and their sense of moral community—yes, moral community—with one another. Here, creating new kinds of cruelty can be the mechanism through which the individual members feel they have found a personal way to be creative. (And who, among us, does not yearn for a way to be creative?)

The Holocaust is not the one and only place where this type of culture has emerged. But, for a start, one can learn how such a phenomenon works by looking at its existence in the Holocaust, specifically among the guards in the Auschwitz concentration camp. I shall also discuss its existence among American troops during the events at My Lai, in the Vietnam War. In both, there emerged a community that supported and encouraged deliberate cruelty; where being cruel received a group mandate; where a distinctive morality, in the form of a Local Moral Unviverse, prevailed and specified how creative cruelty could be performed, enjoyed, and rewarded.

I discovered the reality of a distinctive culture of cruelty while reviewing the record of a trial of former Auschwitz concentration camp guards. The trial took place in Frankfurt, Germany, in 1965; that is, it took place twenty years after the Holocaust ended.[1] Hannah Arendt, who had written the widely read book about the Eichmann trial and who was a distinguished historian and philosopher, was an observer at the trial in Frankfurt. She wrote the introduction to the report about the trial.

Even though Arendt was quite knowledgeable about the Nazi era, she was simply appalled by what she saw and heard in the courtroom. Witnesses detailed deeds the guards had committed that were so horrible that the recounting made some jurors faint. But Arendt was appalled even more by the behavior of these former guards there, in the courtroom, so many years after the horrors had taken place. They seemed pleased with themselves when their gruesome deeds were recounted. They beamed with pleasure when reminded of what they had done. They made friendly bows to the survivors, their former victims, while these individuals presented testimony that would surely serve to convict them.

Arendt found this behavior maddeningly frustrating. She was a sophisticated scholar who had begun to make some sense out of the Eichmann phenomenon, the committing of immense evil without any clear ideological commitment to evil. Yet here in the Frankfurt courtroom she found herself stunned and at a loss for words to explain what was happening. She remained aghast at these guards who, apparently, found joy in being reminded of their cruel deeds.

It was obvious that their deeds were evil, even to the guards themselves. Yet they seemed to derive joy from their deeds, and that joy seemed to be rekindled in the courtroom when their actions were being recalled. What was going on?

The answer came to me when I remembered some early sociology I had learned while in graduate school. That sociology did not deal with evil at all. In fact, in those days no self-respecting "scientific" sociologist would study a topic as archaic and laden with religious fundamentalism as "evil." Sociologists regarded themselves as members of modern science, part of the modern world reaping the fruits of the Enlightenment, whereas notions such as deliberate evildoing seemed to belong to the thinking of ancient times, for which we had nothing but scorn.

Yet I remembered a topic of sociological research that was fashionable in the 1930s and 1940s which offered a clue to understanding deliberate evildoing, even though it never mentioned evildoing. It was the study of the cultures that emerged and persisted in informal groups in factories, to which I alluded in chapter 7. What was found in those studies turns out to have had some uncanny similarity to life among concentration camp guards. It showed, above all, the existence of a system of social living that had its own morality and ways of honoring and sustaining its individual members. In its own way, it was a Local Moral Universe.

Since Henry Ford's day, mass production has been conducted in large factories. The tasks performed by individual workers are highly routinized and repetitive, leaving little room for thought processes and mental initiatives by these workers. They are expected to work with their hands, and a bit with their arms and legs, but not with their brains. Work can be stupefying.

Early social research done on factory operations did not concern itself with the welfare of the workers, however. Most of it was done under the sponsorship of factory owners and managers who wanted to find ways to increase productivity. The objective was to get workers to produce more; there was no interest in the interactions among the workers. Yet it was found, quite accidentally, that even amid the routines of mass production within the confines of the factory, workers tended to develop a social life of their own. It turned out that this social life contained distinctive "informal cultures." Once discovered, these informal cultures were studied extensively.

A typical finding was that a "culture" in any one part of a factory had a set cast of characters. One worker might be the butt of jokes; another was a big talker, who regularly made up stories; another was an uncritical believer of everything anyone said, including the storyteller's obviously fictitious stories; another was a prankster, who regularly played practical jokes on fellow workers.

Informal roles of this type became firmly established, and each worker seemed to develop a well-defined reputation. Each character would repeat his or her particular role behavior over and over again, thereby perpetuating the reputation. Others would not encroach on that character's role. Workers rarely, if ever, switched their roles, since the specialized role a worker carved out for oneself defined one's position in the culture and one's distinctive contribution to the work group.

It amazed me to read how a particular specialized role behavior was repeated over and over again. One could never predict just which prank the prankster would produce next, but one could be sure that the prankster would produce a new prank every few days. Similarly, it was never sure just how the person who was the butt of jokes—the group's *shlemiel*—would next manage to look like a fool, but repeatedly and regularly that person would be the butt of someone's joke. That individual would look like a total fool to everyone in the group, and everyone, including the *shlemiel* himself, would enjoy the episode, despite the *shlemiel*'s expression of genuine anguish.

A typical example of informal worker interplay is called "Banana Time." It is the story of an individual who always brought a banana for his lunch in his lunchbox. The banana was frequently snatched from the lunchbox by one of the other workers. Unexpectedly, this "thief" would hold the banana up in front of the group and, before the hapless owner of the banana could get to him, would gleefully eat the banana while calling out "Banana Time!" The sad owner of the banana would always complain loudly and vehemently, amid the laughter of the onlookers. But he kept bringing a banana each day! And it kept getting snatched from his lunchbox by another worker, who ate it before the owner could get to him. The whole scenario provided entertainment in a highly predictable format. It enriched workers' lives and was a vital part of their informal culture.[2]

To carry out their informal roles, workers, despite their stupefying routines, often are very creative. They are rewarded for their creativity by their fellow workers and, to maintain their reputation, individuals come up with creative inventions quite frequently. They always do this within the confines of their particular, informally developed social culture. The various roles form the social support system for each worker who is, in turn, enabled to do creative things and is rewarded for his or her creativity. All this interaction takes place in a highly regulated work setting, where one would think that there is no creativity at all.

Informal cultures also demonstrate the value of specialization. Each individual performs, creatively and regularly, the themes of the specialized role. That specialization is safeguarded in two ways: The individual repeats, over and over again, the particular specialized ways of behaving, including creativity in a particular zone of behavior, and other people do not intrude into the zone of the specialist. Instead, they honor it by rewarding the specialist with a reputation precisely for the specialized performance of the role. They laugh at the prankster's pranks, they deride the person who is the butt of jokes, and so forth.

Specialization is central to the functioning of the informal culture. It solicits and harnesses distinctive and individualized contributions by each member. Specialization is also central to the reputation of the individual member. It honors one's accomplishments. It specifies and upholds one's worth as a unique individual within one's social context. It provides one with a sense of self that is clearly identified, by oneself and by the other members of that social context.

Now let us return to the postwar trial of former Auschwitz guards. It showed that within the Auschwitz concentration camp these persons had also created an informal culture. Each individual had developed a *specialty* within the role of being a guard. Each one had a distinctive *reputation* among work colleagues, based on that specialty. And each one had earned that reputation through repeatedly displaying the specialty and having the colleagues acknowledge it and not intrude into it.

The unique thing about the Auschwitz guards, what made them different from the American factory workers, was that the *content* of their entire self-created informal culture concentrated on the manufacture and practice of cruelty. Each guard specialized in creating a particular form of cruelty. Each had a reputation—among the victims and among colleagues—for creating and practicing a particular form of cruelty.

To be sure, each guard was an officer at the Auschwitz camp, and was therefore entrusted with a cruel assignment as part of his or her official role. The open objective of Auschwitz was the deliberate murder and mutilation of the body and spirit of its victims, and each guard was assigned specific functions within that enterprise. Each was assigned a role in cruelty.

Yet the striking reality is that many guards went considerably beyond their official roles in cruelty. They personally created a specialty to augment the official cruelty. They invented a type of cruelty particular to themselves, and based their personal reputations on it.

Here are some specific, personally created specialties in cruelty, practiced by individual guards, which were brought out at the trial:

- Hitting prisoners with the edge of a hand in such a way that it either broke their nose or killed them.
- Inventing games, with specific rules, for shooting prisoners as target practice. The inventor was known as William Tell.

- A jovial willingness to shoot prisoners at any time, being extremely trigger-happy, but without inventing or participating in games of shooting.

- Killing prisoners with an injection of phenol into the heart. The medical orderly who developed this specialty went to the sick wards on his own and picked up additional victims when doctors did not send him prisoners fast enough. He killed an estimated 20,000 persons in this way.

- Putting prisoners in cold showers, then sending them out into the cold, then beating them, then sending them back to the showers. The sequence was repeated until death mercifully intervened.

The development and reputation for these specialties were not left to chance. Frequently a guard's reputation was deliberately advertised among prisoners and colleagues. It was bragged about. "In me you will get to know the devil," (Naumann, op. cit., p. 306) said one SS officer to a new prisoner.

A guard's particular specialty was repeated over and over again, in virtually identical form, and often in a way that assured publicity. By contrast, any act of kindness to a prisoner was done in private, when no audience was present. Often the cruel deed was performed in a way that assured that the message—the guard's commitment to deliberate and specific cruelty—was heard loud and clear. When a baby was murdered in front of its mother, for example, the guard had as witness the one who was most devastated by that act, most clear about the message, and most able to attest to its sheer horror.

A notorious reputation for cruelty was developed by Dr. Josef Mengele, a physician at Auschwitz. He prided himself on his specialization in lethal research on prisoners with a physical abnormality, particularly among twins. He had the prisoner with an abnormality killed, and followed this quickly with an autopsy. Dr. Mengele then immediately and personally announced the results of the autopsy. His immediate announcement of the results of the autopsy ensured that it was generally known what he had done. It underscored and perpetuated his reputation for cold-blooded "science," and it gave recognition to his particular specialized form of creative cruelty.

Getting recognition for one's creativity was the issue. It produced the reward. It was the justification for one's cruelty.

The yearning to do something creative may be a universal human attribute. Perhaps each of us needs to be creative, somehow, somewhere. It may be a fundamental way of saying, I am alive. And, obviously, it can go terribly awry.

For most of us, most of the time, creativity is an illusive thing. We rarely find ways to be creative. It seems to me that we have to be creative to find ways to be creative. The American factory workers who spent their work days, indeed their entire working years, in dull, stupefying activities, found creative ways to be creative. In a particular zone of their daily work life, they nurtured creativity for themselves.

To be sure, the creativity of factory workers existed only in certain zones, namely those that had no bearing on the products on which they were actually working. They were allowed no creativity whatever in the design of the product, the price charged for the product, or the material used in making it. They were totally excluded from decision making decisions in these matters. Instead they created a zone where they could be creative, and they nurtured it in deliberate ways.

Creativity was also nurtured among the Auschwitz guards. We are appalled and aghast by the content of that creativity, namely the creation of ever more refined forms of cruelty, but it was creativity. In many ways, it was treated just as creativity is treated in other contexts. For instance, repetition was expected and rewarded. The Auschwitz guards' repeated performance of creative cruelty reminds me of the pianist who is encouraged to perform his or her particular version of Mozart, over and over again, at concert after concert. We express appreciation for that particular version of creative musicianship through requests for its repetition; similary, the Auschwitz guards gave appreciation for the creative cruelty of their colleagues by being aware of, and not intruding into one another's domain of specialized cruelty. Each type of repeated creativity is rewarded by explicit social esteem. (As in the case of the informal cultures among factory workers, the repetition of one's specialty establishes and solidifies one's place in a social community. It is thereby a fundamental reward of one's very existence.)

Now when we go back to the smiles, joy, and satisfaction displayed by former Auschwitz guards as their deeds were being recounted at their trial in Frankfurt, we understand the reason. Each one is reliving pride in his or her creativity, in one's unique and personal contributions of twenty years ago. This pride is not unlike that of a former opera singer who beams with delight upon being told that you heard her at the Metropolitan Opera House thirty five years ago and will always remember her creativity. There is satisfaction and joy in such a reminder, in knowing that others are aware of one's creativity and, through it, one's vitality as a human being. This was once affirmed in one's daily life in an actual community, and is now, in a convoluted way, being reconfirmed at the Frankfurt trials. It is a reason to smile.

Some people may find it upsetting that I apply the term "creative" to evil-doing. In our culture "creative" generally is a positive term, so that some find it intolerable that anyone would use that term to describe the actions of concentration camp guards. Perhaps I am being overly "creative." It seems to me that one can be creative in many ways. One can be creative in wholesome ways, such as creating better human services; in artistic ways, such as creating new works of art or of performing existing works of art in new ways; in scientific ways, by creating new realms of scientific knowledge. One can also be creative in evil ways, by creating new forms of horror, new cruelties, new ways of hurting and harming people.

Evil creativity, like wholesome creativity, produces a novel product, something that has not previously existed. Central to this is a communal, social process. One deals with newness that is appreciated and rewarded by an audience, by people who bestow rewards on the producer of the newness. This is surely what happened among the guards at Auschwitz, both at the time the Auschwitz operations flourished, and twenty years later, as the participants remembered and relived their moments of creativity and the social appreciation they had received at the time.

Creative cruelty is not a German monopoly. It has occurred many times, in many forms. In the village of My Lai during the Vietnam War, in March of 1968, a culture of cruelty emerged, and it, too, was produced and enjoyed in a social context.[3] It differed from the Auschwitz culture of cruelty in that it was short-lived, and specialized roles did not have time to be stabilized or repeated again and again, over a long period of time.

The entire military action at My Lai lasted only about four hours. During that time about four hundred fifty civilians—old men, women, and children—were killed by American soldiers. The action followed a period of intense frustration for the American soldiers. The enemy had repeatedly ambushed and killed American soldiers, only to disappear before the American soldiers could respond. While preparing for the action at My Lai, the American soldiers fully expected that, finally, they would encounter and fight the enemy openly and directly. They had prepared for this confrontation for a long time. The time had come, they believed, when they could release their pent-up frustration and avenge their dead buddies.

They stormed into My Lai with guns blazing. But the expected enemy was not there. Only unarmed civilians were there, women and children and a few old men. All of them were frigthtened and offered no resistance. Some of these were shot immediately. Others were herded together, forced into a ditch, and shot there. Still others became the victims of soldiers who, spontaneously, found new ways of killing. (At least one soldier, however, created his own way of stopping his participation. He deliberately shot himself in the foot, taking himself out of action.)

The record reveals that the American soldiers who took part in this event were not handpicked for their cruelty. They were not a bunch of sadists, social deviants, or misfits who habitually murdered or mistreated people. By all accounts, they were rather ordinary American young men, most of them well brought up, taught to respect human life, and imbued with a sense of decency in dealing with fellow human beings.

Their leader, Lieutenant William Calley, was later put on trial for his role at My Lai. He was convicted and eventually exonerated. The proceedings show that Calley displayed a great deal of zeal and influence upon his men in the course of perpetrating cruelty. However, I do not want to discuss the contribution of leaders. I am here concentrating on the role of the lowly soldier who, at My Lai, contributed his own zeal and creativity to the production of horrors. He did so in a communal way, as part of the nascent and distinctive local morality.

At My Lai, cruelty was not only openly practiced, it was openly and loudly enjoyed. Individual soldiers yelled and bragged about their killings. They bragged not only about how many persons they had killed, but how, in which ways, they had killed. They were bragging about their creativity in the art of killing. They congratulated one another on their newfound ways of killing. They killed human beings and any animals they happened to encounter at the moment. There was *festivity* in the air, and it centered on the celebration of creative cruelty. Cruelty was being enjoyed; it was being valued for its own sake. A culture of cruelty had come into existence.

Unlike the Auschwitz culture of cruelty, as I have already mentioned the one at My Lai was fairly short-lived. It lasted just a few hours. But during that time the production and enjoyment of cruelty achieved a character and a moral momentum of its own. It had fairly ordinary sorts of people participating in cruelty, and doing so with zeal and ingenuity and relish.

Events such as those at My Lai are often written off as battlefield frenzy, as something that can happen in the heat of battle and which is, therefore, really beyond the understanding of normal human behavior. On the contrary, I am suggesting that it is well within the range of normal human behavior. At My Lai we saw a brief flourishing of a culture of creative cruelty. That culture has much in common with the elongated and far more extreme culture of cruelty at Auschwitz, and with informal cultures that celebrate and reward individual creativity in any—even the most benign—group context.

The nascent Local Moral Universe at My Lai was linked to the larger Moral Universe that prevailed in the military and in the American government. On an official level, the soldiers on the ground at My Lai provided the higher military staff with an exuberant—though fictitious—"victory." Among the commanding officers in Vietnam there had been considerable frustration about the failure to devise and implement a plan of action that brought victories in the field and would ultimately conquer the North Vietnamese army altogether. The action at My Lai was to be a decisive vindication of American superiority, and the action was duly reported as a great American victory. The staff officers' strained reputations received some welcome relief.

But beyond that, and more important for my thesis here, My Lai was one of several instances where the local participants, the soldiers in the field, used their local autonomy to invent victories. The higher officers, in turn, were delighted to use their own autonomy to report and publicize these "victories" to the press to bolster their own standing, to further justify their mission, and to inflate the "body count" (the number of enemy soldiers claimed to have been killed). The low-level officers and soldiers needed victories to protect themselves from the incessant pressures from the higher officers. The higher officers needed victories to protect themselves from the political pressures emanating from Washington and America at large, where the Vietnam war was coming under increasingly nervous scrutiny. In a sense, there was collusion between the high-level military leaders and the low-level officers and soldiers in the field. Each created victories using their own autonomy, and in so doing, each contributed to inventing and honoring a unique morality of joyful killing.

The invented victory at My Lai, and its celebration in a culture of cruelty, amounted to a win-win event for the lowly soldiers and commanders both. It was a lubricant that made a larger system work. The enemy army suffered great (imaginary) losses without the loss of any American forces from the fierce (imaginary) enemy. There was rejoicing all around—until news of the ugly side of the events leaked out, exposing the horror of what really transpired there.

At Auschwitz the culture of cruelty among the guards also constituted a lubricant, and a "moral" underpinning, for a system that otherwise could have broken down. Early in the war, during the German invasion of Poland and the Soviet Union, there were the reports, discussed earlier, of German soldiers (including SS men) becoming despondent over their participation in explicit murder. This was before murder was organized into a mass-production system, and some soldiers committed suicide rather than be a party to such murders. Himmler, the head of the SS, noted the existence of a high level of stress among his officers at that time. Wading in blood from the murder of huge numbers of innocent people was stressful. Even at Auschwitz, SS men would occasionally come to their commandant and complain about the horrors in which they were participating. But complaints were the exception. At Auschwitz a highly efficient system of mass-producing murder was in operation, and the appalling fact remains that the system operated with awesome efficiency and full cooperation from the staff.

It would seem that Auschwitz officers learned to support one another through a distinctive culture. No one needed to feel that one was acting by and for oneself. One was part of a distinctive community. One need not confront one's own conscience and personal background in relation to one's current activities; activities were contextualized within a culture of cruelty.

Here cruelty was not only accepted, it was a personally rewarding social activity. A Local Moral Universe sustained and encouraged the participants.

Individual guards were not mere functionaries in a large organization. Amid the large maniacal system of organized murder, SS officers created a system of communal living—the culture of cruelty—where individuals enjoyed distinctive social standing, distinctive reputations, and distinctive rewards. This kept them in step with the larger system's diabolical demands and objectives.

By creating a celebration of cruelty, Auschwitz guards developed a stake in the larger system's murderous objectives. And that larger system, in turn, was harvesting the autonomous contributions of its functionaries to achieve its own objectives. Guards contributed their technical expertise for the production of murder, as well as their total allegiance to a program involving utter contempt for human life.

The culture of cruelty, alas, is not limited to Auschwitz and My Lai. In a widely publicized incident in the early 1990s, Americans learned of the laughter and enjoyment expressed by Los Angeles policemen while they were beating Rodney King, a black motorist who represented no real threat to them. Here was a mini-culture of cruelty or, perhaps, a mere indicator of a larger culture of cruelty in that police department at that time. At about the same time, Westerners heard about ethnic warfare in the former Yugoslavia. There, killings and rapes were often committed joyfully and enthusiastically. Here, I suspect, was another instance of a culture of cruelty embedded in a Local Moral Universe.

In the "inner city" of many large urban American centers the high crime rate and extreme poverty give rise to patterned and socially rewarded physical cruelties linked to personal reputations. These are sometimes based on drug distribution systems, sometimes based on other features of the local underground economy. They are also cultures of cruelty. In this case, a culture of inner-city killing fields is sometimes tolerated by surrounding affluent sectors under a posture of benign neglect. Sadly, there are more instances of cultures of cruelty one can cite.

In summary, cultures of cruelty are contexts within which individuals do cruel deeds. Ordinary sorts of people—who, to start with, are neither particularly evil nor particularly good—may participate in evil enthusiastically when they find themselves under the moral mantle of a culture of cruelty. And, in turn, these cultures may be part of a larger system that tacitly or actively tolerates them because it, too, derives benefits from the horrors being perpetrated.

When we understand more fully how cultures of cruelty work, we may be able to protect ourselves from participating in them. We may be able to do so despite the seductive forces at work within such culture systems. To be sure, a culture of cruelty may provide relief from frustration, as it did at My Lai. It may provide the individual participant a way of being creative, and derive a measure of respect, in one's occupational career within a gruesome organization, as it did at Auschwitz. And, more broadly, it typically provides a social milieu where the cruelties are embedded in rewarding social interchanges that nurture the participants. All these are seductive aspects against which we need to protect ourselves.

Earlier in the book I dwelled on the fact that we humans usually live our lives in the confines of a Local Moral Universe. From that moral universe we derive our basic nurturing and well-being. We cannot exist otherwise. Yet there occasionally emerges a particularly horrifying aberration of a Local Moral Universe, such as a culture of cruelty, where the content of our common morality is mocked while, at the same time, the trappings of a social morality are left in place. These trappings—such as the social reward an individual receives for one's creativity—make cultures of cruelty both appealing and appalling. Yet cultures of cruelty are not beyond understanding. We are apt to accept them meekly and impotently so long as we fail to understand their workings dispassionately. From such understanding we may, in the future, devise weapons against them.

Ordinary people's participation in evil is not beyond understanding. Its beguiling danger is surely real. Understanding these systems—cultures of cruelty and ordinary people's participation in evil—can give us the weapons to oppose them.

CHAPTER ELEVEN

Mind-Set of the Terrorist

The Quest for Transcendence

How could the horrors of September 11, 2001, happen? We are appalled, aghast, enraged, saddened, bewildered. Words fail.

It seems to me that if we are to better understand the perpetrators of such horrors, we must learn new lessons from things that have happened previously. From this we may eventually derive some tools that will protect us. I refer to what we can, and must, learn about cult members and the followers of false messiahs.

First, let us take another look at the Heaven's Gate cult, in the vicinity of San Diego, first discussed in chapter 5. In 1997 thirty-nine Heaven's Gate members committed suicide. We were amazed, surprised and, above all, shocked—just as we were shocked after the earlier mass suicides by cult members at Jonestown in Guyana. Cult members seem to do things that healthy, normal people would never do. We define such people as crazy, as deviants, as utterly different from the rest of us. To preserve our own sanity we have created a cult mythology which, it turns out, continues to deceive us; it causes us to be shocked whenever cult members confront us with mass suicides. Part of that mythology is that cultists who committed suicide are physically isolated from people in the regular human community. Actually, the Heaven's Gate members had "outside" jobs in the San Diego community; they were free to come and go from their compound; they had frequent interactions with the "sane" people in that community. And, through the Internet, they were in active contact with many people beyond the San Diego area. Psychologically, they may have existed in a separate world, but they were not physically isolated.

Our mythology about cults also maintains that cultists who kill themselves in unison must be under the total control of a leader. They are zombies who have no autonomy whatsoever. They simply do what the leader tells them to do. (A *Washington Post* headline, of 30 March 1997, read: "Surrender of Self Is the Key to Cult Life.") We blame it all on the leader. Yet, by all evidence, the Heaven's Gate cultists did not act like zombies, devoid of any will of their own. They engaged in demanding work in their jobs outside the cult's compound. They were respected for their work. They carried themselves with dignity. They adhered to such standard American values as love of fine clothes and cars. Former members of the cult tell of communal living that included much laughter, discussions, and joy. Popular analyses stubbornly ignore these facts and continue the doleful description of cult life as devoid of all personal independence, dignity, and fun.

A fundamental aspect of the conventional wisdom about cults is that we must concentrate on a belief the cultists follow. (Remember what we were told about beliefs of the Muslim suicidal terrorists: that they would receive rewards in the next world.) The Heaven's Gate cultists expected to be picked up by a spaceship and transported to another universe. It does not take much of a leap to regard such beliefs as utterly crazy and empirically beyond proof by any objective or scientific criterion. But is it so very different from some things many of us "sane" people believe? How about a "Heaven," a "Soul," or a "Next World"?

Yet all of this is quite beside the real issue. It is not what people actually believe that counts. It is not a matter of one belief being inherently untrue and crazy, and another belief being inherently true and sane. The real issue is the human yearning for a personally meaningful transcendence. We long to overcome life's turbulence and uncertainties, to come to terms with the death and suffering of loved ones, to discover meaning in our existence amid the pettiness, pain, and exasperation. This lies at the heart of much of the appeal of formal religions. They typically show a way beyond the immediacy in which we find ourselves—beyond its hurts, sorrows and frustrations, while offering some assurance about what lies beyond. In short, they offer the gift of transcending of what most troubles us.

What applies to formal religions applies even more to cults. They, too, claim to give answers to the most troubling questions that confront us. And they do so in what seems to be a most wondrously effective way. This brings us to the heart of the appeal of cults.

Cults do far more than supply answers to fundamental questions. In fact, their "answers" are often quite absurd and ridiculous by every objective criterion. But this does not matter—not to the believer, not to the cultist. What does matter is that members see themselves as actually participating in transcendence, and through it achieving the highest form of self-realization to which they can possible aspire. Stated differently, the cult leader, or the guru, the current "messiah," not only tells followers what is the Ultimate, the grandest, the most noble aspiration (reaching the "Kingdom of God," "salvation," union with the divine, or whatever is the community's vision of the Ultimate). In addition, and most important of all, the leader convinces the followers that it is *through their own contribution* that they will have direct access to the Ultimate. The Ultimate becomes Immediate. And the followers are making it happen. They can do so by their actions, now. The greatest, most profound contribution a member can make to this goal can be the act of donating his or her own life and, even, in the case of some cults (and many a Palestinian parent) donating the life of their children.

This is the mind-set of the cultist, of the terrorist, of the True Believer who is definitively activated. It centers on the conviction that they have access to the Ultimate, which is a most profound enticement. When this is combined with the sense that they personally are helping to make that new Immediacy happen—right now!—it can become an explosive mixture of social dynamite. It has been generated by such false messiahs as Hitler, who managed to recruit a very large segment of the German population into joining the quest for achieving—right now!—Germany's destiny, its grandeur that had been "unjustly" denied by the Versailles treaty after the World War. Here the "messiah" is a person in a threefold way:

1. He is a person who has attributes far beyond those of an ordinary person; he is godlike. He is believed to see further, feel more deeply, act more profoundly than other human beings. Hence he cannot be held accountable by ordinary human standards. It would be sacrilege to do so.

2. He addresses you, the member of the community, personally. You—your own actions, your being—are addressed by the message of the messiah.

3. You are expected to reply to the message by your own actions, your own behavior. You, personally, are a critical participant in the process of reaching the Ultimate.

Consider the first attribute as it relates to Hitler, namely that he is beyond human accountability. Perhaps the most profoundly evil directive in all of human history—the order to actually exterminate millions of Jews— was supposedly given by Hitler verbally. It was not written down. It was not witnessed by anyone. It could not be questioned because it came, supposedly, directly from Hitler. The mind-set of the follower did not permit questioning that order's validity, not to mention its moral basis. It was believed to come from a deity. It was sacred. The mind-set of the followers declared that it was unthinkable not to obey—a statement heard so frequently at the Nuremberg trials.

The crux of the issue, then, is not merely the existence of leaders who are committed to an evil course of action. It is the followers who have the mind-set to really carry it out. They do so through a psychological process that is entirely natural and usually benign. It is the human quest for transcendence, for access to ultimate values through one's own active personal participation. We may abhor its harnessing by false messiahs and cult leaders, but we can understand how the process works. The next issue is to put this knowledge to work in the effort to prevent or abort suicidal and murderous terrorism.

The Second Path

He was described as gentle, shy, quiet, soft, childlike in his innocence, delicate: a nice person. He was born into a middle-class Egyptian family. His father was a lawyer, one sister was a university lecturer, another was a doctor. He was trained as an architect, receiving his education in Egypt and Germany. He had a bright future. He was Mohammed Atta—the person who organized and led the final phase of the September 11 terror raids on America—and who, by all indication, gave his life joyfully for the glory of God while consumed by hatred for America.

Our intuitive response to the September 11 horror is to look for evil. In a Mohammed Atta, whose actions were so evil, there must be explicitly evil personal attributes and beliefs. Surely the attributes of gentleness, delicacy, and niceness must be mere covers for an underlying meanness, viciousness, and brutality that eventually came to the surface in the horrific terror action. How else can we preserve our own sanity in light of what actually happened on September 11 at the World Trade Center in New York, at the Pentagon near Washington, and in a field in Pennsylvania?

Mohammed Atta had indeed come under the influence of Muslim extremism. This extremism espoused rage at Western culture, especially America's, and proclaimed boundless frustration and limitless rage at America's supposedly filthy thuggery. In contrast, Allah stood for sublime purity that was seemingly so clear, so perfect, so attainable, if only one fought against the degenerate and vile evil-doers conspicuously enthroned in America. One's total commitment—one's life—was the least and yet the greatest contribution one could make in the service of Allah, the sublime perfection of this and all future life. The perfection was so real, so palpable, and, most importantly, so attainable—if only one contributed by giving one's own life.

How did the transformation happen? How did a Mohammed Atta come to accept, and be so entrapped in, Muslim extremism? After all, here was a person from a family of comfortable economic circumstances, with faith in advanced education, and with his own exposure to Western education. How could it have happened? In all likelihood Atta embraced Muslim extremism while he was living in Europe. While given access to Western education and the offerings of Westernism, many Muslim Arabs living in Europe were, at the same time, made acutely aware that they were not fully accepted as real Westerners. They were tagged, in subtle and overt ways, as Muslim strangers who did not, and never could, fully belong in the West. This gave rise to smoldering rage among many of these dislocated persons. Thomas Friedman, writing in the *New York Times*, described that phenomenon among Arab Muslims living in Belguim.[1] Friedman considers it a breeding ground for Muslim extremism. The same conditions exist in other European countries.[2] For Mohammed Atta, the alluring exposure to Western ways coupled with the increasing realization that he was denied membership probably became the catalyst for his embracing Muslim extremism.

Yet a mystery remains. How can two vastly disparate realms, containing extreme opposites, coexist in one person, in a Mohammed Atta who lived in the West, peacefully and uncomplainingly attended college, savoring Western life, and yet evidently consumed by total hated for the West? To accept this coexistence of extreme opposites within an individual—without rejecting it as mere sickness—seems to defy all reason and common sense. Specifically, when extreme opposites do coexist within one person, are we looking at what is popularly known as dual or multiple personality (or "doubling" as Robert Lifton discovered) that, by definition, is a pathology, a mental illness? Are the Mohamed Attas of the world aberrant sickies? Or are we doomed to continual incomprehension when we encounter opposites within an individual?

I suggest that we may be adopting the wrong perspective when we assume that extreme opposites cannot possibly coexist within one functioning individual. A far more challenging issue arises if we entertain the possibility that drastic duality may exist even within entirely healthy human beings; that it is not necessarily abnormal for disparate attributes to coexist within one individual. And, if so, can we understand how this works? Can one incorporate such drastic dualities into models of human behavior that we can use for understanding the functioning of ordinary human beings? To answer such questions we must adopt a perspective that opens itself up to the possibility that dualities are part of the natural, mundane, and healthy operation of our daily life—not invariably deep, hidden pathologies but, on the contrary, an essential and commonplace aspect of our ongoing participation in the art of living.

I have tried to illustrate such a perspective in the study of high American military officers, of Holocaust survivors who became prominent writers and who, later, committed suicide, and of African-American professionals in my book *Immediacy*. I suggest that there is such a phenomenon as a Second Path in our lives into which we shunt our daily disgruntlements, frustrations, fears, and rage while, at the same time, keeping up a public posture of relative confidence, competence, and self-respect. The latter posture, the First Path, constitutes our visible way of participating in much of our ongoing social intercourse. Through that First Path we ordinarily project a picture of ourselves as relatively self-assured, poised, in command of our own person and, at the same time, accessible to people around us. By contrast, the Second Path can serve to keep socially unacceptable and disruptive components of ourselves in check and invisible—to people around us and, even, to ourselves. It can thereby serve as a vital safety valve to minimize social disruption.

Yet there is a dangerous aspect to this phenomenon. The Second Path is not only a reservoir where our uncongenialities are quietly stored. There, in that context, these uncongenialities may multiply and grow without restraint, since they are invisible to public view and scrutiny. As a result, when they go do get activated publicly, they may do so with unanticipated ferocity and huge impact. I do not know how common the Second Path phenomenon is. But it seems that when it exists it can be, up to a point, a healthy, adaptive feature in one's ongoing way of conducting one's life. However, the Second Path can also provide a "safe haven" for extreme and evil inclinations, as the Mohammed Atta example illustrates. This "nice, gentle guy" could live and participate in harmonious and peaceful ways in the Western world while, at the same time, nurturing within himself the most vicious propensities against the West. This nurturing of attributes that can be totally at variance with one's public persona is one of the striking characteristics of the Second Path.

In my observation of some high-ranking military officers, I have suggested that these very confident, competent, and deservedly respected individuals may, at the same time, nurture a Second Path of real insecurity. This is totally unmentionable in their public persona, but it can continue to be fed and grow from frustrations and uncertainties in their current and ongoing social context. Let me emphasize, I am not speaking of insecurities that are rooted in one's early life experiences and have, somehow, never been resolved, which is the traditional psychoanalytic conception. Instead, I am speaking of insecurities that are being produced now, ongoingly, and felt in one's current social context. In the case of the high-ranking officer, the insecurities may arise from the narrowing pyramid of career opportunities at the very top of the military hierarchy. If you are a general, how many openings are there for Chief of the Army, the ultimate pinnacle of an army careers? The ease with which one can be knocked out of the running for that single opening, when several highly distinguished fellow officers are also in the running, could also be a source of insecurity. These insecurities are based on stark reality, not fanciful, imagined fears. As the individual sees it, the insecurities grow in the soil of one's present world.

In the case of Holocaust survivors who became prominent writers and who later committed suicide (most notably, Primo Levi), the Second Path may consist of ever increasing survivor guilt. Each new acclaim for one's writings, each new award, is apt to be regarded as further evidence that one is dancing on the grave of loved ones who did not survive. One does not deserve to enjoy life when so many innocent and deserving individuals have been murdered. Here each new success can be interpreted by that writer as more failure, and it thereby generates ever more survivor guilt. The more one succeeds the more vulnerable one becomes. Ultimately the Second Path can overflow, resulting in suicide. Life now seems unlivable. (When my friend, the writer Henryk Grynberg, saw my list of six Holocaust survivors who, after becoming successful writers, had committed suicide, his response was: "Your list is too short."[3]) Returning to Primo Levi, at one point toward the end of his life he confided to friends, "This is worse than Auschwitz." What is worse than Auschwitz—that he won yet another award? We see here a grotesque distortion of reality as the Second Path prevails over the First Path's poised composure and embrace of life.

Similarly, I have suggested that for some African-American professionals, success—by American middle-class standards—can be increasingly stressful to the very individuals who have actually achieved and fully earned that success. For them, too, the Second Path is a reservoir for receiving and nursing ongoing pain and frustrations. These frustrations are based not only on one's harsh early circumstances but on perceived harshness in one's present circumstances—where, in one's current, "successful" life one perceives inequities and pain that white colleagues may not recognize at all but which, to oneself, can be disablingly real.[4]

The Second Path: Some New Thoughts

So far, I have given a quite one-sided picture of the Second Path. In my book, *Immediacy*, I also explore that

> The Second Path may not be all unhealthy or pathological. To be sure it is made up of items the individual regards as inappropriate for bringing out into the open in the situation in which one now finds oneself. These items are shunted into a silent siding, perhaps permanently, perhaps temporarily. Yet these items may be the most honest, the most moral, the healthiest responses to the reality in which the individual currently operates.[5]

There is the case of General George Lee Butler. Upon his retirement from the United States Air Force he began a huge campaign, nationally and internationally, to eliminate the use of nuclear weapons. He enrolled many a prominent citizen in this campaign to awaken the world to the futility and utter immorality of a national policy that would include the actual use of nuclear weapons. Who was General Butler? Before his retirement, he was in command of America's nuclear weapons! In case of war and a presidential order, he would have been in charge of dropping nuclear weapons upon an enemy. Surely he must have harbored his anti-nuclear views before he retired, while he was in charge of actually dropping nuclear bombs. And surely, too, he could not, and did not voice his views (perhaps not even to himself) while he was in that position of responsibility for delivering nuclear weapons. These views were stored in his Second Path, awaiting activation upon his retirement from the Air Force.

There was President Dwight D. Eisenhower, who in his farewell speech upon leaving the presidency warned against the dangers coming from the "military industrial complex." He was implying that, in America, there was a giant lobby that promoted warfare based on its own vested interests. But President Eisenhower gave his warning only upon leaving the presidency. To my knowledge he never gave such warning while he was actually in command of the nation's military establishment. He must surely have harbored his military-industrial-complex fears before he left the presidency, but he did not mention them in the open. They were stored in his Second Path, to be mentioned only as he was leaving the presidency. Had he done so earlier, he might have been able to influence national military policies more profoundly, such as limiting the influence of defense contractors.

There was President Lyndon Johnson. He was virtually run out of office by the antiwar movement because of his escalations of the Vietnam War. He was held responsible for the horrors of that war. He was forced to confront extreme hostility by many of the citizens of his own country. Yet we learn from the private records of Johnson's presidency that Johnson himself shared most of the views of those who opposed the war. He thought the war was immoral and, in practice, unwinnable. In public he repeatedly stated the opposite. That public posture was the First Path. The Second Path contained his profoundly tortured doubts about that war, virtually identical to the views of his opponents.

A deeper question arises: In which sense can the Second Path become a distinct, organized structure in its own right, available for harnessing in a social movement? In its most vicious manifestation, are we not seeing it harnessed, through the Mohammed Attas, where some mobilize suicide-induced-terror as an active technique for waging war?

Most of the time one's Second Path has no clear, publicly visible structure. It is, after all, the repository of stored unmentionables from one's current and past experiences. These unmentionables have accrued from one's responses to day-to-day events in one's life and are, most of the time, securely separated from one's public persona. These stored unmentionables may fade away as past experiences that are outgrown and supplanted by more current immediacies. Or, in contrast, these unmentionables may continue to fester as remembered experiences that are never extinguished but, instead, continually grow and eventually explode into public view, dominating one's First Path.

Each of these two patterns can be a "continuous" process. One is a process whereby each particular unmentionable is supplanted: Following an episode of acute attention to the very recent unmentionable, it is surpassed by attention to new immediacies, leaving little or no residue. The other is a series of cumulative unmentionables that might eventually erupt. I have surely over-simplified both of these patterns. The first is a pattern where a particular episode of an unmentionable can be overcome, where unmentionables no longer fester and threaten the individual's First Path. In the second, the un-mentionables persist as cumulative cancer that may eventually exact a terrible price. In the case of Mohammed Atta, it was probably a case of cumulative growth of festering unmentionables (of hatred of the West while living in the West in ostensible acceptance of the West) that eventually culminated in the calculated terror attack that took over, and transformed, his First Path—and the lives of thousands of innocent people. In a larger sense, Mohammed Atta was a part of a rather systematic mobilization of a Second path that focused fully on hatred of the West.

The Local Moral Universe

The morality to which we subscribe can give our life its most profound guidance and focus. It can show us which of our activities are important, valuable, and significant. It can set them off against those activities which are superficial and trivial, thus clarifying our priorities. Amid the turbulence and superficialities in our daily life, morality can give focus to our actions. It can give us direction and a sense of grounding in things that matter. It can give meaning to what we are doing. It can do so by spelling out for us a larger context under which we exist and to which we may actually contribute. That contribution can, in turn, give us a sense of personal moral virility because we sense that our own activities are morally oriented activities.[6]

Yet morality has its dark side. It can underwrite the most horrible deeds, doing so under a mantle of high and honored morality. It can under-write mass killings of entirely innocent people as well, of course, of the social acceptance of killings of combatants in times of war. It can, and did, under-write mass deprivations, such as preventable and, at times, deliberate cam-paigns of mass starvation, notably the starvation of the kulaks in the former Soviet Union under Stalin, leading to some fourteen million deaths.[7] It can, and did, underwrite the murderous deeds of Hitler's SS as they went about killing millions of innocent individuals. And finally it can, and did, under-write the suicide bombings we saw on American soil on September 11, 2001, and on the soil of Sri Lanka and Israel, to name just a few locations where such suicide bombings have taken place. Before going into these suicide bombings more fully, let me report how I first became aware of the process by which the dark side of morality actually works; how it can become the mind-set of ordinary human beings. Here I must, once again, go back to the famous Miligram experiments in psychology, reformulating its basic premise and, therefrom, reassessing the nature of the results of these experiments.

Perhaps the most imaginative, courageous, and, eventually, most disturbing psychological experiments conducted during the twentieth century were those devised by Stanley Milgram.[8] At the time of the experiments, shortly after the Second World War had ended, Milgram was a junior psychology professor at Yale University. As both a Jew and a professional psychologist, he set himself the task of trying to make sense of the Holocaust, where many a Jewish relative of his had perished. Specifically, Milgram addressed the conventional wisdom that the reason the Nazis were able to carry out a huge program of mass murder was because the Germans were prone to obedience. Given the authoritarian structure of the German family (typically ruled by a father whose authority could never be questioned), the German child was trained to obey orders, and would continue to do so throughout his or her adult life. Hence, if the German leaders ordered the persecution and murder of entirely innocent persons, the German citizen was likely to obey blindly, and to carry out any assignment to bring about this end. Milgram asked himself, if this proneness to obeying orders, regardless of how harsh they were, was a uniquely German characteristic then, would Americans behave differently? They would never blindly obey harsh orders, orders that would inflict suffering on innocent persons, would they? To test this thesis Milgram devised a series of experiments to test whether Americans would be willing to inflict extreme pain and suffering on innocent persons.

Briefly summarized, the Milgram experiments focused on a laboratory situation where individuals were supposedly involved in a teaching process: There was a "learner," a "teacher," and a supervisor. The "teacher" read a series of words which the "learner" was to repeat. If the "learner" made mistakes, the "teacher" would inflict an electric shock upon the "learner." The more mistakes by the "learner," the more severe the electric shocks inflicted upon that person by the "teacher."

Actually, the situation was rigged. There were no electric shocks. The "learner" faked being shocked—often crying out in great agony at the "terrible pain" caused by the electricity. But the "teacher" did not know this! The "teacher" believed that his or her actions were actually inflicting great pain on a perfectly innocent individual. Often the "teacher" would argue with the supervisor, saying that surely one should not be doing this, whereupon the supervisor would insist that, in the interest of science, it was absolutely crucial that the instructions were followed fully and accurately. One was thereby making a vital contribution to science.

The results were most surprising. Despite raising an occasional objection, most of the Americans obeyed the instructions, even when they knew they were hurting an entirely innocent person. Americans were behaving like the stereotypical Germans. Milgram's experiments were repeated on many different populations, even in different countries. The results were almost the same every time. Most people were shown to obey even instructions they knew to be horrifying when presented to them by an authority. In their obedience they would do things they would ordinarily regard as immoral.

Milgram's conclusion was that ordinary people—be they Germans, Americans, or another nationality—are prone to obey authority, even if this means doing things they would ordinarily regard as being utterly wrong. He states:

> With numbing regularity good people were seen to knuckle under to the demands of authority and perform actions that were callous and severe. Men who are in everyday life responsible and decent were seduced by the trappings of authority, by the control of their perceptions, and by the uncritical acceptance of the experimenter's definition of the situation into performing harsh acts.[9]

Milgram's findings suggest that we are dealing with a far deeper disease than Germans being authority-prone. We are all authority-prone.

Yet is seems to me that we must interpret Milgram's experiments as more than centering on obedience to authority. Although, to be sure, obedience to authority was what Milgram meant to investigate—and did indeed investigate—he surely created a situation in the laboratory where a *specific morality prevailed*. It had its own ultimate values: the prime importance of science, its ultimate importance of yielding greater knowledge that can benefit humankind; and the ongoing behavior that must adhere to "scientific" conduct of inquiry, where personal feelings must be excluded in the pursuit of dispassionate, objective knowledge. Along the way the individual participant became part of a team, a social community (temporary, to be sure) that would labor to bring about the grand goal of increasing our scientific knowledge, even if it included having to do some awful things along the way. Science was given top priority, overcoming the participants' personal squeamishness about hurting innocent people. Here, in the laboratory, a distinct morality prevailed, one I have been calling a Local Moral Universe. That Local Moral Universe explicitly excluded values on which one was brought up (notably, that one does not hurt innocent people) while one acted within the confines of an immediate, locally defined moral community. That community had a system of rewards: one's contributions to science, amid one's (brief) membership in the prestigious context of a famous university doing fundamental research. Conversely, one's failure to live up to the norms and rules of this moral community meant one would be the source of great failure in accomplishing worthy objectives.

It might be argued that the Milgram experiments were conducted in an artificial context—a laboratory, far removed from real life. That, in real life, people would not behave in the way that Milgram demonstrated in his laboratory. In response, let us pay attention to a study of actual behavior, by actual people, that actually demonstrates the very same pattern of ordinary people's willingness to inflict horrific injury on entirely innocent people. I refer again to Christopher Browning's study of German police reservists during the Second World War.[10] Browning studied a group of German police reservists who lived in the city of Hamburg, who were somewhat above military age, who were not ideological Nazi zealots, who held regular jobs in their community, and who had hoped to sit out the war by signing up for a police reserve unit. Their unit met periodically for some rather perfunctory military training. To their great surprise, the unit was activated. They were sent to Poland, and, not long after arrival, assigned the task of conducting mass exterminations of entire communities of Jews. It was not a quick, one-time assignment. It was repeated several times, over the course of about a year. After some initial pained efforts by some individuals to lessen their participation in mass killings, the overwhelming majority became increasingly efficient and willing killers. A new mind-set had been created.

The police reservists eventually carried out their murderous tasks with zest and alacrity. Very few refused to participate. One who was reluctant to be a "shooter" identified himself as a weakling, who did not have the courage to carry out this severe task, rather than as a courageous honorable human being who did not want to commit murder. Even he did not question the new mind-set.

It seems that here, again, we see a Local Moral Universe in action. Early on, when the reservists met periodically during their sessions in Hamburg, they had the rudiments of a self-contained community. Subsequently, when they were removed from their homes in Hamburg and were, together, sent to Poland, their nascent sense of being a real community made them into a tight-knit community. It is likely that the real transformation took place when all of them, *together*, were given a specific, horrifying assignment, and inducted into the course of action to carry out this assignment. In the early stages, at least, there was little attention to grand, overall philosophical issues (anti-Semitic issues, for example). Instead, the overwhelming focus was on the immediate task at hand, on time schedules, on allocation of personnel, on getting things done. The emphasis was technical and immediate, such as techniques for shooting that created certain death on the first shot, close-range shots that did not produce unpleasant splattering of tissue onto the shooter, and other horrifying specifics. These were the immediacies that were addressed and came to prevail in the outlook of the participating perpetrators of horrors. They became their mind-set. They emerged from within a specific Local Moral Universe. Here considerations of human decency—of one's participation in the murder of individuals who were entirely innocent—became, quite soon, a distant blur. They were not part of one's current, ongoing considerations and priorities. One's immediate moral world was insulated from these facts of life. It substituted a different, self-contained, and fully functioning moral universe. Here issues entirely different from those they would have entertained previously, at home with their families, prevailed. These locally defined issues dominated the thoughts and actions of the participating individuals. Here an entirely different mind-set held sway.

Now, onto the world of suicide bombers, a world that was brought to forceful attention of the West by the September 11, 2001, events and has been a fairly constant feature in the struggle between groups of Palestinians and Israeli Jews. As a technique to produce terror in a population, the use of deliberate, planned acts of suicide bombing, in which an individual deliberately kills oneself while inflicting death and destruction on others, was not suddenly invented on September 11. It was used long, even centuries, before. In recent history it was perfected as a specific technique for producing terror by the Liberation Tigers of Tamil Eelam (LTTE), in their struggle to obtain a separate ethnic state on the island of Sri Lanka (the former Ceylon, near India). It was practiced in their warfare over a twenty-year period. It was copied by other groups, "by al-Qaeda, the Lebanese militia Hezbollah, and Palestinian groups such as Hamas and the al-Aqsa Martyrs Brigades."[11] Much attention has been paid to the actual suicide bombings carried out by LTTE.

> Since the 1980's the group has conducted some 200 suicide bombings. . . . [They] have attacked civilians on mass transit, at Buddhist shrines, and in office buildings. On October 1997, a suicide truck bomb killed 18 people at the 39-story World Trade Centre in Colombo, Sri Lanka's capital. . . . LTTE fighters wear cyanide capsules around their necks, so they can commit suicide if they are captured. . . . LTTE suicide attacks have targeted political leaders in Sri Lanka and India, including:

- The May 1991 assassination of former Indian Prime Minister Rajiv Gandhi at a campaign rally in India'

- The May 1993 assassination of Sri Lankan President Ranasinghe Premadasa;

- The July 1999 assassination of a Sri Lankan member of Parliament, Neelan Thiruchelevam, an ethnic Tamil involved in a government-sponsored peace initiative;

- A pair of December 1999 suicide bombings in Colombo that wounded Sri Lankan President Chandrika Kumaratunga; and

- The June 2000 assassination of Sri Lankan Industry Minister C. V. Goonarantne.[12]

The total number of victims runs into the high thousands.

Attention to the deeds of suicide terrorism by LTTE must not obscure the fact that they are being produced through, in the confines of, a Local Moral Universe, a system of beliefs, rules, and a morality of its own. It includes elaborate celebration of the suicide bombers as martyrs (their names are apt to be enshrined in a memorial)[13]; quasi religious celebrations of the acts of martyrdom that have occurred; and are a theme of the martyr's resurrection. All this is coupled with veneration of the current leaders of LTTE—military leaders, as well as ideological leaders (about the national liberation objectives, the opposition to the "genocidal policies . . . of the Sri Lankan governments"[14])—and an extensive external network among expatriates (a diaspora) who are cultivated as a source of funds to carry out the ongoing militant actions. In short, in the pursuit of distinctive goals, in the culmination of a distinctive history (which I do not have space to described here) there is a distinctive moral infrastructure, an orientation to life and death that justifies and celebrates, among other things, active suicidal bombings of supposed enemies.

In the suicide bombings carried out by Palestinians against Israelis, we see much similarity to the actions of LTTE. There is the underlying sense of deep grievance among people who are a minority, and who feel displaced and extremely and wrongfully disadvantaged. In the case of the Palestinians, they have lived in dismal refugee camps alongside a prosperous population of Israelis who, in the view of these Palestinians, have usurped their homes. (In the case of LTTE we are not dealing with refugee camps, but merely a sense of displacement and denial of their rightful place.) There is the discovery that suicide bombings can create such terror and fear among members of a dominant power, that they become an equalizer in the otherwise disparity of power.

"Inside the World of the Palestinian Suicide Bomber" is the title of a report by a journalist for the *Jordan Times*, herself a Lebanese and a Muslim.[15] She was allowed to spend four days in the hiding place that prepared suicide bombers for their mission. The report gives an indication of the mind-set of the participating individuals as well as the Local Moral Universe that provides the nurture and facilitation for suicidal bombing action in this part of the world. (I cannot vouch for the veracity of this report, since I have no way of comparing it to other sources. But at any rate, it is worth hearing its features.)

The participants undergo a highly formal and disciplined program of training for what they regard as martyrdom to a sacred cause. The participants were not stereotypical poverty-stricken, mindless youths but, instead, persons who were quite well educated in aspects of Western culture—one was a student of Western art, another was a student of international law—as well as Muslim orthodoxy. They were serious and sensitive, yet indifferent to the suffering they were about to inflict on innocent persons. They had strong support from their families. One said that killing is not his ultimate goal, although it is part of the equation that will produce a message to the larger world that it is an ugly thing to be "forced to live without freedom." In the previous section I emphasized that the suicide terrorist believes he is personally and directly addressing ultimate issues, just as this man is saying. The participants were not totally removed from everyday life. They could mix passionate attention to the latest British soccer team scores with passionate preparation for their suicide action. But surely they were living in a self-contained moral world, where a distinctive set of values prevailed. Where certain issues—such as the loss of innocent lives among their victims—were not confronted or, even, mentioned. Where a particularly distorted view of reality was enshrined, including the glories awaiting you in the next world. That educated persons could believe such things is amazing, but no more so than the beliefs found among American followers of cults (which I discussed earlier in this chapter, as well as in Chapter Five).

So we arrive at the end of a journey into the mind-set of individuals who are prepared to kill themselves in order to kill others. They are sometimes quite sensitive, but also quite brutal. They are courageous in the donation of their own life, and cowardly in the consideration of the lives of their victims. They are sometimes sharply incisive in their consideration of evils in the world that need to be addressed. They are also muddle-headed to an extraordinary extent when it comes to the choice of methods for addressing these evils. All his, I daresay, is made possible by a Local Moral Universe in which the perpetrators of suicidal horrors find themselves. I am not saying that each of the suicide bomber syndromes—be it in Sri Lanka, in Israel, or elsewhere—flourishes in an identical Local Moral Universe. I am saying, merely, that each syndrome exists within the nurture and facilitation of a Local Moral Universe. And, as a first step, we can have insight and understanding of how such Local Moral Universes operate. The next step, of course, is to find ways to disrupt them, to end their cancerous reign, and to perhaps facilitate ways to harness them for promoting human well-being. For this, I invite your suggestions and your help.

Conclusion:
Endings and Beginnings

This book is the third volume of a trilogy. Together, the three books are an attempt at a constructive response to some of the major horrors of the last and present centuries. They spring from the hope that we can end some of our victimhood to human horrors; that such horrors as happened during the twentieth and, already, in the new, twenty-first century might be prevented in the future if we develop a more viable science of human social behavior; and finally, that we can develop such a science, one that will give us new beginnings.

The first book, *Ordinary People and Extraordinary Evil: A Report on the Beguilings of Evil,* addressed the issue of how ordinary people—not zealous fanatical persons, not mentally deranged persons, not socially deviant persons—can participate in horrible acts, and do so with considerable enthusiasm. It developed a social and psychological explanation of how this can happen. Much of its focus is on decision making in everyday life, especially the cumulative effect of small, locally focused decisions, where the larger picture can be entirely obscured and disregarded. Another focus is on the packaging of diverse social programs, as they were in Nazism, whereby persons can be recruited because of their attraction to one particular program within that package. Since the diverse programs are amalgamated, the individual may come to contribute substantially to the remaining programs, even to those to which one has no commitment. Together, the cumulative, locally focused decisions and the packaging of programs can be the route by which entirely decent and sensitive persons can be recruited to using their own discretion, their autonomy, to do horrendously evil deeds.

The second book, *Immediacy: How Our World Confronts Us and How We Confront Our World*, begins from realizing that during the past century there have been in excess of a hundred million violent human deaths on our planet. The human behavior sciences failed to predict, or prevent, or, even, to convincingly explain how the horrors could have happened. This is a colossal failure. It cries out for new ways of developing human social behavior science. We need new paradigms, new ways of looking at human social behavior so that we may understand it better. In response, this book plunges into one new paradigm, and explores its usefulness through a series of essays that apply it to real, practical issues. The underlying conviction is that, just as Einstein taught us that Time has distinctive and indentifiable attributes, so does Immediacy have distinctive and identifiable attributes. These attributes can be core concepts—core scientific constructs—in better understanding the immediate social context in which we humans operate. I have identified and illustrated these attributes in a very preliminary way. When they are refined and sharpened, they can be building blocks for a more viable science of human social behavior. The book does not claim to describe a complete, new science of human social social behavior. But it does, I hope, offer some assistance toward creating such a science.

The present book is both more personal and more universal than the two previous ones. It begins by describing my two journeys in response to surviving the Nazi Holocaust. One journey is that of a survivor who tries to come to terms with his own survival and who must cope with survivor guilt as well as the sense of rootlessness that can go with it. The other journey is that of a behavioral scientist who, after years of psychological denial (part of the first journey) gradually attempts to develop dispassionate ways of addressing social horrors.

This book reiterates some of the first book's themes of ordinary people's considerable contributions to horrors. But it goes further. It emphasizes the moral context under which we humans live our lives much of the time. This context—I call it the Local Moral Universe—sometimes provides the justifying morality, the moral umbrella, for our most magnificently humane activities. Yet the Local Moral Universe can also underwrite horrendously evil deeds. It is therefore crucial to clarify how a Local Moral Universe comes about, how it exists as a distinct and indentifiable entity, and how it impacts human behavior. For good or evil, the Local Moral Universe is a phenomenon in its own right. It can sponsor a culture of sanctity (which I do not examine in this book), and it can sponsor a culture of cruelty (which I do examine in this book). I am convinced that it is a naturally occurring phenomenon whose characteristics can be discovered and mastered—so that we cease being its unwitting victims. The Local Moral Universe is perhaps the most intriguing scientific issue raised in this book. It is also the most unfinished business at hand as we try to make a constructive impact on our future.

Notes

Preface

1. Fred Emil Katz, *Ordinary People and Extraordinary Evil: A Report on the Beguilings of Evil* (Albany, N.Y.: State University of New York Press, 1993), p. 5.

Introduction

1. Christopher Browning, *Ordinary Men: Reserve Battalion 101 and the Final Solution* (New York: Harper Perennial, 1993).

2. Paul Henrickson, "Witness to the Unimaginable," *Washington Post,* 15 November 1998. This is a review of a journalist's book on Rwanda: Philip Gourewitch, *We Wish to Inform You That Tomorrow We Will Be Killed with Our Families* (New York: Farrar, Straus and Giroux, 1998).

3. Andrew Delbanco, *The Death of Satan: How Americans Have Lost the Sense of Evil* (New York: Farrar, Straus and Giroux, 1995), p. 234.

4. R. J. Rummel, *Lethal Politics: Soviet Genocide and Mass Murder Since 1917* (New Brunswick, N.J.: Transaction Books, 1990); *China's Bloody Century: Genocide and Mass Murder Since 1900* (New Brunswick, N.J.: Transaction Books, 1991).

5. Hannah Arendt, *Eichmann in Jerusalem: A Report on the Banality of Evil* (New York: Penguin Books, 1976).

6. Peter J. Haas, *Morality after Auschwitz: The Radical Challenge of the Nazi Ethic* (Philadelphia: Fortress Press, 1988).

1. All in One Day

1. My late sister, who was three and a half years older than I, survived by a different route than I did. She left Germany in 1937, to live with relatives in the

United States (who were unable to sponsor the rest of my family since they themselves were new immigrants). We met again in 1947, after I came to America from England.

2. In recent years I have been advocating, to anyone who cares to listen, for the beautiful songs that come at the end of the Passover Seder—they are essentially children's songs—to be sung at the beginning of the Seder when young children are still sufficiently awake to enjoy them. Is there a personal connection to me—to my non-singing years—that make these songs so central? I wonder.

3. Concerning the power of an inscription: Upon visiting the United States Holocaust Memorial Museum in Washington, the most moving moment for me came when I saw the name of my village inscribed on a wall that listed Jewish communities.

4. Ellen S. Fine, "The Search for Identity: Post Holocaust French Literature," in *Remembering for the Future,* ed. Yehuda Bauer (New York: Pergamon Press, 1988), vol. 2, p. 1479.

5. See Ilya Levkov, ed., *Bitburg and Beyond: Encounters in American, German and Jewish History* (New York: Shapolsky Publishers, 1987).

6. See Michael Marrus, *The Politics of Assimilation* (New York: Clarendon Press), 1971.

7. See, for example, Emile Durkheim, *The Division of Labor in Society,* trans. George Simpson (New York: Free Press, 1960); and *Suicide: A Study in Sociology,* trans. J. A. Spaulding and G. Simpson (London: Routledge & Kegan Paul, 1952). I am returning to Durkheim's theme (and my indebtedness to him) in the focus on the Local Moral Universe in this book and in my book *Immediacy.*

8. Viktor E. Frankl, *Man's Search for Meaning: An Introduction to Logotherapy* (New York: Touchstone Books, 1984), pp. 47, 147.

9. Franz H. Link, "Postmodern as Holocaust Literature: The Example of Raymond Federman," in Yehuda Bauer (editor), *Remembering for the Future,* ed. Yehuda Bauer (New York: Pergamon Press, 1988); vol. 2.

10. Emil Fackenheim, *To Mend the World: Foundations of Future Jewish Thought* (New York: Schocken Books, 1982).

2. The Bitburg Affair

1. Cited in Ilya Levkov, ed., *Bitburg and Beyond* (New York: Shapolsky Publishers, 1987), p. 66.

2. Ibid., p. 79.

3. Surviving the Holocaust

I shall concentrate on Jewish survivors coming to terms with the Nazi Holocaust. Yet much of this discussion can also apply to survivors of other horrors—ranging from Armenians who experienced genocide at the beginning of the twentieth century to Tutsis who experienced genocide toward the end of that century. Virtually all survivors, and many of their descendants, still feel raw pain.

1. Cited in Aharon Applefeld, *Beyond Despair,* trans. Jeffrey M. Green (New York: Fromm International Publishing Corp., 1994), p. 79.

2. Cited in *Tikvah News.* San Francisco, Bay Area, California, 1991.

3. Cited in *Tikvah News.* San Francisco, Bay Area, California, 1992.

4. Viktor Frankl, *Man's Search for Meaning* (New York: Touchstone Books, 1984).

5. Helen Fein, *Accounting for Genocide: National Responses and Jewish Victimization during the Holocaust* (Chicago: University of Chicago Press, 1984).

6. Zygmunt Bauman, *Modernity and the Holocaust* (Ithaca, N.Y.: Cornell University Press, 1992).

7. Stanley Milgram, *Obedience to Authority: An Experimental View* (New York: Harper and Row, 1974).

8. Israel Shahak, " 'The Life of Death': An Exchange," *New York Review of Books,* 29 January 1987, pp. 34–49.

Part III. Dissecting Evil

1. Ilya Prigogine, *From Being to Becoming: Time and Complexity in the Physical Sciences* (New York: W. H. Freeman and Company, 1980), p. 215.

4. Unpleasant Surprises

1. Douglas Birch, "Children pay for adults' vengeance," *Baltimore Sun,* 29 December 1992.

2. From the *New York Times* News Service, cited in the *Baltimore Sun,* 18 May 1993.

3. In *Ordinary People and Extraordinary Evil* (1993), and again in chapter 10 of this book, I discuss the "culture of cruelty" at Auschwitz, where low-level functionaries create their own distinctive ways of being cruel.

5. The Local Moral Universe

1. Christopher R. Browning, *Ordinary Men: Reserve Battalion 101 and the Final Solution* (New York: Harper Perennial, 1993).

2. Stanley Milgram, *Obedience to Authority: An Experimental View* (New York: Harper and Row, 1974).

3. Fred Emil Katz, *Autonomy and Organization: The Limits of Social Control* (New York: Random House, 1968); and *Structuralism in Sociology: An Approach to Knowledge* (Albany, N.Y.: State University of New York Press, 1976); see especially chapter 3.

4. R. J. Rummel, *Death by Government* (New Brunswick, N.J.: Transaction Books, 1994).

5. Pierre van den Berghe, *State Violence and Ethnicity* (Boulder: University of Colorado Press, 1990).

6. Emile Durkheim, *The Division of Labor in Society*, trans. George Simpson (New York: The Free Press, 1960); and Emile Durkheim, *Suicide: A Study in Sociology*. Trans. J. A. Spaulding and G. Simpson (London: Routledge and Kegan Paul, 1952).

7. Helen Fein, *Accounting for Genocide: National Responses and Jewish Victimization during the Holocaust* (Chicago: The University of Chicago Press, 1984).

8. Based on research reported by Robert Jay Lifton, in his book *The Nazi Doctors* (New York: Basic Books, 1986).

6. A Look at Implementation of the Holocaust

1. On some of the personal turbulence confronting one after survival, see the chapter "The Second Path in the Course of Personal Careers," in my book *Immediacy*, where I discuss suicide among Holocaust survivors who became successful writers, notably Primo Levi.

2. Helen Fein, *Accounting for Genocide: National Responses and Jewish Victimization during the Holocaust*. (Chicago: University of Chicago Press, 1984).

3. B. Wytwycky, *The Other Holocaust: Many Circles of Hell* (Washington, D. C.; The Novack Report, 1980).

4. B. M. Dank, review of *On the Edge of Destruction* by Celia S. Heller, *Contemporary Sociology* 8:1 (1979): 129–130.

5. S. M. Lipset and E. Raab, *The Politics of Unreason*. 2nd ed. (Chicago: University of Chicago Press, 1978), p. 484.

6. The moral myopia shown through early social and psychological studies focused on careerism and one's immediate task—on which I shall dwell here in this book. More contemporary myopia, particularly among high-level functionaries in large corporations (such as the use of "creative accounting" methods), focuses on the bottom line and on short-term profits. This myopia often involves extreme dislocation in the lives of their employees, notably, the dismantling of factories in the United States and the moving of production facilities to underdeveloped countries where labor costs are lower and where working conditions may be appalling, by American standards.

7. Stanley Milgram, *Obedience to Authority: An Experimental View* (New York: Harper and Row, 1974). Since this study has so many ramifications, I mention it a number of times in this book. In this chapter my focus is on immediate problem solving.

8. Hannah Arendt, *Eichmann in Jerusalem: A Report on the Banality of Evil* (New York: Penguin Books, 1976); H. Dicks, *Licensed Murder: A Socio-Psychological Study of Some SS Killers* (New York: Basic Books, 1972); and P. H. Merkl, *Political Violence under the Swastika: 581 Early Nazis* (Princeton: Princeton University Press, 1975).

9. Cited by Geoffrey Ward, review of *Lincoln,* by David Herbert Donald, *New York Times Book Review*, 22 October 1995, p. 11.

10. Fred Emil Katz and Harry W. Martin, "Career Choice Processes," *Social Forces* 41:2 (1962): 149–153.

11. Sylvia Ashton Warner, a publicly honored teacher, reports in her autobiography that she had no real commitment to teaching and that she did not enjoy teach-

ing. (S. A. Warner, *I Passed This Way.* [New York: Knopf, 1979]). However, one illustrative example such as that of Warner tells us nothing about the prevalence of this situation. It tells us, merely, that the situation here described *can* happen.

12. Julius Streicher published the vitriolic anti-Semitic newspaper *Der Stuermer*. For a citation of one of his anti-Semitic speeches, see Raul Hilberg, *The Destruction of the European Jews* (New York: Holmes & Meier, 1985), p. 17.

13. Lucy S. Dawidowicz, *The War Against the Jews: 1933–1945* (New York: Bantam Books, 1976). German anti-Semitism is also the central driving force seen by Daniel Goldhagen, in his book *Hitler's Willing Executioners*.

14. R. Hoess, *Commandant of Auschwitz*, trans., C. Fitzgibbon (Cleveland: World Publishing Co., 1959).

15. Fred Emil Katz, *Autonomy and Organization: The Limits of Social Control* (New York: Random House, 1968).

16. R. Hoess, op. cit.

17. E. Crankshaw, *Gestapo* (Moonachie, N. J.: Pyramid Publications, 1977).

18. Max Weber, *The Theory of Social and Economic Organization,* trans. A. M. Henderson and Talcott Parsons (New York: Free Press, 1947).

19. E. Crankshaw, op. cit., p. 141.

7. The Routinization of Evil

1. Viktor Frankl, *Man's Search for Meaning: An Introduction to Logotherapy* (New York: Touchstone Books, 1984).

2. Raul Hilberg, *The Destruction of European Jews* (New York: Holmes & Meier, 1985), p. 14.

3. See, "Impingings of Dormant and Hidden Immediacies," in Fred Emil Katz, *Immediacies: How Our World Confronts Us and How We Confront Our World* (Raleigh, N.C.: Pentland Press, 2000).

4. As I mentioned previously, there are some exceptions, such as Helen Fein's book, *Accounting for Genocide: National Resources and Jewish Victimization during the Holocaust* (Chicago: University of Chicago Press, 1984). Up to recent times, the almost total neglect of the Holocaust in professional sociology is attested to by the fact that a monumental survey of the entire field of sociology—covering its theory, research methods, and applications to human societies—published in 1988, makes no mention of the Holocaust (see, Neil J. Smelser, ed., *Handbook of Sociology* [New York: Sage Publications, 1988]). I, too, am guilty. My own survey of sociological theory also makes no mention of the Holocaust (see Fred E. Katz, ed., *Contemporary Sociological Theory* [New York: Random House, 1971].)

5. Christopher Browning, *Ordinary Men: Reserve Battalion 101 and the Final Solution in Poland* (New York: Harper Perennial, 1993).

6. Their other two children had already been sent off. The oldest had joined a youth movement for emigrating to Palestine; he failed to reach Palestine, and was killed by the Germans. Their middle child had been sent to the United States, to live with relatives, who were unable to sponsor the rest of our family despite their urgent effort to do so.

7. In my book *Ordinary People and Extraordinary Evil,* I also discuss the life and career of Rudolf Hoess. There is an overlap with the discussion here, since the basic material—the life of Hoess—is the same. Hence much of the illustrative material used is the same. However, here the focus is on this man's demonstrating for us the process of routinizing mass murder. He does so through the way he conducts himself at work and at home; and he does so through his particular career style. He thereby demonstrates to us the distinctive social invention—in the form of a career and ways of adapting to ongoing challenges—that goes along with the invention of gas chamber technology to produce the mass production of murder. Routinized mass murder requires both inventions.

In the previous book the story of Hoess is used to demonstrate the life of a mass murderer as bureaucrat. It shows us how the ordinary workings of bureaucracy can be harnessed for the manufacture of mass murder.

8. Bertrand Russell's introduction to Rudolf Hoess, *Commandant of Auschwitz,* op. cit., pp. 17, 24.

9. Ibid., p. 57.

10. Ibid.

11. In the Nuremberg trials of war criminals the obedience-to-authority issue became a major feature. Most of the accused claimed they were merely obeying orders. Most of the judges made much of the notion that some orders ought to be disobeyed, since they were obviously of a criminal nature. It seems to me that the judges failed to learn from Hoess (and others who had swallowed the Nazi ethic). The Hoesses regard obedience as *inherently* honorable, even when one is obeying orders that come from a detested authority, an immoral authority, or an unworthy authority.

12. Pierre Boulle, *The Bridge on the River Kwai,* trans. X. Fielding (London: Random House, 1961).

13. Hoess, op. cit., p. 69.

14. Ibid., p. 76.

15. Ibid., p. 93.

16. Ibid.

17. Ibid., p. 160–171.

18. Ibid., p. 141.

19. Ibid., p. 149.

20. Ibid., p. 163.

21. Ibid.

8. A Career in Doing Evil

1. Robert Jay Lifton, *The Nazi Doctors: Medical Killing and the Psychology of Genocide* (New York: Basic Books, 1986).

2. In the book *Immediacy,* I suggest that in many occupational careers there is a "second path" made up of issues that we cannot confront openly and that we therefore shunt off into a separate zone of our lives. Such shuntings take place quite often amongst people in general. The second path is also discussed in chapter 11, on the mindset of terrorists in this book.